The Politics of Switzerland

Despite Switzerland's small size, its political system is one of the most complex and fascinating among contemporary democracies. The rich, complex mixture of centuries-old institutions and the refined political arrangements that exist today constitute a veritable laboratory for social scientists and their students. Often presented as the paradigmatic case of political integration, consensus democracy and multinational federalism, the Swiss model has become a benchmark case for analyses in comparative politics, political behaviour and other related fields. Written by two leading experts on Swiss politics, this book presents a definitive overview for scholars and students interested in Switzerland's political system at the beginning of the twenty-first century. By focusing on its intricacies but also taking in larger issues of general interest, the broad scope of this study will appeal to all those interested in contemporary European politics and democratic systems.

HANSPETER KRIESI is Professor of Comparative Politics in the Department of Political Science at the University of Zurich.

ALEXANDER H. TRECHSEL is Professor of Political Science in the Department of Political and Social Sciences at the European University Institute, Florence.

D1595825

The Politics of Switzerland

Continuity and Change in a Consensus Democracy

HANSPETER KRIESI

ALEXANDER H. TRECHSEL

CAMBRIDGE
UNIVERSITY PRESS

CAMBRIDGE UNIVERSITY PRESS
Cambridge, New York, Melbourne, Madrid, Cape Town, Singapore, São Paulo,
Delhi, Dubai, Tokyo

Cambridge University Press
The Edinburgh Building, Cambridge CB2 8RU, UK

Published in the United States of America by Cambridge University Press, New York

www.cambridge.org
Information on this title: www.cambridge.org/9780521606318

First published 2008
Reprinted 2010

Printed in the United Kingdom at the University Press, Cambridge

A catalogue record for this publication is available from the British Library

Library of Congress Cataloguing in Publication data
Kriesi, Hanspeter.
The politics of Switzerland / Hanspeter Kriesi, Alexander H. Trechsel.
    p. cm.
Includes bibliographical references and index.
ISBN 978-0-521-84457-4 – ISBN 978-0-521-60631-8 (pbk.)   1. Switzerland – Politics
and government – 21st century.   I. Trechsel, Alexandre H.   II. Title.
DQ212.K74   2008
320.4494 – dc22   2008031947

ISBN 978-0-521-84457-4 hardback
ISBN 978-0-521-60631-8 paperback

Contents

Figures

Tables

Preface

Despite Switzerland's small size, the Swiss political system is in many respects one of the most complex and fascinating among contemporary western democracies. It not only builds upon historical developments that started centuries ago, but the unique structure of its society, the richness of its political institutions, its complex political arrangements and the multifaceted pressures for reform constitute a laboratory for any scholar in the social sciences. Often presented as the paradigmatic case of political integration, consensus democracy, multinational federalism and direct-democratic decision making, the Swiss political system has become a benchmark case for analyses in comparative politics, political behaviour, European studies and related fields.

Surprisingly, however, social scientists and policy experts outside Switzerland rarely include the Swiss case in their comparative work. This is in large part due to the still (quantitatively) meagre research output published in English and the limited availability of data and sources on the Swiss political system. Of course, these two shortcomings interact and create a vicious circle. With the present introduction to Swiss politics, we hope to take a step towards bringing Switzerland into the mainstream of comparative work.

The present volume starts out with the development of the modern state and focuses on the process of state formation within the federalist framework. In addition, the introductory chapter discusses the ambiguous concepts of Swiss nationhood and Swiss political culture. Chapters 2 to 5 introduce the Swiss polity, the structures and institutions of the Swiss political regime. This regime is characterized by a unique combination of institutional structures, which is crucial for understanding its functioning. In these four chapters we provide a thorough overview of the three main political institutions – neutrality, federalism and direct democracy – as well as of the Swiss system of government. Although neutrality, federalism and direct democracy are not exclusive features of Switzerland, it is their combination inside the same constituency which is unparalleled. This institutional framework accounts for Switzerland's status as the paradigmatic case of consensus democracy and offers a structure with an exceptionally large number of veto points.

Having laid the structural and institutional bases for understanding the Swiss political system, we then focus on politics involving the citizens, political parties and interest associations in chapters 6, 7 and 8. The discussions cover fundamental processes in the Swiss political system. Voting behaviour in elections and referendums, the role of interest associations within the policy process, as well as a comprehensive presentation of the Swiss party system and cleavage structure, constitute the main topics discussed in this part of the book.

The remaining chapters 9, 10, and 11 address three major policy domains. We concentrate on the issues which are currently most salient in Swiss politics. First, we discuss economic policies. This is not only one of the most important policy domains in any liberal democracy, but Swiss economic policy has also undergone profound changes in the more recent past. Second, public policies related to social welfare receive particular attention and allow us to put the Swiss model into a comparative perspective. Finally, Switzerland's relationship with the European Union is of utmost importance for the Swiss political system and is therefore carefully discussed in the closing chapter of this book.

For many years, we have taught classes on Swiss politics from undergraduate to PhD level in Swiss, European and American universities. We are grateful to our students who have enriched our understanding of this complex topic by engaging with us in discussions and debates throughout the years. The same goes for our colleagues in the field, many of whom have helped us by providing detailed suggestions and critique to earlier versions of our arguments. They are too numerous to be mentioned here individually but our gratitude reaches out to all of them.

More specifically, we would like to thank a number of persons who have helped us in finding the data and information we used for this book: Dominik Furgler, Roman Kolakovic, Stefan Schmid and Karin Siegwart (Federal Department of Foreign Affairs, Berne), Tobias Zellweger (Research and Documentation Centre on Direct Democracy, Geneva). Furthermore, we acknowledge the substantial feedback on earlier versions of the manuscript provided by Fernando Mendez (European University Institute). Special thanks go to Mel Marquis,

Andrew Glencross and Mario Mendez (European University Institute) who greatly helped us in the copy-editing of the volume. We would also like to thank Gabriella Unger for her professional secretarial assistance. Finally, our gratitude goes to John Haslam from Cambridge University Press. His help was essential for completing this book.

Hanspeter Kriesi and Alexander H. Trechsel
Zurich and Florence

Abbreviations

ACS	Automobil Club der Schweiz/Automobile Club de Suisse
AHV/AVS	Alters- und Hinterbliebenen-Versicherung/Assurance vieillesse et invalidité
ASM/APSM	Arbeitgeberverband der Schweizer Maschinenindustrie/Association patronale suisse de l'industrie des machines
ASTAG	Schweizerischer Nutzfahrzeugverband/Association suisse des transports routiers
AUNS/ASIN	Aktion für eine unabhängige und neutrale Schweiz/Action pour une Suisse indépendante et neutre
CNG/CSCS	Christlich-nationaler Gewerkschaftsbund/Confédération des syndicats chrétiens de Suisse
CSP/PCS	Christlichsoziale Partei/Parti chrétien-social
CVP/PDC	Christlichdemokratische Volkspartei/Parti démocrate-chrétien
EDU	Eidgenössisch-Demokratische Union
EVP/PEP	Evangelische Volkspartei/Parti évangélique suisse
FDP/PRD	Freisinnig-demokratische Partei/Parti radical-democratique
FPS	Freiheitspartei/Autopartei
GPS/PES	Grüne Partei der Schweiz/Les Verts
GBI/SIB	Gewerkschaft Bau und Industrie/Syndicat industrie et bâtiment
GSOA	Gruppe für eine Schweiz ohne Armee
LdU/AdI	Landesring der Unabhängigen/Alliance des indépendants
Lega	Lega dei Ticinesi
LPS/PLS	Liberale Partei der Schweiz/Parti libéral suisse

OECD	Organization for Economic Cooperation and Development
OFCOM	Office of Telecommunications
OFEA	Office of Foreign and Economic Affairs
PdA/PdT	Partei der Arbeit/Parti du Travail
POCH	Progressive Organizations of Switzerland
SAV/UPS	Schweizerischer Arbeitgeberverband/Union patronale suisse
SBV/USP	Schweizerischer Bauernverband/Union suisse des paysans
SBV/SSE	Schweizerischer Baumeisterverband/Société suisse des entrepreneurs
SD/DS	Schweizer Demokraten/Démocrates suisses
SGB/USS	Schweizerischer Gewerkschaftsbund/Union syndicale suisse
SGV/USAM	Schweizerischer Gewerbeverband/Union suisse des arts et métiers
SMUV/FTMH	Schweizerischer Metall- und Uhrenarbeiterverband/Fédération suisse des travailleurs de la métallurgie et de l'horlogerie
SP/PS	Sozialdemokratische Partei/Parti socialiste suisse
SVP/UDC	Schweizerische Volkspartei/Union démocratique du centre
TCS	Touring Club der Schweiz/Touring Club de Suisse
VCS/ATE	Verkehrs-Club der Schweiz/Association transport et environnement
VHTL/FCTA	Gewerkschaft Verkauf, Handel, Transport, Lebensmittel/Fédération du commerce, des transports et d'alimentation
VKMB	Vereinigung zum Schutz kleiner und mittlerer Bauern
VSA/FSE	Verein schweizerischer Angestelltenverbände/Fédération des sociétés suisses d'employés
VSM/SSCM	Verein schweizerischer Maschinen-Industrieller/Société suisse des constructeurs de machines

1 | *The development of the modern Swiss nation-state*

1.1 State formation

Until the French Revolution, the Swiss Confederation remained no more than a loose alliance of thirteen cantons with strong ties to allied territories such as Geneva, Grisons or Valais, plus subject territories (e.g. Vaud, Argovia, Thurgovia, Ticino or Valtellina) of their component units or of the federation as a whole. The Confederation exercised only limited governmental capacity. The only stable institution that the Thirteen and their allies maintained was a permanent assembly of delegates – the Diet, which met regularly in order to discuss matters of common interest, especially of war and peace. Together with the ancient pact from the thirteenth century and some other agreements, the national peace treaties, concluded after the religious civil wars in the sixteenth and seventeenth centuries, constituted the fundamental law of the Confederation (Körner 1986: 398). Most importantly, in the first peace of Kappel in 1529, which had put a temporary end to the war between the cantons that had converted to the new Protestant creed and the cantons that remained Catholic, the belligerents had promised to no longer interfere in each other's religious affairs. The formula chosen already stated the principle of what would later become a 'defensive' kind of federalism. The second peace of Kappel confirmed the preceding formula in 1531: each camp promised to respect the religious choices made by the other one. As far as common affairs were concerned, the first national peace treaty introduced one more innovation: the powerful Protestant canton of Zurich obtained agreement from the majority of the Catholic cantons that, for common affairs, future decisions would no longer be taken by majority vote but by a procedure called 'amicabilis compositio' (amicable agreement) at the time, i.e. by a consensual mode which gave every canton a right of veto. The contrast with the surrounding absolutist monarchies was striking. Christin (1997: 203f.) concludes that the federalist structures such as the ones adopted by the Swiss Confederates or the Dutch Republic were better able than the absolutist monarchies to deal with the challenge of religious confrontation and to find compromises which allowed very diverse territories to coexist peacefully over a long period: the weakness of the central state, the sovereignty of the member states in religious affairs and the institutionalization of procedures for negotiation and arbitration opened the way to political equilibria and complex pacification systems which combined the recognition of cantonal peculiarities with the preservation of the common interest.

The old regime of the Swiss Confederation collapsed when Napoleon's troops swept through the Jura and conquered its territory. During the French occupation (1798 to 1802) the basic principles of a modern state, modelled after the highly centralized French pattern, were introduced, just as elsewhere in the occupied territories in Europe. But, contrary to the Netherlands, where the French occupation replaced the existing underdeveloped central state with a durable unitary structure, the centralized state did not last for very long in Switzerland. Upon the withdrawal of the French troops in 1802, multiple rebellions broke out. Only Napoleon's intervention and the imposition of a new constitution in 1803 kept the country together. With this so-called 'Mediation act', Napoleon restored considerable autonomy to the cantons. After the defeat of the French, the Swiss returned almost completely to the old confederate order in 1815. The subsequent drive for Swiss unification led by the Radicals (the liberals) was opposed by seven Catholic cantons – Lucerne, Uri, Schwyz, Unterwald, Zoug, Fribourg and Valais – who wanted above all to defend their cantonal autonomy and who eventually formed a mutual defence league (*Sonderbund*) to protect their interests. The conflict ended in military confrontation – first in a kind of guerilla warfare (1844–5) and then in a short, unbloody civil war (1847) between the radical majority of cantons and the cantons of the *Sonderbund*. The war lasted for twenty-six days and left hardly more than a hundred dead (Andrey 1986: 590). Following the defeat of the conservative forces, the Diet of the Confederation elaborated the first federal Constitution in 1848, which represented a cautiously liberal compromise between the victorious Radicals and the Catholic Conservative losers of the war. Ratifying the new Constitution proved to be a difficult endeavour. While in some cases (Fribourg and Grisons) the cantonal Parliaments decided, most cantons had to refer to a popular vote. Nine out of the twenty-five cantons rejected the Constitution by majorities reaching up to 96 per cent (Kölz 1992: 609). In the canton of Lucerne, the Constitution was only adopted because the persons not voting were counted among its supporters. In spite of this opposition, the Diet adopted the new Constitution in the autumn of 1848. As observed by Tilly (2004: 197), '[m]ilitary, diplomatic, and popular confrontations from 1830 to 1847 came close to shattering the Swiss federation forever. Switzerland could easily have split into two separate countries, one mainly Protestant, the other almost entirely Catholic. It could also have split into multiple clusters of cantons . . . But Switzerland survived as a direct result of its war settlement.'

The hard-won new Constitution established a federal system, not a unitary state. The cantons lost their sovereignty, but they retained important powers. The price the victors paid for the acceptance of the new state by their adversaries was a far-reaching decentralization of political authority. The new centre was to be weak: the essence of political power rested with the cantonal authorities, which allowed the Catholic losers a large measure of control over their own territories. For many Radicals, the number of concessions that had to be made was too great and they subsequently pressed for a more centralized state. But they met with great resistance: a first reform package containing no less than nine proposals dealing mainly with questions of citizenship and civil liberties was rejected by a popular vote in 1866. Similarly, a first attempt to totally revise the Constitution was rejected in 1872. It failed because of joint opposition from the Catholic cantons and the French-speaking Protestant cantons. The attempt to unify the civil and penal codes proved to be the main obstacle. Two years later, a modified proposal, which took into account the critique of the French-speaking Radicals with respect to the unification of the two legal codes, was adopted by a majority of the population and all cantons except for the seven Catholic cantons of the former *Sonderbund* and the equally Catholic Appenzell Inner Rhodes and Ticino. As in 1848, the population was once again divided between a Radical part and a Catholic Conservative part (Kölz 2004: 624).

The new Constitution of 1874 definitively broke down the economic boundaries between the cantons. Among other things, it introduced the freedom of commerce and trade and improved the freedom of residence. Overall, the new Constitution was business-friendly and in favour of progress. It was also a democratic Constitution, since it introduced the institution of the optional referendum. Calls for more direct democracy had been made in Switzerland since the 1830s, when the veto was first introduced in Saint Gall and Basle-Country. Several cantons followed these examples in the early 1840s, but the wave was quickly stopped after the cantons dominated by Radicals realized that the use of the veto (an early version of the popular referendum) could contribute to the fall of a Radical government, as it did in the case of Lucerne in 1841. A motion demanding the veto thus was turned down in Zurich in 1842. It was only in the 1860s that the democratic move-ment, a broad coalition of farmers, artisans and workers, gained more momentum. After its initial success in the canton of Zurich in 1867–9, the paradigm of direct legislation spread decisively to other cantons and was also introduced in the new Federal Constitution. However, the new Constitution did not usher in a centralized state. It also did not fundamentally change the statute of the cantons. The dream of many a German-speaking Swiss Radical to create a national unitary state following the French example had been frustrated (Kölz 2004: 625).

The Constitution of 1874 still provides the fundamental framework for the Swiss federal state. The basic federalist structure remains the same, the only change concerns the numerous shifts of competences from the cantons to the federal government which took place in the course of the following 125 years. Although numerous, these shifts were by no means guaranteed in advance, and always implied intense political struggles between the centralizing reformers and the defenders of the cantonal prerogatives. As Lüthy (1971: 31) pointed out, Swiss federalism has always been an 'anti-centralism', which considered the federal government if not an enemy, then at least a necessary evil which one had to live with but not give in to. From then on, the federal government had to play the role of a stop-gap, i.e. it had to assume all those tasks which the cantons were no longer capable of assuming, but would still cede only reluctantly to the problem-solver of last resort. Chapter 3 will follow these shifts in more detail.

In the aftermath of 1874, the political climate deteriorated, since the Catholic Conservatives did not accept the progressive, centralizing and secular goals of the new Constitution. With the optional referen-dum, they now had obtained a powerful weapon to mobilize against the radical legislation which attempted to implement these goals. Until the partial revision of the Constitution in 1891, no less than nineteen proposals were attacked by optional referendums, of which two-thirds were successful (Kölz 2004: 633). In 1891, a partial revision introduced the popular initiative into the Constitution. This revision was a reaction to the grievances of the Catholic Conservatives. At the same time, their first representative was elected to the Federal Council. These concessions allowed for the integration of the Catholics into the Swiss nation-state, which led them to abandon their obstructionist use of the optional referendum.

Until World War II, the continuous modifications of the distribution of competences in the federalist state as well as the numerous popular initiatives led to 140 partial revisions of the Constitution of 1874. The key ideas of the Constitution were no longer recognizable, the language appeared outmoded and several of its elements out of date, while there remained glaring omissions in other respects, for example with regard to the bill of rights (Kölz 2004: 906f.). The general sentiment that there was need for a new Constitution grew stronger in the 1960s, and after thirty years of tinkering a new text was adopted by popular vote in 1999. The new Constitution brought the old text formally up to date, but included only a few substantive changes. A total revision in the classic sense would have had little chance of success. To avoid a cumulation of oppositions, the government chose a 'modular system' of reform: as a first step, the old Constitution was to be rewritten to bring it formally up to date; subsequent steps would revise those chapters that were most in need of reform – popular rights, the Federal Court and the system of government, to mention but the most obvious ones. Since then, only the reform of the Federal Court has been adopted, in a popular vote in March 2000.

According to the French standards of Badie and Birnbaum (1982: 212), Switzerland has 'neither a real centre, nor a real state'. Although they exaggerate somewhat, there is a kernel of truth in their quip. One and a half centuries of stepwise centralization of legislative competences have reinforced the federal government, but it still has to confront powerful cantons who jealously guard their prerogatives. Not least among these is the power to tax. There is probably no better indicator of the continuing weakness of the Swiss central state than the distribution of public revenues over the three levels of the federal state: the federal government gets only about one-third of this revenue, while the municipalities obtain somewhat more than a quarter and the

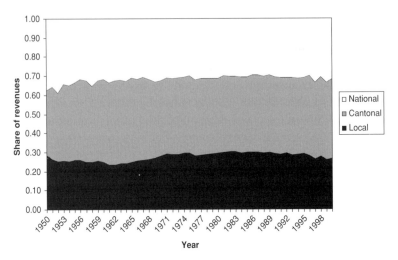

Figure 1.1 Shares of public revenues obtained by the three levels of government (percentages)
Source: Federal Ministry of Finance, Berne, 2004.

cantons 40 per cent. As shown by figure 1.1, this distribution of fiscal power has hardly changed at all over the post-war period.

1.2 Nation building

Religion mattered in the process of European nation building, and the Reformation constituted a first major step in that direction. However, language, as the most obvious and pervasive expression of identity and distinctiveness, became even more important for nation building in Europe and elsewhere. Switzerland is one of the few European countries where *religion* constituted the crucial issue for the formation of the modern Swiss nation, while language hardly mattered at all, despite the fact that the Swiss are divided into four different language communities (speaking, respectively, French, German, Italian and Romansch). In 1848, the new Radical state elite came from all language communities, and the main criterion used in recruiting them was their participation in the Radical movement. Wimmer (2002: 246) argues that when they founded the modern Swiss state of 1848, the elites from all parts of the small country knew one another rather well thanks to the activities of an associational network in which they were embedded: 'After their rise to power, they were able to rely on this densely woven network of relations stretching all over the country, penetrating deeply into the society, and transcending class and linguistic boundaries.' For Wimmer, Switzerland is a perfect illustration of his thesis that 'nation-building takes an inclusive, trans-ethnic form when the networks of civil society organisations are dense enough to allow the new political elites controlling the modern nation-state to legitimise their rule and to mobilise political support without having to resort to an ethnic constituency and the practice of ethnic favouritism and clientelism' (2002: 241).

These networks of civil society were, however, essentially elite networks and did not integrate the population at large consisting of the different language communities. Moreover, Wimmer overestimates their integrative character since they did not extend to the Catholic Conservatives, who essentially withdrew into their cantonal 'homelands' where they kept an independent power base. The federalist structure of the country allowed for a large degree of self-regulation of the different cultural communities. In Switzerland, federalism constituted a functional equivalent to 'pillarization', i.e. the formation of separate organizational infrastructures by each culturally defined community, in other culturally divided European societies such as Austria, Belgium and the Netherlands. Federalism and pillarization not only create culturally segmented communities but also contribute to their peaceful coexistence in the new nation-state. Lehmbruch (1967: 33ff.) has already observed the analogy between these two mechanisms in his comparison of Switzerland and Austria, where he compared the Swiss 'sectionalism', i.e. the territorial and horizontal integration of federalism, with the formation of '*Lager*', i.e. the pillarization or vertical integration of Austria.

However, under the impact of the process of industrialization, the territorial segmentation of religious groups started to break up. In Switzerland, industrialization gave rise to the emigration of hundreds of thousands of Catholics from their 'homelands' in the Catholic cantons to the new industrial centres in predominantly Protestant regions. In the diaspora, these Catholics made direct contact with other religious communities and with socialism. As shown by Altermatt (1991) and, in a comparative perspective, by Righart (1986), it was at this point that the process of pillarization, i.e. the construction of the Catholic organizational structure, began. Both authors point out that this process was mainly driven by Catholic elites in the diaspora of the predominantly Protestant cantons, whereas the traditional elites in the Catholic 'homelands' long resisted the formation of a Catholic organizational infrastructure in the union movement and in party politics. The traditional elites were sceptical of the constitution of a mass party because this would imply an extension of political participation and a certain democratization of decision making. To some extent, the pillarization process was also a democratization process, which explains this resistance. To the traditional elites, pillarization seemed to be only a second-best solution which they adopted once their traditional strategy of building up their regional power bases had lost its meaning in a transforming society.

Some authors (Siegenthaler 1993: 323; Ernst 1998: 234) maintain that the successful national integration at the federal level was in fact a precondition for the regional decentralization of the state. Such authors not only overestimate the success of the nation-building effort by the Radicals but also tend to entertain a much too harmonious conception of the resulting state. Although the mechanisms of territorial and social segmentation allowed for the appeasement of the religious conflict, they nevertheless at the same time imposed serious constraints on national integration at the mass level. This is not to say that the process of federal nation building did not continue parallel to the stepwise expansion of the federal government's legislative competence. The industrialization process and the rise of nationalism in neighbouring countries – German and Italian unification, and the establishment of large continental and colonial empires – reinforced the process of federal nation building in Switzerland (Froidevaux 1997: 35). The new nationalism of the late nineteenth century had interconfessional characteristics, which now appealed to the Catholics too (Siegenthaler 1993: 325; Jost 1998: 67). Thus, the year 1891 not only marks the important partial revision of the Constitution and the entry of the first Catholic Conservative into the Swiss government, but also the creation and institutionalization of the Swiss national holiday (1 August), commemorating the anniversary of the original pact between the Confederates of 1291.

Nationalist historiography blossomed, 'portraying late medieval wars as episodes in an eternal fight for independence against the mighty evil lords of the surrounding empires' (Wimmer 2002: 235). The myth of the heroic past of the Swiss was celebrated by the commemoration of historic battles such as the battle of Sempach of 1386, the erection of monuments, the organization of national exhibitions (Zurich 1883, Geneva 1896, etc.), the foundation of the national archives, the national library, a national commission for art and a national museum, and the displaying of historical paintings such as the famous Marignano frescoes of Hodler in the national museum. Additional icons of the new national myth included depictions of Alpine nature – the Swiss Arcadia in the Alps – the direct-democratic tradition and Helvetia, the Swiss version of the 'maiden with the shield' (Nagel 1999), who still today adorns the most frequently used Swiss coins. The ideologues of Swiss nationalism used existing customary practices – folksongs, physical contests, marksmanship – to construct an invented tradition of a novel type for the purposes of uniting the different component parts of the Swiss nation (Hobsbawm 1992: 6). Although it was a newly invented tradition, it gradually resonated with the Swiss public and served to forge a sense of 'unity in diversity'. As pointed out by Smith (1991: 22), 'it is myths of common ancestry, not any fact of ancestry (which is usually difficult to ascertain), that are crucial'. The question, of course – as Birnbaum (1997: 28) is careful to add – is why some myths and some dreams about common ancestors reinforce nationalist mobilization while others do not.

After the religious divide, it was mainly the *class conflict* that posed a problem for national integration. Swiss labour relations have not always been as peaceful as they were in the post-war period. Indeed, the strong polarization of classes before and during World War I culminated in the declaration of a general strike in 1918. The three principal demands of the strike were the introduction of proportional representation, the 48-hour working week in all public and private workplaces and the introduction of an old-age pension system. Faced with the challenge of the general strike, the government addressed the strike committee with an ultimatum and mobilized troops. The strike committee capitulated unconditionally and ordered the end of the strike. The government, in turn, answered this 'sense of responsibility' with the opening of negotiations about the three basic demands of the strike. Proportional representation was introduced immediately after the strike: in 1919, the new National Council, the lower chamber of Parliament, was elected according to the proportional system. The main beneficiaries of this new electoral system were the Social Democrats and, above all, the new Farmers' Party – the precursor of today's Swiss People's Party (see chapter 6) – while the Radicals and Liberals lost almost half of their seats. A reduction of working hours was also introduced in 1919, although this measure was later repealed during the economic crisis of the early 1920s. As for the old-age pension, this reform was technically adopted by means of a new article incorporated in the Constitution in 1925, but it took until 1947 to implement this most important pillar of the Swiss welfare state.

The other two crucial events for the integration of the labour movement into the Swiss nation were the conclusion of the peace accord in the metal industry in July 1937, which brought an 'integral peace' to Swiss labour relations, and the co-opting of the Social Democrats into the Swiss government in 1943. Faced with the fascist threat, national coalition governments including the Social Democrats had been formed in other European countries long before World War II. In Switzerland, however, the parties of the right were not ready to include any representatives of the left until late in the war. Only after the decisive turn in the war during the winter of 1942–3 – a turn marked by the German defeat at Stalingrad – was the governing coalition ready to accept the first Social Democrat into the government. After a brief interlude without a member from the left during the 1950s, the government in 1959 finally took the form of a long-lasting grand coalition according to the 'magic formula' which includes members of the four largest parties, including two Social Democrats (see chapter 5).

1.3 Switzerland: a nation-state?

Even in its sacralized and mythological form, the Swiss federal nation remained imbued with the spirit of *civic nationalism*. Thus, in 1875, the liberal Swiss constitutional lawyer Carl Hilty formulated the nature of the Swiss nation in these terms (quoted by Im Hof 1991: 169; authors' translation):

Neither race, nor tribal cooperation, nor common language and custom, nor nature or history have created the state of the Swiss Confederation. It has been formed rather as a contrast to all these great powers, originating in an idea, in a political thought and a will of increasing clarity and is based on it still today after 500 years of existence, just as it was on the first day.

A nation based on political will – this was the voluntarist essence of the renewed federal nationalism. Moreover, the reference to a mythical past not only served to forge a community of sentiments between the different parts of the Swiss nation, it also provided the narrative fidelity for the democratic movement which mobilized to radicalize liberal ideas in the second half of the nineteenth century. This movement tied its claims for direct democracy to the older heritage of the popular myths about the direct democratic general assemblies (*Landsgemeinden*) in the Alpine cantons and the general councils in city cantons. The protagonists of the democratic movement framed the new paradigm of direct democracy as nothing but a modernization of tradition (Kriesi and Wisler 1999).

Beneath the civic nationalism at the federal level, we find an ethnic conception of nationhood and citizenship at the cantonal and communal level. As Smith (1986: 149) has pointed out, concrete cases of nationhood and nationalism contain both civic and ethnic elements 'in varying proportions at particular moments of their history'. In Switzerland, the two elements are clearly associated with the different levels of the federal system. As Centlivres and Schnapper (1991: 158) suggest, at the federal level, the political unification preceded and conditioned the development of common sentiments of nationhood, which implies that the federal conception of the Swiss nation is closer to the French republican model. At the cantonal level, by contrast, the sense of belonging to a community with a common culture and a common origin preceded the formation of a political unity, which implies a conception of nationhood and citizenship closer to the German ethnic model.

Thus, the multicultural Swiss nation is in fact composed of diverse ethnic groups, each relatively homogeneous within itself. Switzerland constitutes a successful federation of 'nations'. Its citizens are welded together by *a common political culture*, i.e. by a common attachment to a set of fundamental political principles and institutions – most notably, as we have already mentioned, federalism and direct democracy, and, in addition, neutrality – buttressed by a set of myths about past heroic struggles to defend these principles against outside aggressors. However, this common political denominator is minimal. Its purpose is precisely to allow the different cultural groups that compose the Swiss nation to be culturally different from one another. Within a common procedural framework, the different constituent cultures of the Swiss nation lived their own way of life and tended *to ignore one another*. 'Live and let live' was the motto, which allowed the coexistence of different religious and language communities. As Denis de Rougemont (1965: 175), an astute observer of his own country, noted in his essay on the history of 'a happy people': 'compartments, this is the key word for Switzerland. Geographical or social, historical or sentimental, statutory or initiatory ones, all very close to one another and yet so closed. Without any doubt, there it is, the Swiss mystery.' Moreover, he stresses the differences between the Swiss peoples: 'in fact our federation constituted itself and functions well without the peoples of our diverse cantons needing to know one another, or to establish personal relations or even to love one another as brothers; in fact, they are as different from one another as the Burgundians from the Rhinelanders, or the Swedes from the Italians'.

It is certainly no accident that the ethnic or communitarian element of the Swiss nation is tied to the local or cantonal level. Just as they have jealously tried to guard their political prerogatives, the cantons and the municipalities have also tried to retain the right to define the national identity of their citizens. Just as Swiss state formation has stopped short of the creation of a strong centre, Swiss nation building has not achieved the degree of standardization we find in other European nation-states. The civic conception of Swiss nationhood and the pride in one's exceptional political institutions did not preclude a restrictive, assimilationist conception of citizenship, which closely resembles the German conception before it became considerably less restrictive in the mid 1990s. According to such a conception of citizenship, it is possible for immigrants to become part of the national community and obtain full rights as individuals, but only under a strict set of conditions, one of which is the willingness to give up one's original ethno-cultural allegiance. The Swiss conception, which is closely tied to the self-perception of the territorially segmented cultural communities composing the Swiss nation, is diametrically opposed to the multiculturalist conception of the Dutch, which builds on the long tradition of pillarization, i.e. the coexistence of different cultural groups within the same territory (see Koopmans *et al.* 2005).

The Swiss naturalization law, adopted at the height of European nationalism in the wake of World War I and only marginally modified since, renders acquisition of Swiss citizenship very difficult (Froidevaux 1997: 51). The Swiss naturalization procedure is characterized by three particularities (Centlivres and Schnapper 1991: 153; Kleger and D'Amato 1995: 266). First, Swiss citizenship is acquired by becoming a citizen of a local community. Second, while the cantonal and communal naturalization procedures vary from one canton and municipality to another, they are never of a purely administrative nature (Helbling and Kriesi 2004). They often involve a decision by communal legislative assemblies, and in some municipalities they even involved decisions by popular vote until very recently. Third, it is the commune's responsibility to assess the suitability of an applicant to become a Swiss citizen. This assessment considers especially the applicant's integration into the local community, their familiarity with Swiss lifestyle and habits, and their conformity with Swiss law. Still today, the naturalization procedure is notoriously slow, cumbersome and, not least, often rather costly for the applicant.

Given the internal diversity and the lack of a 'thick' common culture, *external pressure* provided the glue that has preserved Swiss unity. It was at its most extreme during World War II – the historic moment which more than any other event forged the Swiss nation – although external pressure continued to consolidate Swiss unity during the Cold War, when the communist threat and the massive immigration of workers from southern Europe served as functional equivalents to the Nazi menace during World War II. It was only with the fall of the Berlin Wall and the dissolution of the communist regimes in Eastern Europe that, in the Swiss perception, the external pressure lifted. The Swiss then found themselves in the geographical heart of a continent no longer at war but integrating at a rapid pace. Faced with this new reality, and suddenly lacking any foreign threat, the Swiss public to some degree actually experienced a sense of loss.

This surprising reaction has to do with the fact that Swiss multiculturalism within a common institutional framework came at a certain price. Mutual ignorance within and abstentionism without – these were the implications of the Swiss national identity. Externally, the minimal common denominator did not allow for more than a minimal involvement in international affairs. As we shall see in chapter 2, Swiss neutrality had, primarily, an internal function: it contributed to the coexistence of the country's various component parts. Today, in an increasingly interdependent world, in a world of regional integration, of expanding international regimes and globalizing markets, both of these components of Swiss national identity are called into question. The Swiss are forced to resituate themselves with respect to one another and in relation to the rest of the world.

As Theiler (2004) points out, the new situation constitutes the greatest challenge for the *German-speaking Swiss*. More than any other population in Western Europe, German-speaking Switzerland ranks highly on all four main correlates of euroscepticism – Germanic or Anglo-Saxon (as opposed to Latin) cultural roots, a successful political legacy, economic privileges and cultural predominance in a culturally divided country. The French-speaking Swiss, by contrast, share only two of these four predictors, since they constitute the Latin minority. However, according to Theiler, the predicament of the German-speaking Swiss in an evermore integrating world goes even deeper. His argument has two sides: on the one hand, he argues that given the 'thin' common culture, Switzerland's position vis-à-vis the European integration process in particular is more vulnerable than that of its more mono-cultural neighbours. Given that, at the federal level, Switzerland is predominantly if not exclusively based on civic foundations, if these civic foundations are taken away, Switzerland 'will be no more'. As we will argue in chapter 11, the Swiss institutions are hardly threatened by a possible Swiss membership of the European Union (EU). Yet the threat may still be perceived as real and, as Theiler argues, the perceived threat may be particularly important for the German-speaking Swiss because of their more negative perceptions of the EU which, in turn, result from the already mentioned cumulative impact of some more general factors. Finally, German-speaking Switzerland is in a cultural position that differs sharply from its francophone counterpart and is quite unique in Europe. The key issue is language: Swiss-German lacks a standardized written idiom, which means that German-speaking Swiss are bilingual in the sense that they speak Swiss-German but use standard German for writing. In other words, the German-speaking Swiss find themselves in a peculiar linguistic position vis-à-vis their northern neighbour. The cultural boundary between them and the Germans is problematic and insecure. Language separates the German-speaking Swiss from the Germans, but it is also language that keeps them tied together. Theiler (2004: 648) interprets this particular situation in psychoanalytic terms and suggests that small cultural differences give rise to 'a process of continuous self-differentiation and often subconscious fears of insufficient separation from and damaging exposure to the other category'. Seen in this light, the German-speaking Swiss position with regard to Germany is fundamentally different from that of the French-speaking Swiss with regard to France. To complicate this predicament further, the German-speaking Swiss must negotiate this relationship without the backing of an institutional safety net: the flipside of the federal

Swiss 'state without a culture' is a Swiss-German culture without a state. As a result of their cultural insecurity, large sections of German-speaking Swiss society have adopted a generally defensive and often inward-looking and isolationist stance.

With the increasing secularization of modern society, the traditionally dominant religious conflict has lost much of its force and no longer threatens the unity of the country. But given the divergent sensitivities of the major language communities with respect to the changing international context, *language* is becoming more important for Swiss national integration than it was in the past – with the possible exception of World War I, when the French-speaking Swiss sympathized with the Entente, while the German-speaking Swiss were quite germanophile. Language is also becoming more important because of the increasing political importance of *the public space*, which is segmented by language: members of the major language communities generally only use the television, radio and press of their own respective communities (Kriesi *et al.* 1996). Moreover, rather than following the TV programmes of the other Swiss language communities, the members of the several Swiss language groups pay considerably more attention to the programmes of their respective foreign neighbours who speak the same language. In other words, French-speaking Swiss watch francophone Swiss television and French stations, while the German-speaking Swiss watch germanophone Swiss television and German and Austrian programmes. Although linguistically segmented, the public space need not lack unity. It may still be a national space, if the issues debated are the same in all the different language segments and if the lines of political conflict are not segmentally specific. To the extent that all language groups debate the same national issues (e.g. within the framework of a direct-democratic campaign), and to the extent that the political camps opposing one another on the various issues are the same in all language groups, politics can still result in national closure (Ernst 1998: 230). To be sure, given the linguistic segmentation of the public space, public debate about common issues in the different language communities may possibly develop in opposite directions. However, as Tresch (2008) has recently shown in a painstaking comparative analysis of the debate about Switzerland's policy with respect to the European Union in the two major language regions, there is hardly any systematic differentiation between the two regions.

1.4 Conclusion

Switzerland has often been represented as an ideal model of 'unity in diversity' for European integration. In spite of the difficulties which we have just described, we believe that there is some truth in this observation. The development over a period of one and a half centuries of an ambiguous combination of a mainly cultural or communitarian nationhood at the regional level with a civic or political nationhood at the central level holds out some promise for European integration. The Swiss example of a *'federation of nations'* may indicate the way forward. There is no guarantee that this recipe will work, of course, as the failure of Yugoslavia amply illustrates. Like Switzerland, Yugoslavia was built around a federation of nations, and a common cultural-historical experience (Smith 1991: 146). But the Swiss example holds out the promise that it might work.

In many ways, today's Europe resembles the Swiss Confederation of the early nineteenth century, on the eve of the creation of the federal state. In the Swiss case, the federal state together with universal suffrage (for males) was imposed by a liberal elite, which subsequently created a national myth of the civic, republican type to shape the national identity of the populations of all the cantons. In the European case, the elite created a political structure, which so far lacks the political institutions for the appropriate integration of the European populations, and which also still lacks a civic myth that would assist in the creation of an appropriate common, federal identity for the different populations at the European level. The Swiss experience suggests that, in order to be successful, the construction of a common European myth must employ ancient materials in order to create a new type of tradition that resonates well with the past experiences of the different European nations. Suffice it to say that the history of Europe offers many possibilities from which to add the required 'historical depth' to the invention of a common European tradition.

The Swiss precedent also suggests that there are limits to the common European experience. Just as in the Swiss case, unity may come at the price of external political abstentionism and far-reaching internal decentralization of political authority. Again following the Swiss example, state formation at the European level may stop far short of the traditional model of the European nation-state. Neutrality in foreign affairs and multilevel governance with a relatively weak centre may be a possible recipe for European state formation. There are plenty of indications that this is exactly the direction in which the European polity is heading.

In many ways, however, the Swiss model is not sufficiently complex. This can be illustrated with the question of *language*. It is true that Switzerland has been capable of integrating different language communities based on the principle of territoriality. This principle implied that only one language was to be spoken on a given territory, but that the language could vary from one territory to the next. In order to communicate with one another, the members of the different language communities are supposed to understand (if not to speak) both of the two major languages (French and German). The European Union of course embraces many more languages than Switzerland, and in the EU there are more than just two major languages. The Swiss solution will obviously be impossible in this case. India may constitute a more adequate point of reference in this respect. As Laitin (1997) points out, India is a multilingual state where citizens who wish to have a broad range of mobility opportunities must learn at least three languages plus a possible fourth: English and Hindi are necessary for communicating with the central state; the language of the member state is necessary for communication with the corresponding administration; and minorities in a member state may continue to use their native language. In Europe, a similar language constellation is taking shape. European citizens in the future are likely to have multiple languages and multiple cultural identities, just as they are likely to have a multilayered national identity. Our point is that, in the European context, they will most closely resemble the citizens of a European state that has never really achieved political and cultural closure – the citizens of Switzerland.

2 | Neutrality

2.1 Introduction

Neutrality constitutes one of the three fundamental institutions characterizing the Swiss political system. Today, only a few states in the world can be considered 'neutral' and in Europe only Austria, Finland, Ireland, Liechtenstein, Sweden and Switzerland belong to this category. Switzerland's neutrality, however, is the most longstanding. Historians of neutrality, such as Paul Schweizer (1895) and Edgar Bonjour (1965), believe that the sources of Swiss neutrality reach back as far as 1515, the year in which the Swiss armies suffered a major defeat against the armies of François I, King of France, at the battle of Marignano. More recent research on the history of neutrality challenges the assertion of such a longstanding tradition, showing that the latter is disputable (Suter 1999). Scholars agree, however, on the crucial role of the Congress of Vienna in 1815 in relation to Swiss neutrality. It was during this watershed event, as the map of Europe was being redrawn in the aftermath of the Napoleonic wars, that Swiss delegate Charles Pictet de Rochemont succeeded in persuading the great European powers to recognize and guarantee Switzerland's self-imposed 'permanent and armed neutrality' (Widmer 2003).

Since 1815, the principle of neutrality has unquestionably been the keystone of Switzerland's foreign policy. Equally unquestionable is the fact that neutrality never constituted a goal *per se* but was considered to be a means to an end, or rather two ends: preserving Switzerland's independence from external threats and maintaining internal unity. For nearly two centuries, neutrality was – and remains – the ineluctable guiding principle of Switzerland's relations with other states, polities and supra- or international organizations. The *conception* of neutrality, however, varies across time. As we will argue in this chapter, the traditional conception of neutrality has nowadays become obsolete. At the same time, the novel understanding of Swiss neutrality is in constant need of demonstrating that the shell of neutrality has not yet been emptied.

2.2 The traditional meaning of neutrality

In spite of its importance, the principle of neutrality is not granted full constitutional status. A proposal to insert neutrality among the primary goals of the federal state was rejected on the grounds that neutrality was merely a means to secure Switzerland's independence and might therefore need to be abandoned as circumstances changed. Right from the beginning of the federal state, neutrality therefore was – and still is – above all a strategic instrument and not a rigidly defined fundamental principle. It should be noted that neutrality nevertheless was consecrated, somewhat through the back door, in two articles of the Federal Constitution of 1848 (Kölz 1992: 577).[1] The content of these constitutional provisions has survived intact to the present day. Indeed, the Federal Constitution of 1999 still contains a concurrent competence between Parliament[2] and the Federal Council[3] to maintain Switzerland's neutrality (Auer *et al.* 2006: 52ff.). Nonetheless, neutrality remains undefined in the Constitution, which allows for flexibility regarding its interpretation.

The content of neutrality can be conceptually divided into two categories: neutrality law and neutrality policy. Neutrality law established itself as customary law throughout the nineteenth century until parts of it were codified in the two Conventions of The Hague[4] in 1907 (Federal Council 1993a: 8). These Conventions continue to be the key reference up to the present day. In addition to the Conventions of The Hague and customary international law, other conventions contain provisions applying to neutral states such as, for example, the four Geneva Conventions of 1949 on the Protection of Victims of War (Federal Council 1993a: 8). Among all sources of neutrality law, 'international customary law is [today] regarded as the decisive source of law

---

[1] Articles 74.6 and 90.9 Federal Constitution of 1848.
[2] Article 173.1a Federal Constitution.
[3] Article 185.1 Federal Constitution.
[4] Convention respecting the rights and duties of neutral Powers and Persons in case of war on land, 18 October 1907 ('V. Hague Convention'); Convention concerning the rights and duties of neutral Powers in naval war, 18 October 1907 ('XIII. Hague Convention').

for the contemporary law of neutrality' (Interdepartmental Working Group 2000: 11).

Neutrality law confers certain *rights* to neutral states *in times of war between states*. It is crucial to stress that it refers to relations 'between states', since neutrality law does *not* cover internal conflicts such as civil wars. The law of neutrality prohibits attacks on neutral states, as it prohibits belligerents to move troops, ammunition or provisions across neutral territory. Neutral states have the right to trade goods – including armaments – with any other state, belligerent or not. Neutrality law also imposes two basic types of *obligations* upon neutral states (Interdepartmental Working Group 2000: 12). First, neutral states have the duty not to intervene militarily in a conflict (prohibition of *direct* military assistance), and second, they must not provide support for the military operations of the parties to such a conflict (prohibition of *indirect* military assistance). The obligation to respect the prohibition of *direct* military assistance is at the core of neutrality law. With regard to the prohibition of *indirect* military assistance, the White Paper on Neutrality (Federal Council 1993a: 8) states that a neutral state is not permitted 'to assist belligerents by furnishing them with troops or arms. It is forbidden to place its territory at the disposal of the belligerents for military purposes, whether to install operational bases, to move troops through it, or nowadays even to overfly it. The neutral state is obliged to ensure the inviolability of its territory with a suitably equipped army.' This latter obligation traditionally constituted the foundation of Switzerland's security policy and has been used as a justification for the existence of a Swiss army whose primary goal is to defend the country's independence. In addition, article 9 of the Hague Convention respecting the rights and duties of neutral powers and persons in case of war on land obliges neutral states to observe the principle of non-discrimination with regard to potential restrictions or bans on the export of war material to belligerent states. According to Gabriel (1990: 18f.), this obligation caused major problems to Swiss neutrality during the twentieth century.

In addition to subscribing to neutrality *law*, neutral states also pursue a neutrality *policy*. Switzerland's neutrality policy can be characterized by two fundamental elements which date from 1815 and which do not derive from international law: (1) Switzerland's neutrality is *permanent* and (2) it is *self-imposed*. These two elements have had major effects on neutrality policy over the past century. Concerning the first, Switzerland has chosen – for political reasons – a permanent rather than an *ad hoc* form of neutrality applicable only in times of war. The permanent character of Swiss neutrality requires a coherent policy in times of peace ('anticipatory effects'), aiming at the protection of Switzerland from any political maelstrom that could lead to an involvement in armed conflict. Instruments employed to achieve this goal have traditionally comprised Switzerland's non-alignment, its abstention from participation in supranational defence organizations such as NATO and its non-participation in economic sanctions. The second basic element – self-imposition of Swiss neutrality – leads to certain *flexibility*. Indeed, Switzerland's neutrality policy is not only self-imposed but self-*defined* and accommodates continuous adaptation of policy across time.

Gabriel (1994: 9) distinguishes three essential forms of neutrality policy: *integral* neutrality, *differential* neutrality and *super-integral* neutrality. An integral neutrality policy is constituted by three elements: first, a neutral state falling in this category must have adequate military forces in order to defend itself (armed neutrality). Second, the neutral state must not enter into any form of military alliance (military non-alignment), and third, it must refrain from participating in any type of economic sanctions. On various occasions throughout the twentieth century, Switzerland chose – or was forced – to abandon integral neutrality by adopting the differential type of neutrality policy, which differs from integral neutrality in that the neutral state may choose to participate in economic sanctions. During World War I, a conflict of dimensions never before seen in Europe, the Swiss government was impelled to participate in the economic sanctions taken by the Entente against Germany and Austria–Hungary. In the aftermath of the Great War, the Paris Peace Conference of 1919 led to the creation of the League of Nations, designed to promote international peace and security. Most neutral states participated in the League and the Swiss government, in its message to Parliament concerning Switzerland's own accession, insisted on the fact that a new orientation of neutrality policy had become 'unavoidable' (Federal Council 1919: 42). Switzerland would retain its right of non-participation in wars but would need to participate in economic sanctions decided by the League. In the 1920 referendum vote, a majority of the people and a very thin majority of cantons decided to join the new organization (Dupont 1992: 255). Switzerland's differential neutrality between the two World

Wars underwent a serious crisis in 1935 when all members of the League of Nations were supposed to participate in sanctions against Mussolini's Italy following its invasion of Ethiopia. Not all members of the League participated with equal fervour in the sanctions and the Swiss government only half-heartedly and very partially contributed to the sanctions against its big southern neighbour. In the spring of 1938, the Swiss government notified the League of Nations of its intentions to revert to a policy of integral neutrality, thus abstaining from any type of sanctions – including economic measures – taken by the League (Jost 1986: 742).

Switzerland purported to maintain its integral neutrality throughout World War II, although recent revelations by an independent expert commission on Switzerland's role during the war confirmed a series of grave neutrality violations (Independent Commission of Experts Switzerland – Second World War 2002: 508). These revelations came fifty years after the end of the war, in connection with heavy international pressure on Switzerland to shed light on the scandal of Nazi gold in Swiss banks. It goes without saying that Switzerland's efforts to finally come to terms with its past contributed to a severe loss of prestige with respect to Swiss neutrality.

In the aftermath of World War II, Switzerland maintained a policy of integral neutrality throughout the Cold War. However, this posture drew harsh criticism from the Allies, and the pressure on Switzerland's neutrality policy in the economic realm increased. In particular, the US would not tolerate Switzerland indiscriminately trading with any economic partner. For instance, Switzerland was forced to align itself with the guidelines of the Coordinating Committee on Export Controls (COCOM) set up by the US in the aftermath of World War II. Among other things, Switzerland would not be able to serve as a platform for technology transfers to the Soviet Union.

Nevertheless, Switzerland's neutrality policy during the 1950s may be described as *super-integral*, meaning that in addition to the characteristics of integral neutrality, the country adopted the principle of non-participation in any supra- or international organization with a political vocation potentially impacting on Switzerland's impartiality. Membership of the United Nations, the Council of Europe or the EC was – according to this third form of neutrality policy – not permitted. However, this super-integral neutrality did not last very long, as in 1963 Switzerland became a full member of the Council of Europe.

Integral neutrality remained the preferred policy of Switzerland right up to the fall of the Berlin Wall and the end of the Cold War. In terms of longevity, this form of neutrality policy prevails over other forms in the history of the federal state. Integral neutrality has been abandoned, however, with the breakdown of the bipolar world order. Since the 1990s, Switzerland has again pursued a differential neutrality policy.

In sum, Switzerland has always adhered to a pragmatic approach with regard to its neutrality policy. Under pressure, or when offered new opportunities, it altered this policy, adapting it to the circumstances of the international context. Today, however, the leeway for Swiss neutrality policy has dramatically diminished.

2.3 Swiss neutrality today: orphan of its substance?

Traditionally, neutrality has fulfilled five functions in Switzerland (Riklin 1991, 1992): (1) an *integration* function, fostering internal political cohesion in a multicultural national context; (2) an *independence* function, enabling the government to lead a relatively autonomous foreign and security policy; (3) a *trade* function, enabling Switzerland to maintain trade relationships throughout times of war; (4) an *equilibrium* function, representing a contribution to political stability in Europe, by protecting the Alpine crossings and by constituting a 'buffer zone' (together with neutral Austria) between the blocks during the Cold War; and finally (5) one can distinguish a *service* function, again 'offered' to the international community by providing so-called 'good offices' such as humanitarian missions, providing neutral grounds for the establishment of international organizations, mediation between countries and mutual representation of states that do not entertain diplomatic relations, etc. Adopting a conceptual perspective derived from international relations theory, Goetschel (1999: 120) conceptualizes the first four functions as 'realist' and the fifth as 'idealist'. These five traditional functions of neutrality could not remain immune from the profound changes in the international context following the end of the Cold War.

Neither could neutrality law. We identify three reasons for the weakened role of neutrality law: its exclusive focus on interstate conflict, the evolution of UN security mechanisms and the pro-active attitude of NATO during the Kosovo conflict. First, neutrality law – as mentioned before – applies exclusively to armed conflicts between two or more states. Besides the fact that the conceptual distinction between internal and international conflicts is not always straightforward – conflicts of secession come to mind – armed domestic conflicts in the world are proliferating. In addition, international terrorism, 'wars against terrorism', organized crime, economic warfare and conflicts related to migration and immigration are developments generally missed by neutrality law. These new threats, and in particular international terrorism, require international cooperation. To invoke neutrality for not actively cooperating in combating terrorism would hardly be tolerated by the international community, since opting out of such cooperation could hinder the fight against such menaces (Brunner 1989: 112f.). Since 11 September 2001, the Swiss government has therefore repeatedly declared that Switzerland would not remain neutral with regard to terrorism.[5]

Second, the role of neutrality law has been weakened by the increasingly important system of collective security set up by the United Nations and contained in chapter VII of the UN Charter (action with respect to threats to the peace, breaches of the peace and acts of aggression). This system enables coercive measures against aggressors to be decided upon by the UN Security Council. In such cases, the law of neutrality is not applicable. Whether the law of collective security or the law of neutrality is applicable in an armed international conflict therefore depends upon a decision of the UN Security Council (Interdepartmental Working Group 2000: 12). In international conflicts, the principle of 'solidarity with the victim of an aggression' plays an increasingly important role – and probably a more important one than that played by the principle of neutrality.

Third, neutrality law was invoked by Switzerland and Austria during the 1998 Kosovo conflict. Both permanently neutral states refused to allow NATO aircraft to fly over or to move troops through their respective territories. For Switzerland, this was a difficult decision. NATO's military operations against Yugoslavia were not based on any resolution by the UN Security Council and, with such a resolution constituting the only mechanism to formally disable neutrality law and participate in military operations, the federal government considered the law

---

[5] Joseph Deiss, former Minister of Foreign Affairs, cited by the *Neue Zürcher Zeitung*, 25 October 2001.

of neutrality applicable (Interdepartmental Working Group 2000: 15). While certainly coherent from a legal point of view, this attitude nevertheless raises significant ethical questions. In the Kosovo conflict, the UN Security Council was unable to pass a resolution (due to Russia's veto) allowing international military action against Yugoslavia. The main argument behind the NATO raids was that in a situation where genocide, crimes against humanity and manifest violations of human rights occur, the international community needs to react despite the absence of an explicit UN mandate. International law does not – yet? – provide for a legal basis for military assistance to victims without a resolution of the UN Security Council. However, with the Kosovo conflict, this issue became salient and with the non-UN authorized invasion of Iraq by the US and UK forces, this issue is now given even greater attention. As a result of the controversial Swiss decision in the Kosovo conflict, the question of whether or not a strict interpretation and application of neutrality law still should – and above all can – remain consistent with the ever-increasing importance of international solidarity has to be raised (Gabriel 1999).

The end of the Cold War as well as more recent developments in the international context have had a profound impact not only on neutrality *law*, but also on Switzerland's neutrality *policy*. This then ultimately challenged the traditional functions of neutrality. First, with the Soviet empire dissolved, the need for a neutral buffer zone in Europe was no longer of the same importance. The *equilibrium function* was therefore emptied of its content. Second, the end of the bipolar world order led to a strengthening of the UN security mechanism. The invasion of Kuwait by Iraqi forces in 1990 was unanimously condemned by the UN Security Council, which took action by employing economic and military sanctions against Iraq. In contrast with the Austrian government, the Swiss Federal Council refused to participate in any military action. However, Switzerland did fully participate in the economic sanctions. According to Schindler (1990), the federal government did not have any option other than to endorse the economic sanctions against Iraq even though Switzerland was not, at this point, a member of the UN. The decision to participate in the sanctions was a significant reorientation of Switzerland's neutrality policy: for the first time since the sanctions taken against Italy by the League of Nations, the Swiss government reverted to *differential* neutrality. This reorientation was subsequently bolstered by the federal government's Report on Swiss Foreign Policy in 1993 (Federal Council 1993b). Participation in economic sanctions is now considered to be compatible with Swiss neutrality as 'in principle the law of neutrality is silent on duties in the economic sphere and, furthermore, for Switzerland to stand aside would be equivalent to partisanship in favour of the law-breaker' (Interdepartmental Working Group 2000: 4). Subsequent participation by Switzerland in non-military sanctions includes: Yugoslavia (1992); Libya (1992); Haiti (1993); Sierra Leone (1997); Angola/Unita (1998) and Afghanistan/Taliban (2000). In the economic realm, the Swiss government also participated in sanctions not imposed by a UN Security Council resolution but by the European Union. With the European Free Trade Association (EFTA) and states associated with the EU supporting the EU sanctions against the Federal Republic of Yugoslavia (1998) and Myanmar (2000), Switzerland could not stand apart and followed its European neighbours.

The evaluation of the Iraq/Kuwait crisis of 1990/1 led the Federal Council in 1993 to reconsider its stance with regard to military actions. Although the Federal Council refused to join in any military action during the First Gulf War, the Swiss government now considers that participation in coercive measures adopted by the UN Security Council is compatible with Swiss neutrality. Indeed, Switzerland allowed the United Nations Protection Force (UNPROFOR) military surveillance aircraft to overfly Swiss territory in 1993 (Yugoslavia). The same was true for the Organization for Security and Cooperation in Europe (OSCE) mission in Kosovo (Kosovo verification mission) in 1998. In addition to granting permission for the overflight of its territory, the federal government allowed Implementation Force/Stabilization Force (IFOR/SFOR) military personnel and material to transit through Switzerland during the Bosnia conflict in 1995. The same rights were granted to the UN-mandated Kosovo Force (KFOR) after the Kosovo war in 1999.

With the new role of the UN since the end of the Cold War, the *service function* of Swiss neutrality policy is also clearly weakened. As Marquis and Schneider (1996: 72) show, the importance of this function has been overestimated by public opinion. Their analysis shows that in a worldwide comparison, Switzerland's mediation efforts represent only 0.3 per cent of the 1,540 mediation efforts that took place since World War II. Almost one-third of these 1,540 mediation efforts were undertaken by the UN, followed by states in the Middle East, the US and other European states (including the EU). In addition, recent

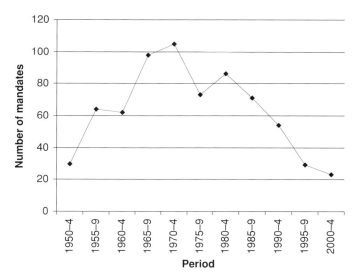

Figure 2.1 Number of Swiss mandates as a protecting power, 1950–2004
Source: Re-compilation of data from Trachsler (2004: 41).

data on Switzerland's mandates as a protecting force show that their erosion started in the mid 1980s and has continued up to the present (figure 2.1).

As Trachsler (2004: 40f.) notes, this trend holds equally true for other traditional protecting forces, such as Sweden, and it is not necessarily to be regretted, since it indicates a certain normalization of relations among former enemies. Switzerland has also actively contributed to this trend by not accepting a number of proposed mandates. Similar trends can be observed with regard to international arbitration efforts, once a flagship of Switzerland's 'good offices'. On the other hand, international conferences still play a significant role and Geneva remains the seat of many important international organizations.[6]

---

[6] Such as the United Nations Office at Geneva (UNOG) along with the specialized organizations within the UN system (World Health Organization, International Labor Organization, International Telecommunication Union, World Intellectual Property Organization, World Meteorological Organization). Other international organizations, outside the UN system, also have their seats in Geneva (e.g. World Trade Organization, International Organization for Migration, Global Fund, European Free Trade Association, Inter-Parliamentary Union, European Organization for Nuclear Research, International Air Transport Association).

European integration, allegedly the biggest challenge to current neutrality politics (Kriesi 1998a: 41), puts the *trade function* of Swiss
neutrality under pressure. Until the 1980s, a common belief among
policy makers and experts was that neutrality was incompatible with
accession of Switzerland to the EU. Since the publication of the federal government's report on foreign policy in 1993, this perception
has changed. The federal government repeatedly stressed that Switzerland could – without any conditions attached – preserve its neutrality
should the country become a member of the EU. Of course, should
the EU strengthen the military cooperation among its members and
even 'progressively adopt a common defence policy' (article 11.4 of
the Treaty Establishing a Constitution for Europe), neutrality would
hinder Switzerland's efforts to take part in such an endeavour. However, the federal government emphasizes that 'if a solid EU security
mechanism should one day prove of value and offer the Swiss the same
security as neutrality, then Switzerland could abandon its neutrality.
In view of the establishment of such a system, neutrality would lose
its *raison d'être*' (Federal Council 1999a: 383, authors' translation).
The federal government's affirmation of the fundamental compatibility of neutrality with Switzerland's attempts to strengthen its ties with
the EU came too late for the 1992 referendum on the accession to the
European Economic Area (EEA) Treaty. Studies show that the argument that Switzerland would lose some of its sovereignty was one of
the determining factors in the narrow rejection of the treaty at the polls
(Kriesi *et al.* 1993: 49). Therefore, according to Kriesi (1998a: 44), one
of the traditional functions of neutrality – assuring Switzerland's trade
potential in times of war – now limits this faculty in times of peace. One
may add that this sombre picture has partly brightened. In several referendums which took place since 2000, and in particular those on the
first and second round of the bilateral agreements between Switzerland
and the EU (in 2000 and 2005 respectively), clear majorities of voters
approved the agreements, considerably enhancing the country's trade
opportunities with the EU. However, as we shall see in more detail in
chapter 11, newer research shows the residual impact of Swiss voters'
perception of neutrality on their attitude towards an eventual accession
to the European Union (Christin and Trechsel 2002).

Neutrality's *independence function*, enabling the government to lead
a relatively autonomous foreign and security policy, is nowadays challenged by the rapid developments in the field of military technology as

well as the proliferation of international terrorism. The federal government has quite radically changed its security policy since the end of the Cold War, heavily reducing Switzerland's military potential through two major programmes ('Army 95' and 'Army XXI') and putting the emphasis on cooperation. Its most recent report on security policy even bears the title 'Security through cooperation' (Federal Council 1999b). With regard to neutrality, the Swiss government concludes that maintaining such a policy should not harm Switzerland's security, as the speed of modern warfare – especially of air power – has dramatically increased. Today, military cooperation with allies cannot be improvised and should therefore be anticipated and prepared for in order to foster the country's security (Federal Council 1999b: 43). And this option has been chosen on several occasions, particularly on the occasion of Switzerland's participation in NATO initiatives such as the *Partnership for Peace* (1996) and the *Euro-Atlantic Partnership Council* (1997). Since 1990, Swiss 'Blue Berets' (UN military observers) were sent to the Middle East, to the former Yugoslavia, Georgia and Tajikistan. Since 1996, Switzerland has also supported the NATO-led operations in Kosovo with the Swiss Company (SWISSCOY) contingent of 'Yellow Berets', a pure logistics unit. In the referendum of June 1994, a majority of 57.2 per cent of voters rejected a revision of the Swiss military law that would have enabled Swiss soldiers abroad to be armed ('Blue Helmets'), which meant that the SWISSCOY troops in Kosovo ironically had to be put under the protection of Austria, one of the neutral states in Europe. The federal Parliament considered this situation to be strange enough to warrant launching a new attempt, in 2000, for a revision of the military law. Two political groupings – one a pacifist movement, the other a right-wing association defending Switzerland's neutrality and opposing UN membership – challenged this further attempt to arm Swiss military personnel during peacekeeping missions abroad. In a referendum vote in June 2001, a very narrow majority of 51 per cent of the voters this time accepted the revision of the law. Consequently, since October 2002, the SWISSCOY troops in Kosovo have been armed.

The independence function of neutrality became further weakened in the post-9/11 era as international – and above all US – pressure mounted for intensified cooperation in the 'war against terrorism'. To pursue a totally independent foreign and security policy within a world order where not only the current hegemon – the US – but also

Switzerland's western allies are constantly exposed to terrorist threats is inconceivable for a small state in the heart of Europe: 'Neither terrorism nor the "War against Terrorism" stop at the Swiss border' (Barthelmess 2003: 157).

2.4 The future of neutrality: living with the empty shell

Since the end of the Cold War, the federal government's conception of neutrality has radically changed. First, its interpretation of neutrality law has become much more flexible, with an occasional backslide, such as during the Kosovo conflict. Furthermore, from a security perspective, neutrality law never guaranteed invulnerability during a conflict. In the past, neutral states – such as Norway – vainly waved the flag of neutrality law when it became clear that Nazi Germany was planning to invade the country – and indeed, Germany did attack on 9 April 1940 (Kersaudy 1987). It used to be convenient for neutral states to hide behind neutrality law in order to avoid participating in international action in times of war. However, nowadays rigid interpretations of neutrality law have become politically perilous. Therefore, in all official reports on foreign policy, neutrality, European integration, security policy and UN membership that have been published over the past decade, references to neutrality law generally emphasize its limited scope in today's world. Also, neutrality law is now believed to be fundamentally compatible with Switzerland's efforts to become more integrated and even play a more pro-active role on the international stage. The White Paper on Neutrality even stresses that, under international law, 'Switzerland is at liberty to give up its neutrality *unilaterally*' (Federal Council 1993a: 6).

Second, the traditional functions of neutrality have been undermined by Switzerland's return to a policy of differential neutrality and the important changes in the world order that have taken place since the end of the Cold War. At first sight, the only function that may have survived this development is the domestic (or integration) function of neutrality (table 2.1).

Survey results show that two-thirds (67.1 per cent) of the Swiss electorate is either very proud or quite proud of Switzerland's neutrality. While pride reflects a present attitude, based on a retrospective evaluation, the 'importance for the future' item gives us some indication about citizens' prospective evaluation of neutrality. Almost three out of four

Table 2.1 *Pride and importance of neutrality for the future of Switzerland*

Pride	%	(n)	Importance	%	(n)
very proud	28.9	(250)	very important	40.2	(348)
quite proud	38.2	(331)	quite important	33.7	(292)
not very proud	23.3	(202)	not very important	21.4	(185)
not proud at all	7.2	(62)	not important at all	3.9	(34)
don't know	2.4	(21)	don't know	0.8	(7)
Total	100.0	(866)	Total	100.0	(866)

Source: Eurobarometer in Switzerland Survey (2001). The data have been reduced to Swiss citizens who are 18 years old or older.

Swiss citizens believe that neutrality is quite important or even very important for the future of the country. Most recent data also show that the principle of neutrality enjoys very high levels of acceptance over time: in 2004, they continue to reach the levels attained during the Cold War, when neutrality embodied one of the most popular maxims of Swiss politics (Haltiner and Wenger 2004: 132). Today, 75 per cent of the electorate still holds the opinion that neutrality represents a paragon to aspire to and is symbolically linked to the 'state of Switzerland' (Haltiner and Wenger 2004: 136). In view of these results, one might gain the impression that the integration function of neutrality continues harmlessly to operate just fine, even though the conception of neutrality has radically changed.

However, after several major ballot proposals that would have opened up Switzerland's foreign policy ended in popular rejection,[7] it became apparent that holding on to neutrality may help domestic integration but may simultaneously hinder Switzerland's external relations. A number of observers of Swiss politics pointed out that a new salient cleavage emerged during the 1990s which pits those favouring a more open foreign policy against those who prefer to hold on to Switzerland's traditions (Moser 1996; Wernli *et al.* 1994; Kriesi *et al.* 1993; Kriesi 1998a; Brunner and Sciarini 2002; Hug and Trechsel 2002; Christin *et al.* 2002). In popular votes on foreign policy issues, among others, the 'openness–tradition' cleavage is important, although this cleavage

---

[7] UN membership in 1986, EEA Treaty in 1992, Blue Helmets in 1994.

cannot be reduced to the attitudes of the electorate towards neutrality. Also, as Gabriel and Fanzun (2004: 34f.) argue, the traditional asymmetry in Swiss foreign policy – strong economic integration vs weak political integration – cannot be explained on the basis of neutrality alone. Finally, this asymmetry has unmistakably been reduced since the beginning of the third millennium – despite the impressively strong attachment of the electorate to neutrality. All recent popular votes on foreign policy or security policy[8] have been won by the government, notwithstanding the arguments of the opponents that neutrality would be harmed in case of acceptance. For Mauer (2003: 64), this shows an ever greater openness of the Swiss electorate for security through cooperation.

In 2002, Switzerland became a full member of the United Nations and it is now among the fifteen countries contributing most to the UN budget (Federal Council 2004a: 44). Since 2002, Switzerland has also been able to participate in the military peacekeeping efforts of the international community. The two rounds of bilateral agreements with the European Union constitute a major step in Switzerland's European integration effort. According to Christin and Trechsel (2002: 432), the attitude towards neutrality would not constitute the number one obstacle to future membership of the European Union. In fact, their study shows that the effect of how citizens perceive the consequences of EU membership for the national economy is four times stronger than its consequences for neutrality.

In sum, we argue that the traditional asymmetry in Switzerland's integration in the world has clearly been reduced in the recent past. With the exception of EU membership, Switzerland's political integration is today comparable to its neighbour Austria. Studies show that the Austrians' attachment to neutrality is very strong, reaching similar levels to those measured in Switzerland (Gärtner and Höll 2001). However, this has not prevented Austria from assuming a pro-active role within the UN: Austria was twice a member of the Security Council, where its voting record 'was not characterized by abstentions, but overwhelmingly by the casting of a yes or no vote, i.e. a clear positive or negative opinion' (Kreid 2001: 40). Furthermore, in 2001, the scale of

---

[8] Bilateral agreements I (2000), law on armed peacekeeping forces abroad (2001), UN membership (2002) and Army XXI (2003), Dublin/Schengen agreement (2005), extension of the agreement on free movement of people (2005), cohesion funds (2006).

Austria's involvement in UN peacekeeping operations was greater than that of any of its fellow EU member states and attained seventh place worldwide (Kreid 2001: 43).

Paradoxically, although the Swiss hold on to neutrality, they seem not to be aware that they hold on to a rather empty shell – not unlike the Austrians. To be sure, it is not the federal government that will draw attention to this state of affairs, as it can effortlessly live with such a situation. If – besides becoming a member of NATO – no other major political integration step is problematic from a neutrality perspective and the voters continue to accept these steps at the polls, then Swiss neutrality indeed has a future.

3 | Federalism

3.1 The gradual consolidation

We now turn to federalism, yet another fundamental institution that underpins the Swiss political system. As discussed in chapter 1, Switzerland's modern federal state was created in 1848 following the two consecutive collapses of the former Confederation. Similar to the transition from the Articles of Confederation to the Federal Constitution of the United States in 1787, the transition from the Confederation to the federal state in Switzerland was revolutionary in the sense that it abolished the unanimity principle and replaced it by a system of qualified majority for amending the supreme law. In both cases, this 'federalist deficit' – the unanimity principle for constitutional change – could therefore be overcome (Trechsel 2005). However, in 1848, the federal level of government in the newly created state was extremely weak, as the cantons were able to preserve significant parts of their power. According to Stepan (1999), Switzerland – together with the United States and Australia – fits into the category of 'coming together' federalism, where the creation of the federal state is based on a largely voluntary agreement. The creation of the Swiss federal state is based on the logic of relatively autonomous units that 'come together to pool their sovereignty while retaining their individual identities' (Stepan 1999: 23).

The constitutional design for altering the interlevel distribution of power is, in the Swiss case, particularly favourable to the *status quo*. First, the residual power lies with the cantons, i.e. competences that are not explicitly delegated to the federal level remain at the subnational level.[1] Any attempt to centralize a competence, new or old, has to pass the hurdle of a formal revision of the Federal Constitution. Second, and as we shall see in further detail in chapter 4, amending the Federal Constitution requires a referendum in which both a cantonal and

---

[1] Article 3 Federal Constitution.

electoral majority need to be attained for the amendment to succeed (double majority).

This particular set-up very effectively delayed, if not overtly hindered, centralizing efforts in many policy fields. Nonetheless, the federal level of government was able to gradually acquire new competences. To start with, a unified economic area was created in 1848 with, among other measures, the abolition of intercantonal tariffs, centralized postal services and a federal monopoly on the Swiss currency. During the second half of the nineteenth century, the federal government acquired authority over the telegraph system and competence to legislate in matters concerning the railways while receiving new competences in the domains of penal and civil law. Later, in 1947 and 1978, the federal government was also given additional tools to define macro-economic policies. Despite this slow but steady centralization of competences aiming at the establishment of a national economic area, cantonal prerogatives remain strong. For example, cantons are free to choose their own budgetary and fiscal policies.

Compared to most European experiences, the development of social security mechanisms at the federal level was slow. Every innovation in the sphere of social security had to run the gauntlet of the referendum, regularly unleashing conflicts between centralizers and anti-centralizers. As a result, the majority of these innovations date from the post-World War II period. In addition to its late implementation, the Swiss social security system 'was and remains highly devolved' (McKay 2001: 110). The second half of the twentieth century also saw the emergence of federal competences concerning the protection against new risks for citizens and the environment, such as civil protection, protection of the environment in general, consumer protection, data protection and so on. Finally, in the more recent past, the federal level was given competences over infrastructures, namely in the fields of telecommunications, public highways and railways, nuclear energy and scientific research.

This creeping centralization of competences was accompanied by an extension of federal instruments in the fiscal realm. During the nineteenth century, the federal government had to rely on very limited resources. These resources mainly came from customs duties, profits generated by the postal services and cantonal contributions. It is only from the end of World War I that this situation progressively improved. New federal taxes on tobacco, beer, income and capital as well as the predecessor of the value-added tax (VAT) regime were introduced. Again, however, this process was cautious and lengthy. For instance, VAT[2] did not replace the former tax on the turnover of goods until 1993, and then only after three attempts that were rejected at the polls (Armingeon 2004: 664). Also, federal direct taxation and the VAT regime are limited in time, requiring periodic renewal by the people and the cantons.[3]

3.2 Cantonal autonomy vis-à-vis the federal level

Despite the creeping centralization of competences as well as the extension of federal taxation, the Swiss cantons continued to retain a large degree of autonomy vis-à-vis the federal authorities. Twenty-six political systems, functionally analogous though different in structure, coexist with the federal level. The model is one of a segmented differentiation of the political system, based on territorial criteria (Nüssli 1985: 93ff.). Following Aubert (1983: 211), the autonomy of the cantons manifests itself in five ways:

1. *The constitutional autonomy of the cantons is explicitly guaranteed (article 47, Federal Constitution).* This does not imply, however, that the cantonal landscape must remain static. As the creation in 1979 of the twenty-sixth canton – Jura – proved, the system provides for a certain flexibility, although the overall stability of the territorial boundaries is very strong.

2. *Cantons can organize themselves autonomously.* Each canton has its own constitution and its own set of popular rights. Each defines its political, administrative and judiciary authorities and their respective functions, and has a certain leeway in the definition of its electorate. Furthermore, each chooses its own schooling system, its own fiscal system and so on. Cantons are obliged to obtain a federal guarantee for their constitutions. This, in turn, obliges each canton to have a written constitution that must respect a certain number of criteria, such as the obligation to organize itself according to democratic principles. The Federal Constitution also requires the cantons to submit their constitutions – and any further amendments – to the approval of their

---

[2] At the time of writing, the maximum VAT rate was 7.6 per cent, a very low rate by international standards.

[3] In a federal referendum vote on 28 November 2004, 73.8 per cent of the voters and all but one canton accepted a minor modification and prolongation of this system until 2020.

respective electorates. Moreover, the cantonal electorate must be given the possibility to initiate constitutional change through the instrument of the popular initiative (see Auer *et al.* 2006: 63ff.).[4]

The cantons can freely choose the form of their government within the limits set by the Federal Constitution. The so-called *Landsgemeinde*, a citizens' assembly, has been abolished or replaced by modern parliaments in all but two cantons (Glarus and Appenzell Inner Rhodes, where citizens' assemblies and parliaments coexist). The number of deputies in cantonal parliaments varies from 55 (Obwalden) to 200 (Berne, Vaud and Argovia), generally following the pattern of 'the less populated and the more socially homogeneous a canton, the lower the number of seats' (Auer and Delley 1986: 98). The composition of cantonal governments varies as well (between 5 and 7 members) and so do the structures of cantonal administrations and the judiciary (see Germann and Weis 1995 for details).

Finally, cantons are free to define their electorates. Therefore, active and passive voting rights for women have been introduced at different moments in time depending on the cantonal legislation. Also, in two cantons (Neuchâtel and Jura), denizens have certain voting rights if they fulfil a number of criteria (e.g. length of residence). Finally, in 2007 the canton of Glarus lowered the age for active voting rights at the communal and cantonal levels to 16. This was a first in Switzerland, setting off debates for similar reductions of the voting age in a number of cantons (Zurich, Berne, Grisons) and at the federal level.

3. *Cantons freely choose their political authorities.* The federal government cannot interfere in the selection of cantonal authorities nor can it impose a certain electoral system as long as the cantons conform to the democratic standards set out by the Federal Constitution (see above).

4. *Cantonal legislation is not politically controlled by the federal authorities.* Cantonal legislation has to conform to federal law. However, within the constraints of federal law, the cantons are free to legislate as they please.

5. *The autonomy of the cantons is closely linked to article 3 of the Federal Constitution,* which reserves the residual competences to the cantonal level. One should add that cantons dispose of their own financial resources, complemented by federal transfers.

---

[4] For further details on direct democracy at the cantonal level, refer to chapter 4 in this volume.

3.3 Federal dependency at the cantonal level

Compared to most federal systems, the autonomy of the Swiss cantons vis-à-vis the federal level of government is rather significant. By contrast, the autonomy of the federal level in relation to the cantonal level is quite limited, as cantons, together with the people, constitute the two fundamental organs on which the federal state is based (article 1 of the Federal Constitution; see also Auer *et al.* 2006: 25). The cantons play an active role during the formulation and decision stages of the federal legislative process (see chapter 8 for details). Two major institutions enable the cantons to co-decide on federal legislation: the Council of States (i.e. the Upper House of the Federal Parliament) and the cantonal majority for certain types of referendum votes.

The structure of the Federal Parliament is based on the model of *perfect bicameralism*, with both chambers, the *National Council* and the *Council of States*, having equal rights. Chosen in 1848, this solution constituted a compromise for resolving the most salient problem in the process leading to the adoption of the first Federal Constitution (Kölz 1992: 554f.). Today, the representation of the people is assured by the 200 deputies within the *National Council*. Since the federal elections of 1919, National Councillors are elected according to the system of proportional representation, with the cantons forming the electoral constituencies. This means that the number of seats for each canton corresponds to the size of its population, except for the fact that even the smallest cantons obtain at least one MP in the National Council. The cantons are represented by the 46 members of the *Council of States*. Each canton has two seats, with the exception of the former 'half-cantons'[5] (Obwalden, Nidwalden, Basle-City, Basle-Country, Appenzell Inner Rhodes and Appenzell Outer Rhodes) which have only one seat (see also chapter 5). It is worth noting that the representation of the cantons in the Council of States is imperfect. Unlike the German *Bundesrat*, the Swiss Council of States is not composed of delegates of the subnational entities. While in Germany the governments of the *Länder* are directly represented in the *Bundesrat*, the Swiss cantons

---

[5] With the adoption of the new Federal Constitution in 1999, the six former 'half-cantons' have become 'cantons' (see also Auer *et al.* 2006: 330). It is only with regard to their representation in the Council of States and their weight in the calculus of the cantonal majority in referendums that they differ.

merely serve as electoral constituencies for the popular election of the members of the Council of States. Therefore, the latter represent their respective electorates rather than the interests of the canton (see also Lüthi 1993; Kriesi 1998a: 60).[6]

The cantonal level of government also plays a major role in the direct-democratic realm above all when a *double majority* is required for certain referendum votes (see chapter 4). In such referendums, every canton has one vote (which corresponds to the popular majority in each canton), with the six former half-cantons having only half a vote. Cantonal and popular majorities rarely collide, but with the 'inflation of votes requiring a double majority' (Germann 1994: 138f.), together with the increasing demographic disparities between large and small cantons (Vatter 2007a: 84), the rate of collisions or quasi-collisions has drastically increased over the past three decades. More recently, a number of models have been proposed to reform or even abolish the cantonal majority in direct-democratic decision-making processes (Germann 1975; Hess and Trechsel 1993; Vatter and Sager 1996). So far, none of these models has been adopted.

The Federal Constitution grants cantons a set of further instruments for directly participating in the elaboration of federal legislation. Similar to the right of any MP to launch a parliamentary initiative, any canton can at any time initiate a legislative process through its right to present the Federal Parliament with a petition (*Standesinitiative*, article 160 al. 1 Federal Constitution). Nonetheless, and despite the fact that cantonal petitions have been used more frequently since the 1970s (see Linder 1999: 142), the study by Sciarini *et al.* (2002: 12) shows that only 1 per cent of all bills between 1995 and 1999 resulted from such an initiative.

Furthermore, eight cantons can launch a referendum procedure against a federal law (article 141 al. 1 Federal Constitution – see also chapter 4). Since its introduction in 1874, this instrument has been used only once: in 2003, coordinated by the Conference of Cantonal Governments (CCG), eleven cantons – in conjunction with a popular demand for a referendum signed by 57,000 citizens – made use of this procedure. The target of this referendum was a package of fiscal

---

[6] Note that roll-call voting in the Council of States is exceptional and since 1947 was called for successfully only on four occasions, thus preventing us from empirically testing this claim (see also Von Wyss 2003).

reforms that was, in the end, rejected by two-thirds of voters on 16 May 2004 (see chapter 9).

In comparison to the German system of federalism, often presented as the one most similar to the Swiss version, Braun (2003: 67f.) stresses that the cantonal governments, despite their role in the federal policy formulation process, do not represent veto players to the same degree as the German *Länder*. One could argue, however, that the Swiss system allows cantons to become serious veto players as soon as they *coordinate* their action. The recent referendum of the cantons on a fiscal reform, refused by the people on 16 May 2004, serves as an illustration of such a coordinated veto action.

3.4 Cooperative federalism

As we have seen, cantons have a large say in federal policy making. Furthermore, with respect to the implementation of federal public policies, the role of the cantons is of utmost importance. This holds first of all with regard to the enforcement of federal law, as the Swiss cantons are in charge of administering justice, most notably in the areas of civil and penal law. The federal courts only intervene on appeal. More generally, unlike the US model of 'dual federalism' (Wheare 1946), where each level of government has a number of competences resulting in policies implemented at the same level (i.e. at the federal and state levels respectively), the Swiss model corresponds to the 'cooperative type' of federalism (Elazar 1962). In cooperative federal arrangements, policies can be formulated at the federal level but are implemented at the subnational entities of the state. Generally speaking, European federal states, as well as the EU, belong to this type of federalism, which stresses a 'division of labour' and the functional relationships between the levels of government (Braun 2000: 4).

Thus, in Switzerland, the implementation of federal policies has traditionally been delegated to the cantons.[7] Although the federal government maintains a predominant position in the drafting of legislation, from constitutional provisions to federal laws, directives and other types of legal acts, in the concrete application of these legal

---

[7] Note that this is not always the case: Kissling-Näf and Wälti (2007: 565–71) distinguish between two additional modes of implementation – see chapter 6 for details.

Table 3.1 *Expenditures for public policies (percentage 1998)*

Policy fields	Federal government	Cantons	Communes	Proportion of overall federal expenditures
International relations	*100*	0	0	2
National defence	*93*	5	5	5
Public finances and taxation	*78*	42	34	7
National economy	*74*	*56*	11	5
Transport	*64*	40	21	11
Social security	*52*	44	23	21
Justice and police	7	*70*	27	5
Education	14	*64*	42	18
Health	1	*63*	48	12
General administration	19	39	*45*	6
Culture and leisure	13	32	*58*	3
Environment and regional development planning	15	29	*75*	4
Total expenditures	39	48	33	100

Source: Wälti (2003: 98).

regulations – i.e. policy implementation – the cantons play a vital role. In the great majority of policy domains, the federal level is dependent on the cooperation of the cantons and, to a lesser extent, on the communal administrations for the implementation of the centrally designed programmes.

For various policy domains, table 3.1 shows the distribution of public expenditures over the three levels of government. Only in the fields of international relations and national defence does the federal government regulate the implementation process on a (nearly) exclusive basis. All other policy fields are characterized by a strong degree of cooperation between the different levels of government, although the federal level tends to dominate in the fields of public finances and taxation, the national economy, transport and social security. By contrast, the cantons play a dominant role in the fields of justice and police, education and health, while the 'third layer' of government, the nearly 3,000 municipalities, dominates the areas of general administration, culture and leisure as well as the protection of the environment and regional development planning.

The high level of cooperation in the accomplishment of public tasks has created, over time, a very complex web of financial flows and organizational coordination among levels of government. The question of whether this web leads to a higher degree of centralization or whether, on the contrary, it has a decentralizing effect, is a matter of much dispute. We believe that both tendencies can be observed, but with significant variation across policy fields (Vatter 2007b: 217). Overall, however, recent studies show that the traditional perception of Switzerland's public sector as one that is characterized by a relatively low level of centralization is not entirely accurate.

3.5 Assessing Swiss federalism

The literature on federalism highlights numerous pros and cons of federal arrangements as compared to more unitary models of government. In the Swiss context, Aubert (1983) mentions five major advantages of federalism:

1. Swiss federalism *is assumed to protect minorities*. Lijphart (1977) most prominently argues that power-sharing structures in consociational countries (including in federal systems) may enhance conflict resolution (see also Christin and Hug 2003). It is true that, unlike other federations, the modern Swiss federal state has not been subject to disruptions such as ethnic violence, overt repression of minorities, etc. Traditionally, religious and linguistic cleavages were accommodated by federalist mechanisms. However, demographic changes and a marked process of secularization tend to dilute the ability of the federalist system to ensure the protection of minorities. For instance, while Catholic minorities in the mid nineteenth century were territorially concentrated in a number of religiously homogeneous cantons, the current distribution of Protestant and Catholic citizens is more equal across cantonal boundaries. With the de-territorialization of religious minorities, the formal institutions and mechanisms of Swiss federalism cannot offer the same degree of protection any more. The same applies for other minorities, including political ones such as women, homosexuals, elderly citizens, handicapped citizens, etc., for which federalism never offered protection in the first place. As Bächtiger

and Steiner (2004) argue, federalism is only one factor among several that led to the relatively successful management of conflicts in the Swiss multicultural context: informal aspects of the fundamental institutions as well as the identification of the actors with the latter need to be taken into account in order to understand this overall favourable outcome.

2. Swiss federalism *brings citizens closer to the political authorities*. According to this argument, federalism, through the multiplication of political authorities at the subnational level, allows citizens more immediate access to administrative authorities and improves their chances to get involved in politics, e.g. to be elected. Critics believe, however, that such improved access only works in very small territorial units (Kappeler 1996). Moreover, one could add that even in very centralized states, a local level of government exists, offering similar forms of 'immediate' access to politics. In other words, federalism may not provide – in and of itself – a fundamentally closer relationship between citizens and politics. As we shall see in the next chapter, it is above all direct democracy at all three levels of the state which brings people closer to politics in the Swiss model. And it is indisputable that the federal structure, combined with the large autonomy of the subnational units with respect to the centre, allowed for innovation, multiplication and the spread of institutions of direct democracy.

3. Swiss federalism *diffuses power*. According to this argument, federalism enables a more flexible, better-adapted implementation of federal policies at the cantonal level and functions as a brake on centralizing trends. However, the fundamental problem in Switzerland is not excessive political centralization but rather a lack thereof, above all for reasons related to the efficiency of policy implementation. Here, both the size of the subnational units as well as their socio-economic heterogeneity is of utmost importance. Zurich, the largest canton, accounts for 17 per cent of the Swiss population and has over eighty times more inhabitants than the smallest canton, Appenzell Inner Rhodes (Federal Statistical Office 2003). In comparison, this ratio places Switzerland among the most heterogeneous federal states in terms of size of population: California, the largest jurisdiction of the US, is more than seventy times larger than the smallest, Wyoming. In Germany, North Rhine-Westphalia is twenty-seven times larger than the *Land* Bremen. In Austria, the *Land* Niederösterreich is only six times more populated

than the Burgenland. Only the EU has a larger ratio than Switzerland, with Germany having more than 200 times the population of Malta.

Of course, the size of the administrative apparatus of a canton is linked to its size in terms of inhabitants. Whereas in 2001 the canton of Zurich employed over 20,000 persons, the canton of Appenzell Inner Rhodes counted 136 employees (IDHEAP/BADAC 2004). Other important discrepancies exist with regard to the economic capacities of cantons. The index of financial capacity, established by the Federal Department of Economic Affairs (2003), shows a value of 227 for the canton of Zug compared to a value of 30 for the canton of Valais.

In view of such discrepancies it is not surprising that the capacity of the cantons to participate in federal policy formulation and implementation processes varies significantly. The smallest cantons cannot profit from economies of scale and are simply not capable of fully executing some of the federal programmes. Indeed, the volume of certain administrative tasks increases with population size, but other tasks, such as a cantons' participation in federal consultation procedures and the systematic implementation of some of the federal regulations, are independent of the size of a given canton. Federal subsidies, fiscal equalization among cantons, coordination among cantonal ministers and intercantonal treaties (so-called *concordats*) constitute the traditional mechanisms for overcoming these structural problems to which cantonal administrations are exposed. However, in a number of policy domains such mechanisms no longer suffice. Recently, in the fields of health policy, police activities and university education, horizontal cooperation among cantons has intensified. For other tasks, such as the implementation of social security, cantonal pension agencies together with private pension agencies have started to pool their IT resources into large conglomerates (Mänz and Trechsel 2004).

4. Swiss federalism *offers a playground for experimentation*. Compared to the autonomy of the German *Länder*, the autonomy of the cantons in the implementation of federal legislation is much greater (Braun 2003: 72). Numerous studies of public policy implementation in Switzerland have shown that the cantonal variations concerning policy outcomes are therefore quite important. Such variations are often problematic, especially in areas where the absence of harmonization creates perverse effects that may completely distort the initial aims of a federal programme. The study of Delley *et al.* (1982) on regional planning serves as an illustration of this problem. Recent studies stress

the variability of policy outcomes in a number of fields. Battaglini and Giraud (2003) show that the implementation of federal legislation on unemployment varies not only in its extent but also in its orientation. The authors explain this variance in terms of differences in cantonal 'policy styles'. Sager (2003), in his study of the federal programme on alcohol prevention, shows strong variance in cantonal implementation strategies. At the same time, he indicates that 'secondary harmonization processes' (Kissling-Näf and Knoepfel 1992), i.e. vertical and horizontal cooperation mechanisms, can at times reduce the gap in the outcomes. Balthasar (2003), who investigates such secondary harmonization processes with regard to the implementation of the federal law on health insurance, observes that the federal government uses new instruments such as policy evaluations to promote cantonal harmonization in the implementation phase.

Although these studies emphasize the difficulties of harmonizing the implementation of federal policies, one should not underestimate the important potential for experimentation. This potential may at times become visible when the cantons' interest in innovation is promoted by the federal government through, above all, logistic and financial incentives. Recent innovations in the field of electronic voting may serve as an example. Initiated by the Federal Chancellery in 2001, a project for experimentation with e-voting was designed in collaboration with three cantons (Geneva, Zurich and Neuchâtel). This project allowed these cantons, and in particular the canton of Geneva, to test remote voting over the internet in several pilot runs and to gain valuable insights and international attention. Also, with the cantons of Zurich and Neuchâtel developing alternative models of electronic voting, the federal level, as well as the rest of the cantons, can profit directly in terms of knowledge and expertise from the different approaches tested in the pilot cantons. As this example indicates, federalism may provide a true laboratory for policy innovation (see Auer and Trechsel 2001; Trechsel and Mendez 2005; Trechsel 2007a).

5. Federalism *promotes competition among the subunits of the federal state.* Several observers (see for example Moser 1991) stress the need to better exploit the potential for competition offered by federalism. In their view, fiscal competition among cantons is beneficial for the economy because such competition makes it possible to attract new companies and to offer more favourable conditions for emerging businesses. According to Scharpf (1994: 56f.), fiscal competition

Table 3.2 *Pride and importance of federalism for the future of Switzerland*

Pride	%	(n)	Importance	%	(n)
very proud	22.7	(197)	very important	31.5	(273)
quite proud	46.7	(404)	quite important	45.5	(394)
not very proud	21.7	(188)	not very important	17.8	(154)
not proud at all	4.2	(36)	not important at all	2.7	(23)
don't know	4.7	(41)	don't know	2.5	(22)
Total	100.0	(866)	Total	100.0	(866)

Source: Eurobarometer in Switzerland Survey (2001). The data have been reduced to Swiss citizens who are 18 years old or older.

between the regions in the European Union is increasing. However, he also points out that the Swiss cantons can compete efficiently at the international level only if they have a minimal size. Furthermore, fiscal competition between cantons can lead to unwanted effects and even a ruinous 'race to the bottom' in the fiscal domain (Scharpf 1988: 245).

3.6 Conclusion: reforming Swiss federalism

As with neutrality, federalism is an institution dear to the Swiss. Recent survey results show that over two-thirds (69.4 per cent) of the Swiss electorate is either very proud or quite proud of federalism (table 3.2). Moreover, with regard to the prospective evaluation of this institution, a large majority (77 per cent) of the Swiss electorate believe that federalism is very important or quite important for the future of the country. But as with neutrality, the current institutions of federalism and their functioning have come under pressure, despite marked institutional attachment. Both external and internal developments challenge Swiss federalism and its prospects for becoming and remaining a modern form of government.

The pressure of internationalization does not affect the *principle* of Swiss federalism. Switzerland's ever-increasing linkages with the EU do not fundamentally interfere with the functioning of federalism. Furthermore, many observers, in addition to the federal government itself (Federal Council 1999a: 319ff.), argue that Swiss federalism would not be weakened if Switzerland were to join the EU. Indeed, other

Table 3.3 *Attachment to the canton*

	%	(n)
strongly attached	33.9	(294)
quite attached	41.9	(363)
not very attached	20.0	(173)
not at all attached	3.9	(34)
don't know	0.2	(2)
Total	100.0	(866)

Source: Eurobarometer in Switzerland Survey (2001). The data have been reduced to Swiss citizens who are 18 years old or older.

federal states belonging to the EU, such as Austria and, in particular, Belgium and Germany (who were both founding members of the Community), have demonstrated that there is no particular conflict between EU membership and the maintenance of a federalist system. On the contrary, as Scharpf (1994) points out, the German *Länder* actually benefit from the introduction of a supranational layer of government, and the greater overall importance of regions resulting from the integration process has been pointed out by Mayntz (1989). Nevertheless, Germann (1994) believes that Swiss federalism would have to be restructured and 're-dimensioned' if Switzerland joined the EU.

Needless to say, re-dimensioning the cantons through the creation of larger entities or 'regions' is nearly impossible in Switzerland, above all because territorial changes must be submitted to the referendum process. The Swiss electorate's attachment to the cantons is still quite strong: three out of four citizens are either strongly or quite attached to their canton (table 3.3). The most recent attempt to change the cantonal landscape was launched by two popular initiatives in the cantons of Geneva and Vaud. The initiative called for a merging of the two cantons, essentially for administrative and financial efficiency reasons. On 2 June 2002, large majorities of voters in both the canton of Geneva (80 per cent) and the canton of Vaud (77 per cent) rejected these initiatives. Earlier attempts to merge cantons, e.g. Basle-City and Basle-Country, were also consistently rejected at the polls.

Despite the reluctance of the electorate to change the territorial boundaries of the cantons, the merging of *communes* has become frequent over the past decade, as a result of which the number of communes in Switzerland has been significantly reduced (Federal Council 2001: 2312). Conscious that such communal regroupings are not sufficient for 'modernizing' Swiss federalism, the Federal Council launched a vast reform project in the early 1990s. This project is characterized by three principal aims. First, a reform of fiscal equalization mechanisms is envisaged in order to mitigate the current financial distortion among the cantons. Second, the project aims at disentangling the tasks and responsibilities between the federal and cantonal levels of government. Third, new forms of vertical and horizontal cooperation and financial mechanisms are proposed (Federal Council 2001: 2314). The overall outcome of this package, which arguably constitutes the most ambitious and drastic reform proposal in current Swiss politics, is still uncertain. Nonetheless, its principles were recently accepted by both the people (64 per cent) and the cantons (i.e. 23 cantons out of 26) in a referendum vote on 28 November 2004. The transformation of these principles into federal laws will take time and may be further delayed by possible referendums. Despite the uncertainty about the final success of this reform, the first and probably most important step has been taken with the acceptance of the constitutional amendments. The success of this first step shows that Swiss federalism can be reformed in spite of direct democracy in general and the mechanism of the double majority in particular.

4 | *Direct democracy*

4.1 The institutions of direct democracy

This chapter deals with the third and in many ways most crucial institution of the Swiss political system: direct democracy. The instruments of direct democracy are not exclusive to the Swiss, in fact an ever growing number of democratic regimes use the referendum device and forms of popular initiatives (Butler and Ranney 1994; Gallagher and Uleri 1996; Budge 1996; Mendelsohn and Parkin 2001). However, nowhere are these more developed than in Switzerland. A comparative glimpse at the (numeric) importance of direct democracy at the national level reveals that Switzerland comes first among all 47 Council of Europe member states (Schmitter and Trechsel 2004: 80). Between 1960 and 2003, a total of 321 referendums were held at the national level in Switzerland. This exceeds by a factor of six the total of those coming second and third on this list, i.e. Liechtenstein (58 referendums) and Italy (57). Also, and unlike anywhere else, the Swiss institutions of direct democracy embody a truly system-formative device, greatly impacting on party competition, government, Parliament, the legislative process and policy making at all levels of the federal state.

Well before the creation of the federal state in 1848, various forms of direct-democratic institutions existed at the cantonal and municipal levels. Although early forms of local democracy go back as far as the twelfth century, it was primarily through the reception of ideas stemming from the French Revolution that direct democracy was extended, modernized and institutionalized at the cantonal level (Kölz 1992). Its transfer to the federal level took place gradually, although most of the fundamental instruments were in place by the end of the nineteenth century.[1]

---

[1] In the following we base ourselves on the contribution by Trechsel and Kriesi (1996) who present the institutions of direct democracy in chronological order (table 4.1).

Table 4.1 *Swiss federal institutions of direct democracy*

Institution	Date of introduction	Promoter	Nature of the object of the vote	Majority required
Mandatory constitutional referendum	1848	–	constitutional amendment	double
Mandatory constitutional referendum on the principle of a total revision of the Constitution	1848	–	question of principle	simple
Popular initiative for a total revision of the Constitution	1848	100,000 electors	question of principle	simple
Optional legislative referendum	1874	50,000 electors or eight cantons	federal law	simple
Popular initiative for a partial revision of the Constitution (precisely formulated)	1891	100,000 electors	Constitution	double
Popular initiative for a partial revision of the Constitution (formulated in general terms)	1891	100,000 electors	question of principle	simple
Counterproposal to a popular initiative for a partial revision of the Constitution (precisely formulated)	1891	–	constitutional amendment	double

Optional referendum for international treaties	1921 (extended in 1977)	50,000 electors or eight cantons	international treaty	simple
Mandatory referendum for unconstitutional, 'urgent' laws applicable for more than one year	1949	–	urgent law	double
Optional referendum for constitutional, 'urgent' laws applicable for more than one year	1949	50,000 electors or eight cantons	urgent law	simple
Mandatory referendum for certain international treaties	1977	–	international treaty	double
Popular 'general initiative'	2003	100,000 electors	Constitution or law	simple
Counterproposal to a 'general initiative' framed by Parliament as an amendment to the Constitution	2003	–	Constitution	double
Counterproposal to a 'general initiative' framed by Parliament as a law	2003	–	federal law	simple

Note: all federal forms of direct democracy are binding, not consultative. A simple majority denotes that a proposal needs to receive only a majority of votes cast; a double majority denotes that both a majority of the votes cast and a majority in at least half of the cantons are needed. Also note that at the time of writing, the amendments to the Federal Constitution adopted in 2003 by the people and the cantons concerning the newly created 'general initiative' and its forms of counterproposal have not yet been enforced.

The Constitution of 1848 already contained the mandatory referendum for constitutional amendments,[2] which submits any amendment of the Constitution to the approval of a double majority of both the people and the cantons. The requirement of a double majority is a direct consequence of the country's federal structure and was initially designed as a safeguard against the 'tyranny of the majority' by the most populated cantons. As we have seen in chapter 3, this increasingly creates tensions between the democratic and the federal principles: the growing asymmetry in population within the cantons gives a powerful power of veto of a relatively small proportion of the people. The Constitution of 1848 also contained a very limited version of the popular initiative, whereby a fraction of the electorate – 50,000, now 100,000 electors – can simply demand a vote on the principle of a total revision of the Constitution.[3] Such a vote only requires a simple majority of the people to pass, as agreement with the principle does not, in itself, alter the Constitution.

In 1874, the Constitution was – for the first time – totally revised. One of the most significant changes made was in the realm of popular rights, with the introduction of an optional legislative referendum. The introduction of the optional referendum was a consequence of a broad democratization movement at the cantonal level that had led to the consecration of this instrument in a number of cantons during the 1860s (Linder 2007: 102f.; for a detailed account, see Kölz 2004: 614ff.). Also, the optional referendum was seen as a compensatory mechanism for the centralization of competences contained in the Federal Constitution of 1874 (Auer *et al.* 2006: 265). The holding of a referendum on any change to federal legislation can be requested by 50,000 voters[4] or eight cantons within a period of 100 days[5] after the publication of the law. Such a referendum only requires a popular majority for the modified law to be subsequently enforced.

The institutions of direct democracy were greatly extended in 1891 with the introduction of a popular initiative for the partial revision of the Constitution. Such initiatives can take the form either of a fully

---

[2] Article 140 Federal Constitution.
[3] Article 138 Federal Constitution. Such a vote also has to take place if a procedure to totally revise the Constitution is supported by one chamber of the Federal Parliament while refused by the other (article 140c Federal Constitution).
[4] Until 1977, the required number of signatures was 30,000.
[5] Until 1996, the period for collecting the necessary signatures was ninety days.

formulated proposal or, alternatively, of a proposal that simply states a
general goal of changing the Constitution.[6] Both forms require 100,000
signatures to be gathered within a period of eighteen months.[7] Parliament then examines the validity of the initiative, decides on its political
desirability (issues a recommendation to accept or reject the text), and
must submit it to the vote of the entire electorate. The parliamentary
review process only takes into account a very limited number of mainly
formal requirements for the validity of an initiative. Hence, the invali-
dation of a popular initiative is extremely rare. The Federal Parliament
may, however, formulate a counterproposal to the initiative (unless it is
formulated in general terms), in which case the electorate must choose
between the adoption of either one of the two proposals or the *status
quo*. As noted above, since formulated initiatives and counterproposals
aim at a partial revision of the Constitution, a double majority must be
attained for their adoption. In the case of an initiative that simply states
a certain aim, Parliament can either accept or reject it. In the first case,
the Federal Parliament elaborates a constitutional amendment which
translates the aims of the initiative and which must be submitted to
the verdict of the electorate and the cantons. In the second case, the
popular initiative is submitted to a popular vote and, provided that
it is supported by a simple majority of the people, the proposal must
be implemented by Parliament in a concrete constitutional amendment
(which, consequently, must be submitted to the approval of both the
people and the cantons).

As mentioned earlier, by the end of the nineteenth century, all major
forms of direct-democratic instruments – the mandatory and optional
referendum, the popular initiative and the counterproposal – were in
place. Subsequent modification of the institutional landscape merely
extended these instruments. A first extension of the optional referendum was adopted in 1921 when international treaties of unlimited
duration were included in the set of legal acts to be submitted to the
referendum process.[8] Since 1977, the optional referendum has also
applied to international treaties that cannot be revoked or that cause
a multilateral legal harmonization. At the same time, a majority in
Parliament obtained the right to submit any other international treaty

---

[6] Article 139 Federal Constitution.
[7] Until 1977, the required number of signatures was 50,000 and no
signature-gathering period was prescribed.
[8] Article 141 Federal Constitution.

to the optional referendum process. In 2003, this latter provision was abolished and replaced by a provision stating that 'any international treaty containing important legal provisions or causing the elaboration of federal laws' must be submitted to the process of the optional referendum. Moreover, since 1977, joining an international organization of collective security, such as NATO, or a supranational community, such as the EU, has been subject to approval by a double majority in a mandatory referendum.[9]

As Linder (2007: 105) notes, since 1874, the optional referendum has been able to severely delay the enactment of certain federal laws. This led the federal government, especially during the economic crisis of the 1930s, to abusively apply the 'urgency clause', whereby federal legislation could bypass the referendum procedure. In 1949, thanks to a popular initiative, the initial potency of the referendum device was restored. From this point on, mandatory referendums have had to be held on any urgent law that is not in conformity with the Constitution and whose validity exceeds one year. If the urgent law is in conformity with the Constitution but is intended to remain in force for more than one year, then it has to be submitted to the optional referendum procedure.

In 2003, the institutions of direct democracy underwent limited reform. Besides cosmetic changes in the sphere of treaty referendums (see above), the constitutional amendment of 2003 introduced a novel form of popular initiative, the so called 'general initiative'. Its logic is the same as that of the non-formulated popular initiative for a partial revision of the Constitution. What is new, however, is the fact that now Parliament may also formulate the goals of the initiative in a simple law (unless the goals of the initiative *de facto* require the amendment of the Constitution). The law is then submitted to a popular vote requiring a simple majority. Another novelty is the fact that if the Federal Parliament agrees with the principles of the general initiative, it can not only frame the latter but even oppose a counterproposal (functionally an alternative proposal). In this case, both proposals are submitted to the vote.

These most recent changes confirm the general pattern of incremental extensions of direct democratic mechanisms at the federal level, based on earlier experiences at the cantonal level: the 'general initiative' first appeared in the Constitution of the canton of Jura in 1978 before it spread to several other cantons during the 1980s and 1990s (Trechsel

---

[9] Article 140 Federal Constitution.

and Serdült 1999: 72f.). Note however that for reasons of complexity the Federal Parliament decided, in 2007, not to implement the 2003 institutional change. A proposal for reverting to the constitutional status quo ante is currently (2008) pending in Parliament. Generally, direct-democratic institutions in the cantons are much more developed than those at the federal level. For instance, cantonal electorates have extensive rights to decide upon purely administrative matters and above all upon the levels and attribution of public revenues and expenditures. Besides its complexity, the institutional landscape at the cantonal level is marked by strong dynamics, caused by frequent adaptations and innovations in the realm of the referendum and initiative devices (see Trechsel and Serdült 1999). The direction these dynamics have taken over the past three decades shows, *inter alia*, a general trend away from mandatory referendums towards more optional and even Parliament-initiated types of referendums. It is worth noting that in general, direct democracy is more fully developed (and used) in the German-speaking Swiss cantons, with the French-speaking cantons relying on a stronger tradition of representative democracy (Trechsel 2000).

At the communal level, the institutions of direct democracy are also well developed. Overall, however, they tend to be slightly less varied at the local level than at the cantonal level (Bützer and Micotti 2003: 22; Bützer 2007a). Historically, the consolidation of direct-democratic institutions at the communal level set in rather late compared to the cantonal and federal levels. Also, the municipalities' scope for changing their institutions is in many cases rather limited (above all in the French speaking cantons), due to constraining legislation at the cantonal level (Bützer 2005, 2007a, 2007b).

The trend of a gradual extension of direct democracy at the federal level was never reversed. However, several attempts aimed at deepening or accelerating this trend failed, such as the two proposals to introduce (in 1872) or extend (in 1961) the popular initiative's scope to federal laws, the proposal for introducing a referendum on hydraulic concessions (1956), on bonds (1956), on nuclear armament (1963), on highway construction (1978), on the construction of nuclear plants (1987) and on the opening of accession negotiations with the European Union (1997). Most recently, in 2000, the proposal for introducing a 'constructive referendum' – a procedure somewhat similar to a 'popular counterproposal' to a law elaborated by Parliament – was rejected by two-thirds of voters and all the cantons.

4.2 The logic and use of referendums and popular initiatives

Like no other political institution, direct democracy opens up the political system while greatly reducing the autonomy of the state vis-à-vis society. It also introduces, as we will further see in chapter 8, a certain measure of *unpredictability* into the decision-making process, giving the electorate the last word over federal policy making. It is important to note that this unpredictability varies according to the instrument under consideration. Swiss direct democracy's fundamental instruments – the referendum and the popular initiative – follow different logics, exhibit dissimilar usage and produce different effects.

The *referendum* intervenes at the *end* of the decision-making process, or at least at the end of the direct-democratic stage in this process. Above all it serves a *veto* function, allowing a majority of the people and/or the cantons to block policy proposed by the Federal Parliament.

Table 4.2 shows that between 1848 and 2007, 543 popular votes were held at the federal level. Four out of every ten votes (221) were mandatory referendums, of which over two-thirds were accepted by the people and the cantons. It should be noted that the success rate of mandatory referendums fluctuated across time. Between the birth of the federal state and the introduction of the optional referendum in 1874, all but two[10] proposals were rejected. This radically changed when the Catholic Conservative opposition started to make use of the optional referendum instead of concentrating its efforts on the mandatory referendum to reject federal policies. Subsequently, the success rate of mandatory referendums rose abruptly: since then, roughly three-quarters of all mandatory referendums have been accepted. Nevertheless, this also means that the federal government and Parliament cannot count on a guaranteed success when mandatory referendums take place. Indeed, some of the most central reform projects and international agreements were rejected by the people and the cantons. For example, as mentioned in chapter 3, the development and consolidation of the welfare state in Switzerland was significantly delayed by the constitutional referendum. The same happened to essential steps for democratization, such as women's suffrage, which was not introduced at the federal level until 1971 (Linder 2007: 110).

---

[10] The two exceptions were the adoption of the Federal Constitution in 1848 and the 1866 bill concerning the rights of Jews and naturalized citizens.

Table 4.2 *The use of direct-democratic institutions from 1848 to 2007*

Period	Total votes			Mandatory referendums			Optional referendums				Popular initiatives				
	Total votes	Accepted	Refused	Total votes	Accepted	Refused	Submitted	Total votes	Accepted	Refused	Valid	Withdrawn	Total votes	Accepted	Refused
1848–1873	11	2	9	11	2	9	–	–	–	–	–	–	–	–	–
1874–1880	11	5	6	3	2	1	63	8	3	5	–	–	–	–	–
1881–1890	12	5	7	4	3	1	75	8	2	6	–	–	–	–	–
1891–1900	24	10	14	9	6	3	74	10	3	7	5	0	5	1	4
1901–1910	12	8	4	5	4	1	59	4	3	1	4	1	3	1	2
1911–1920	15	12	3	9	8	1	57	3	2	1	9	0	3	2	1
1921–1930	28	11	17	10	8	2	94	5	1	4	8	1	13	2	11
1931–1940	23	10	13	8	8	0	73	9	2	7	21	5	6	0	6
1941–1950	21	9	12	7	4	3	104	7	4	3	11	8	7	1	6
1951–1960	42	18	24	22	14	8	205	11	4	7	23	12	9	0	9
1961–1970	29	16	13	14	12	2	213	8	4	4	16	8	7	0	7
1971–1980	87	47	40	47	36	11	278	18	11	7	40	11	22	0	22
1981–1990	66	27	39	25	18	7	259	12	6	6	45	14	29	3	26
1991–2000	106	55	51	36	28	8	504	36	25	11	54	11	34	2	32
2001–2007	56	26	30	11	6	5	312	21	17	4	18	7	24	3	21
Total	543	261	282	221	159	62	2,370	160	87	73	254	78	162	15	147

Sources: Federal Chancellery (Berne), c2d (University of Geneva) as well as own calculations (25 June 2007).

With regard to the optional referendum, table 4.2 shows that of the 2,370 bills that were submitted to the optional referendum process, less than 7 per cent (160) led to a popular vote following a successful signature-gathering process.[11] Also, on average, less than every second bill was rejected at the polls. These numbers give the impression that the optional referendum produces only marginal effects. Neidhart (1970), however, contends that the most considerable effects are of an *indirect* nature. According to Neidhart's famous hypothesis, the optional referendum hangs like a sword of Damocles over the whole legislative process, potentially ruining entire bills. Consequently, institutional mechanisms have developed, both formally and informally, to reduce this risk, transforming Swiss democracy into a *negotiation democracy*. Negotiations take place in informal arenas at the beginning of a legislative decision-making process (chapter 8) where political actors that may credibly threaten this process with the referendum device are invited to negotiate a pre-parliamentary compromise. The aim of this is, of course, to find a sufficiently strong compromise, allowing the future bill to be enacted as law without a popular vote.[12] Empirical studies have been able to show the effectiveness of a large parliamentary consensus: the higher this consensus, the lower the probability of a referendum (chapter 8). The consensus-seeking mechanisms that have been found over time clearly open up the political system: any actor that can credibly launch a referendum is invited to negotiate the bill during the pre-parliamentary stages of the decision-making process. Herein arguably resides the most important effect of the referendum device: it leads, along with federalism, to the establishment of 'concordance' or 'consensus democracy' (Linder 2007: 113) in which governing is carried out 'under the shadow of the referendum' (Papadopoulos 2005).

The optional referendum predominantly served as an instrument of conservative right-wing organizations. From a rational perspective, it is strategically sound for these actors to fight changes to the *status quo*, which is preserved if the referendum succeeds. Kriesi and Wisler (1996) confirm this assumption for the period from 1945–78. However, their data for the period from 1979–89 show a different picture: here, the

---

[11] As Sciarini and Trechsel (1996: 212) show, this proportion remained surprisingly stable (see chapter 8).

[12] As we will see in chapter 5, the optional referendum even accounts (partly) for the partisan composition of the federal government.

political left used the referendum more frequently than right-wing organizations. This state of affairs is above all due to Parliament's tendency to avoid far-reaching reforms, opting instead for minimal changes. If these minor reforms pass, then a new, more profound reform proposal becomes unlikely for a long period. Also, certain reform projects adopted by Parliament may represent a 'step backwards' from the point of view of left-wing organizations, leading to a situation in which the probability that they will launch a referendum is high.

In contrast to the referendum, *popular initiatives* generally occur at the *beginning*[13] of the decision-making process. Through the launching of initiatives, societal actors can put issues on the political agenda that the government and Parliament fail to politicize. Additionally – if put on the ballot – the initiative obliges the entire electorate to take a binding decision at the polls. In this sense, the Swiss initiative device indeed opens up the political process. Even so, the system-opening function of the popular initiative should not be overestimated. Table 4.2 shows that popular initiatives rarely result in *direct* successes at the polls. Despite the dramatic rise in the usage of this instrument since the beginning of the 1970s – though only in absolute, not relative terms – when compared to the two forms of referendums, only 15 (i.e. 9 per cent) of the 162 initiatives on which the electorate has had to decide have so far been accepted by both the people and the cantons. On the other hand, the direct success of initiatives varies over time. The success rate of initiatives was relatively high in the late nineteenth and early twentieth centuries, followed by a sharp decline. Between 1928 and 1982, only a single initiative was accepted at the polls. During the past twenty-five years, the success rate of initiatives has sharply increased and half of all successful initiatives (i.e. 8 out of 15) have been accepted (chapter 8). Traditionally, the popular initiative was predominantly used by the political left. In the past, right-wing and extreme right-wing organizations only rarely made use of the initiative, generally without great success. This has changed since the 1990s, as the ascent of the Swiss People's Party (chapter 6) was

---

[13] Note that popular initiatives can also fulfil the function of a 'supplementary' or 'secondary' referendum, i.e. they can be launched once a decision-making process (including a referendum vote) has failed to go in the direction desired by the initiators. It follows that initiatives may be formulated at the very end of a political decision-making process, fulfilling a reactive rather than an initiating function.

accompanied – and arguably aided – by the launching of numerous popular initiatives at all levels of the federal state.

Despite their relatively feeble chances at the polls, initiatives produce a number of *indirect* effects. These effects are two-fold, as they may not only impact on the political process and legislative output, but also have a 'boomerang-effect' on the initiators. Regarding the first dimension, we can distinguish three types of indirect effects. First, initiatives may encourage Parliament to elaborate a *counterproposal*. With a success rate of over 60 per cent, counterproposals constitute an effective instrument to take the wind out of the sails of a (usually) more radical initiative. It should be noted, however, that both the frequency and success rate of counterproposals have clearly decreased over the past two decades due to a change in the actual voting procedure.[14] Second, unsuccessful initiatives may produce what Linder (1999: 260) calls a 'flywheel effect': roughly one-third of all initiatives leave some trace in later legislation. Third, initiatives may play a 'canvassing' role (Linder 1990: 261). Initiatives may be launched as a means to pursue a 'permanent election campaign', independently of electoral cycles. In addition, they may be deliberately launched immediately preceding elections as a pure campaign tool.

Regarding the indirect effects of initiatives on the initiators Epple-Gass (1988) shows that the latter are exposed to three types of restraints. First, an initiative may only touch upon a single topic, therefore restraining the initiators in their political programmes. Second, the launching of an initiative is resource-intensive and thus has a tendency to restrain initiators in their action repertoire. Engaging in the adventure of an initiative usually leads to a concentration of the initiator's political action where even more radical forces within the movement or party need to comply. Also, initiators may become 'addicted' to this type of instrument, seduced into successive launchings of initiatives. Third, initiatives may generate centralizing and bureaucratizing effects on the organizational structure of the initiative committee. Facing limited resources, initiators are forced to organize themselves effectively, usually concentrating and coordinating in a vertically integrated way.

---

[14] Until 1987, a simultaneous vote on an initiative and its counterproposal prohibited voters from accepting both texts. Since then, voters have been able to accept both proposals while expressing their preference in a subsidiary question should both texts be accepted.

To sum up, let us emphasize the impressive increase in the overall use of direct-democratic instruments (table 4.2). The majority of all popular votes at the federal level occurred over the last three decades. The increasing popularity of referendums and initiatives can largely be attributed to the growing complexity of modern politics. With most direct-democratic institutions dating back to the nineteenth century, nowadays they face novel issues such as globalization, new forms of energy, environmental protection, technological developments, etc., all of which require legislative action. The resulting increase in legislative action positively affects the probability of direct-democratic decision making.

4.3 Voting in direct-democratic processes

Debates about direct democracy's potential for enhancing the democratic legitimacy of political decisions have preoccupied political theorists for decades (Trechsel 2006). Furthermore, direct democracy continues to be promoted by some and rejected by others for reasons related to the ability of citizens, rather than their representatives, to take such decisions. The assessment of the electors' competence is therefore at the epicentre of most theoretical and empirical studies on direct-democratic votes. In Switzerland, political science offers contradictory results. Earlier studies based on survey data found rather disillusioning levels of voter competence within the electorate (Gruner and Hertig 1983): only one out of six voters could be qualified as 'competent'. Recent studies are more optimistic (Kriesi 1993; Bütschi 1993), showing that nearly half of all survey respondents could be considered to possess a satisfactory degree of voter competence. Using the same dataset as Bütschi but limiting the sample to actual voters, Trechsel (2006) finds the inverse of Gruner and Hertig's results: based on these data, only one out of six actual voters can be said to be incompetent. Despite these large differences, there is an agreement regarding the main factors influencing voter competence: on the one hand, the level of education, and on the other, the complexity of the bill. The more educated the voter, and the more familiar the bill, the greater the likelihood that higher levels of competence will be attained. Also, if a voter feels directly affected by the bill, his or her level of competence will rise even though the issue under consideration can be qualified as complex. In addition, voter competence positively correlates with the voter's degree of general interest in politics, trust in political institutions, social integration and socio-economic status.

While voter competence plays an important role in the assessment of direct democracy, so does turnout in referendums. In comparative politics, Switzerland is often presented as an outlier due to its infamously low level of electoral turnout (Franklin 2004: 92ff.). The same applies to participation in direct democracy where average turnout levels currently vary between 45 and 55 per cent. Just as often, a connection is made between low turnout levels and the high frequency of referendum votes. However, this alleged relationship is imperfect, since, despite the fact that the number of referendums continues to climb, turnout levels have discontinued their downward trend and even rebounded. Recent studies show that the factor 'knowledge of the content of the bill' has the greatest power in explaining political participation at the polls (Kriesi 1993, 2005). If the voter is informed about a proposition, he or she is more likely to participate, with less informed – and hence less competent – voters tending to abstain. Furthermore, Mottier (1993), Marques de Bastos (1993) and Caramani (1993) demonstrate that participating in referendum votes is highly *selective*. The majority of voters only occasionally participate, with small minorities either always voting or predominantly abstaining. These studies show that the selectivity of participation depends above all on the expected effects of the bill, as well as the voter's personal interest in it.

Finally, the factors determining the voters' *choice* at the ballot box are extremely complex. A broad range of variables is potentially relevant, such as social, economic and political cleavages, campaign effects, the media, government and party recommendations, the degree of political consensus within the elite, and the nature of the bill. Regarding cleavages, ever since the groundbreaking work by Rokkan in the 1960s (Lipset and Rokkan 1967; Rokkan 1970), this field has become one of the classical paradigms of electoral research. Several studies attempted to unravel the 'structural cleavages' determining referendum votes in Switzerland. Sardi and Widmer (1993) found that traditional cleavages such as 'class', 'religion', 'language' and 'gender' had only a minimal impact on voting behaviour. A closer look at individual ballots reveals that the effect of some cleavages varies across issue areas. For example, analyses of the vote on the European Economic Area (EEA) have shown a clear predominance of the linguistic cleavage (Kriesi *et al.*

1993). Overall, however, the linguistic cleavage tends to lose some of its impact on direct-democratic choice (Kriesi *et al.* 1996), although the French- and Italian-speaking parts of Switzerland find themselves more often on the losing side in absolute terms. Other votes, such as that on the abolition of the army, were dominated by the urban–rural cleavage (Nef 1989). Finally, several studies have shown that the results of certain ballots were influenced by the openness–closure cleavage. According to Christin *et al.* (2002: 259), this cleavage has an impact in particular on issues related to foreign policy, immigration policy, asylum policy, institutional reforms and, to a lesser degree, on issues related to labour conditions. For these authors, it seems that the influence of cleavages varies from case to case, or at least from issue area to issue area, without following a general pattern. Thus, it is plausible that a given cleavage may have a decisive impact on one vote only to prove entirely irrelevant in the next, held a few months later (Trechsel and Kriesi 1996: 201).

Besides traditional and newer cleavages, other factors have an impact on the voters' political choice in direct-democratic decision processes. Passy (1993: 225) found that the citizens' level of competence is correlated with the direction of their vote. Indeed, a majority of 'incompetent' voters simply abstain from voting, through a mechanism of 'self-censorship' (Kriesi 1998a: 127). However, 'incompetent' voters who do participate often adopt a conservative, *status quo*-oriented stance. This finding is not as dramatic as it looks, as Passy could show that a *systematic* rejection of public policies (deviating from the *status quo*) does not occur: there was only one case (out of 61 under consideration) in which the outcome would have been different had incompetent voters not participated.

During referendum campaigns, voters are exposed to numerous messages from elites and fellow citizens. Initial investigations by Hertig (1982) came to the conclusion that campaigning effects may be of such importance that a popular verdict could be 'bought'. However, more recent studies warn against such a conclusion and emphasize that the issue remains unresolved at best (Linder 1990; Longchamp 1991; Papadopoulos 1994a). Kriesi (2005), drawing on a vast set of recent data, comes to the conclusion that the government camp is usually able to pursue a winning strategy by outspending the promoters of a popular initiative. However, the inverse is not true. Even if the promoters of a popular initiative are able to outspend the government's camp, their chances of success are rather poor. This finding confirms research on popular initiatives in the American context, where it could be shown that it was easier to 'buy' a 'no' to an initiative than to buy a 'yes' (Gerber 1999). With regard to referendums, Kriesi (2005) shows that the relationship between campaign investments and outcomes at the polls depends on the fragmentation of the political right and the campaign intensity. If the fragmentation of the right is high, if the balance of the campaign tips against the government and if the campaign becomes intense, then the camp that outspends the other is more likely to win the popular vote. However, Kriesi's overall assessment is that the direction of the campaign and the outcome of popular votes are not as strong as has often been maintained.

Most research supports the overall importance of voting campaigns for the process of public opinion formation. Trechsel and Sciarini (1998) have shown that four out of five actual voters make use of the print media, 75 per cent rely on television, 60 per cent on radio broadcasting and 59 per cent on the brochures issued by the federal government prior to a vote as sources of information. Actual voters also consult on average more than four sources of information, which is consistently more than the number of sources consulted by abstainers. This finding does not contradict the aforementioned difference in competence between participating voters on the one hand and non-voters on the other. Since participating voters are generally more competent than non-participants, it is not surprising that the former make use of a broader range of information sources.

Furthermore, according to Trechsel and Sciarini (1998), more than half of the voters declare that either no source of information, or else the point of view of *ad hoc* groupings, churches, or interest groups, which only occasionally take part in voting campaigns, had an impact on their voting behaviour. One-fifth of the voters consider themselves entirely independent of all opinions and recommendations voiced in the public arena. By contrast, one out of seven voters claims to be most influenced by the position of the Swiss government. On the whole, political parties perform rather poorly. Their recommendations are taken into account by even fewer voters than those of the government. Employer organizations and labour unions, as well as trade and farmers' associations, do worse still; their influence can be described as marginal.

The most recent study of voter competence, campaign effects and political behaviour at the polls comes to the conclusion that neither the pessimistic theoreticians nor the participationist theorists of direct democracy have drawn fully accurate conclusions. Using a large dataset combining aggregate and individual level data for 150 popular votes, Kriesi (2005) shows that a more objective assessment of the situation lies somewhere between these extremes. His 'realist theory of direct democracy' begins from the critics' premises that (a) political elites constitute the driving force in public opinion formation and (b) that citizens are politically uninterested and uninformed. However, Kriesi shows that, despite these initial conditions, citizens are able to efficiently make direct-democratic choices at the polls. They do so by using four different types of *simplifying strategies* or *cognitive shortcuts*. First, the most obvious strategy is simply to abstain. Kriesi's results confirm the previously mentioned studies on competence and participation: the higher the voter's competence, the higher his or her probability of showing up at the polls. For those who participate, a second strategy consists of a 'heuristic of the *status quo*' and Kriesi's results show that the level of information of a voter and his or her openness to policy change are indeed positively correlated. Alternatively, voters may choose a third strategy of simplification: they may trust the government's recommendations and vote accordingly. Again, Kriesi empirically shows the existence of such a strategy among voters. Finally, relying on the most important strategy of simplification, voters choose to follow the recommendations of the political elites, such as parties, interest associations and social movements. When using this strategy, voters will rely on the recommendations formulated by the political actors to whom they feel closest. The impact of these recommendations on voting behaviour varies quite significantly according to the different forms of coalitions that characterize the campaign preceding the vote as well as according to the type of direct-democratic institution used (chapter 8). In addition, Kriesi shows that a complex interaction exists between the various forms of heuristic cues and shortcuts used by voters. His realist theory of direct democracy, while completing the set of 'broken promises' of direct democracy (Papadopoulos 1998: 161– 89), does not confirm the most pessimistic assumptions brought forward by theoreticians of (direct) democracy such as Schumpeter (1947), Bobbio (1987) and Sartori (1987). The recommendations of the political elites have a non-negligible impact on the voters' choice at the polls, but elites are unable to completely control the overall outcome of a vote. The uncertainty referred to above, despite being reduced by the various strategies of simplification, still persists.

Table 4.3 *Pride and importance of direct democracy for the future of Switzerland*

Pride	%	(n)	Importance	%	(n)
very proud	44.1	(382)	very important	60.4	(523)
quite proud	45.7	(396)	quite important	33.3	(288)
not very proud	6.1	(53)	not very important	4.5	(39)
not proud at all	2.0	(17)	not important at all	0.9	(8)
don't know	2.1	(18)	don't know	0.9	(8)
Total	100.0	(866)	Total	100.0	(866)

Source: Eurobarometer in Switzerland Survey (2001). The data has been reduced to Swiss citizens who are 18 years old or older.

4.4 Conclusion

Direct democracy is in many ways the most crucial political institution in Switzerland, exerting a profound impact on its political system. It fundamentally differentiates the Swiss political system from other democratic polities. This uniqueness is not so much due to the existence of direct democracy *per se* – as we have seen, referendums and initiatives exist elsewhere – but rather to its longstanding history at all levels of the federal state, its broad institutional development, its frequent use and, as a consequence, its truly system-transformative effects. As noted above, the establishment of Swiss consensus democracy and its by-products, such as the weak role of parties (chapter 6), the strength of interest associations (chapter 9), the slow but inclusive decision-making process (chapter 8) and the form of Swiss government (chapter 5) are due, to a large extent, to the predominant role of direct-democratic institutions. The political culture in Switzerland, highly participatory in form and based on an almost religious worshipping of the people's empowerment over its representatives, can also primarily be attributed to the referendum and the initiative. Not surprisingly, compared to the other two fundamental institutions discussed in chapters 2 (neutrality) and 3 (federalism), direct democracy inspires the deepest attachment by far among the electorate (table 4.3).

Further investigations reveal that a large majority of Swiss citizens prefer the *status quo* over any form of institutional change related to direct democracy – with a majority of those open to change asking for a further extension of the referendum and the initiative (Trechsel 2004). As we have seen, several extensions of direct democracy have taken place at the federal level, while any attempt to reduce its scope has so far foundered. At the cantonal and municipal levels, direct democracy may be constrained, if only on rare occasions (Trechsel 2000). Also – and this differs fundamentally from direct democracy in the US – interventions by courts are seen as a violation of the (quasi-)sacred people's will. This has become apparent in the aftermath of a recent and highly controversial decision taken by the Federal Court to ban referendums on the naturalization of individual citizens (Helbling and Kriesi 2004; Trechsel 2004).

Today, however, it is not courts, but the internationalization – and in particular Europeanization – of Swiss politics that is seen by a number of observers as constituting the most serious threat to the survival of Swiss-style direct democracy. Needless to say, Switzerland's potential accession to the European Union could not occur without consequences for the referendum and initiative processes. The *principle* of direct democracy would not be threatened by Switzerland's accession to the EU (Tanquerel 1991; Linder 1999; Federal Council 1999a: 327ff.). However, a certain loss in the field of direct legislation would be unavoidable (Jacot-Guillarmod 1990; Epiney *et al.* 1998: 342ff.; Epinay and Siegwart 1998: 137f.). A number of studies have tried to retroactively and counterfactually measure this loss by analysing the EU-compatibility of referendums and initiatives of the past. Only in a small minority of cases (11 to 14 per cent) would a federal referendum have inevitably collided with EU law. For cantonal referendums, a clear conflict would have arisen in only 5 per cent of cases, confirming the *limited losses* to be expected in the realm of direct democracy (see Federal Council 1999a). Although such counterfactual evaluations should be taken for what they are – stimulating proxies at best – we would nevertheless argue that direct democracy would not be fundamentally constrained by EU law if Switzerland acceded to the EU. However, our view is not reflected in public opinion. Christin and Trechsel (2002) have shown that the degree of attachment to direct democracy has a significant impact on citizens' attitudes towards the EU. While objective losses of direct democracy may be limited, the perceived constraining effect of EU membership among the electorate remains significant.

For precisely this reason, a number of observers do not stress the potential constraining effect of EU membership on direct democracy, but rather the inverse: in their view, direct democracy threatens the Swiss political system's ability to open up, to join international organizations and to fully integrate into the EU (Germann 1994). Most recent developments nevertheless de-dramatize such claims: as we have seen in chapter 2, significant steps towards a political opening up of Switzerland (such as UN membership and bilateral agreements with the EU) have successfully made it past the hurdle of popular decision making.

5 | *The Swiss system of government*

5.1 Introduction

This chapter provides an overview of the Swiss system of government and its two branches, the legislative and the executive. We will first present the structure and functioning of the Federal Parliament before having a closer look at the Federal Council, the executive body of the Confederation. This will be followed by a discussion of the relationship between the two and the current problems they are facing. We will conclude this chapter with an assessment of possible options for reforming the Swiss system of government.

5.2 The Federal Parliament

In chapter 3 the reader was provided with the most basic information concerning the set-up of the Federal Parliament. In this chapter we go further and present a more detailed picture of the Swiss Parliament's structure and role. The Federal Parliament is the highest authority of the Confederation, subject to the rights of the people and the cantons.[1] In academic literature, a classic distinction is made between parliaments of work and parliaments of debate. While the latter could characterize the British House of Commons, where major political decisions are taken following plenary discussions, the Swiss Parliament clearly belongs to the first category: it is a parliament of work; the bulk of work is undertaken within committees, outside the plenary chamber (Linder 1999: 195; Ochsner 1987). Other chief examples of parliaments of work include the US Congress and the European Parliament. According to Lüthi (1987: 88), Swiss MPs spend more than 70 per cent of their time working for parliamentary committees.[2]

---

[1] Article 148.1 Federal Constitution.
[2] Each chamber has 12 identical committees (10 legislative committees and 2 control committees). Committees of the National Council are composed of 25

The Federal Parliament is neither a permanent nor a professional body. In 1848, a very lean parliamentary model was adopted according to which MPs only meet in the plenary assembly for four three-week long sessions per year. Until recently, the majority of MPs were unpaid[3] 'amateur politicians', dedicating most of their time to their main professions. A recent study shows that among parliaments in countries belonging to the Organization for Economic Cooperation and Development (OECD), the Swiss Parliament has the second lowest value of an index of parliamentary professionalism (Z'graggen and Linder 2004: 18). At the same time, as this study reveals, the functioning of the Swiss Parliament is cheap: the annual costs for the Swiss Parliament are the lowest among the OECD countries considered. This model tenaciously survived all major attempts aiming at the establishment of a more permanent and professional parliament, as present in most modern, liberal democracies. Despite the absence of structural changes, MPs became more and more professional over time. According to Riklin and Möckli (1991), MPs dedicate about half of their time to the Federal Parliament. Other political activities take up an additional 10 per cent of their time. The study by Z'graggen and Linder (2004) shows that, today, Swiss MPs spend more time on their parliamentary work than their Austrian, Belgian, Luxembourgish, Norwegian, Portuguese and Spanish counterparts. The Swiss Parliament could therefore be best characterized as 'semi-professional'. One should note, however, that this apparent increase in professionalism (when measured by the time spent by MPs on parliamentary work) stands in sharp contrast to the structural weakness of the parliamentary administration. In the OECD, on average, there are 3.5 collaborators per MP. In Switzerland, this ratio is by far the weakest, as there are only 0.6 collaborators per MP (Z'graggen and Linder 2004: 54). Today, a large majority of MPs clearly favour a structural reinforcement of the administrative, technical and professional

members, while those of the Council of States count 13 members each. In addition, there are a number of special committees, common to both chambers. Three committees are clearly more important than the others: the Foreign Affairs Committee; the Committee for Economic Affairs and Taxation; and the Finance Committee (Kriesi 1998a : 184).

[3] MPs do not receive any salary for their parliamentary work, although they do receive compensation for their expenses.

resources at their disposal (Krüger *et al.* 2001). However, Swiss voters do not desire costly reforms of Parliament: in 1992, they turned down such a proposal. That same day, only the proposal changing the structure of parliamentary committees was approved at the polls. As a consequence, the Federal Assembly as a whole lacks time, information and professional competence and is consistently disadvantaged compared with the government and the federal administration.

Not surprisingly, such a structural weakness renders MPs more dependent on know-how generated by alternative societal and economic structures, ultimately making Parliament more permeable to the influence of interest associations and private interests. Studies have shown that 31 per cent of all MPs actively represent the interests of trade unions, farmers' associations and employers' associations (Kerr 1981). The lobbying efforts of businesses are equally – and increasingly – visible: at the end of the 1980s, MPs on average held approximately six seats on executive boards of private companies (Hug 1989: 85). Another effect of the particular parliamentary structure is the overrepresentation of certain professions among MPs, such as attorneys, businessmen, medical doctors, university professors but also farmers.

Despite this structural weakness, the Federal Parliament fulfils, as do other parliaments, a number of important functions. The *elective function* of the Swiss Parliament is, at first sight, rather strong. Indeed, the Federal Assembly elects the seven members of the Federal Council, the Chancellor and Vice-Chancellor of the Confederation, judges of the Federal Courts and, in times of war, the General of the Army. As Germann (1996: 229) points out, however, the elective function of the Federal Assembly is somewhat 'atrophied' due to the limited political choice it is given when electing the government. Important informal constraints, such as the 'magic formula' (see below) according to which the partisan composition of the government is fixed, as well as the need for linguistic, religious and, to a lesser extent, gender proportionality, leave the Federal Assembly a very limited choice when it comes to the election of members of the government. Very recently, the elective function of the Swiss Parliament has, however, been reinforced. As a result of the important changes in the structure of the party system (chapter 6), the Federal Assembly in 2003 did not re-elect one of the incumbent Federal Councillors. By doing so, it changed the pattern of partisan forces within government, further (though only temporarily[4]) increased the gender gap within the Federal Council and for the first time elected two Federal Councillors from the same canton (i.e. Zurich).

Second, the *recruitment function* of the Federal Assembly is not as strong as in the UK, where (almost) every member of the cabinet is an elected MP, but it is stronger than in the USA, where only a minority of 'ministers' (i.e. members of the President's cabinet) have previously been members of Congress. However, among the twenty-eight Federal Councillors elected since 1970, only four have never held a parliamentary seat at the federal level prior to their election into government.[5] For members of government, previous experience within the Federal Parliament is therefore a quasi-necessary condition for being elected to the Federal Council.

Third, the *legislative function* of the Federal Parliament is weaker than in most other liberal democracies, and this is not only due to the constraints imposed by direct democracy (see chapters 4 and 8). As we shall see in more detail in chapter 8, although both chambers of the Federal Parliament can initiate legislation, their agenda-setting role within the decision-making process strongly decreased during the 1990s (Sciarini *et al.* 2002: 11). Also, according to a study by Kriesi (1980), the political elite consider the parliamentary stage to be less important than earlier stages in the legislative decision-making process. A newer study, however, shows that Parliament increasingly modifies drafts of legislation prepared by the government (Jegher and Linder 1998: 90). In addition, the study shows that the magnitude of these modifications has slightly increased. With one out of two governmental drafts modified by the federal chambers and with these modifications being more sustained, the authors conclude that the traditional view of a weak and destitute Federal Parliament is not appropriate. They agree with Lijphart who, in his international comparison, described the

---

[4] On 14 June 2006, Ruth Leuthard was elected into the Federal Council, replacing Joseph Deiss.

[5] The four exceptions are Ruth Dreifuss, Ruth Metzler-Arnold, Micheline Calmy-Rey and Eveline Widmer-Schlumpf, i.e. four out of only five women that have ever held a mandate within the Federal Council. Thus, while male members of the government have held previous parliamentary mandates at the federal level, their female counterparts are recruited predominantly from the extra-parliamentary arena.

Federal Assembly as the 'second most powerful legislature' (Lijphart 1984: 79).

Fourth, the Federal Parliament exerts a *control function* over the government and its administration. Though MPs elect the government, they lack the possibility to dismiss the latter *in corpore* and Parliament cannot impeach or recall individual members of the Federal Council. Despite this structural lack of control, Parliament has a number of instruments at its disposal allowing it to monitor and, if necessary, sanction the government and the administration. MPs can check on governmental activities by means of questions, interpellations and hearings, or through the intervention of two permanent supervisory committees common to both chambers which specifically control executive, administrative and judicial activities.[6] In exceptionally important and obscure cases on which light needs to be shed, the two chambers can set up a common Parliamentary Commission of Investigation (PCI). So far, such a PCI has only been formed on four occasions,[7] although each time notable weaknesses have been revealed within the system of parliamentary control mechanisms and control processes among the state organs in general.

On the whole, when estimating the importance of Parliament by having a closer look at its various functions, most observers come to the conclusion that the Swiss legislature is very weak. According to traditional views, its elective function has been limited, its recruitment function has been weaker than in parliamentary systems, its legislative function has been severely hampered by both direct democracy and structural limitations, and its control function has been comparatively narrow in scope. Recent contributions nuance this weakness somewhat. In the light of new developments, it can be argued that in the absence of structural reforms, the Federal Assembly has initiated a *process of emancipation*. This process is linked to the profound changes in

---

[6] The Finance Committee supervises the financial management of the federal state, while the Control Committee exerts the 'high supervision' over the activities of the Federal Council, the federal administration, the federal courts and other organs entrusted with tasks of the federal state (Article 169 Federal Constitution).

[7] These PCIs were formed in the context of the scandal of the 'Mirage' fighter planes (1964), the scandal concerning the secret police, its filing methods and the functioning of the Federal Department for Defence (in this case, two PCIs were created: one in 1989 and the second one a year later) and in the context of a scandal surrounding the Federal Pension Fund (1996).

the party system that have occurred since the 1990s (chapter 6), leading to more competitive, polarized and confrontational politics within the Swiss legislature. This manifests itself in narrow parliamentary majorities that have succeeded in departing from informal rules that were set in stone for decades (such as the partisan composition of government), in the choice of the vast majority of Federal Councillors within its own ranks, and in the more frequent and profound amendments by Parliament of governmental proposals. However, this parliamentary emancipation varies across policy fields. In certain areas, the impact of internationalization seriously weakens Parliament while at the same time reinforcing the government (Fischer *et al.* 2002). In other policy fields, such as social policy, Häusermann *et al.* (2004) were able to show that the role of Parliament has become more proactive in the most recent past (chapter 8).

The changing partisan landscape also affects the party discipline of MPs. In the literature, and in comparison to the situation in other liberal democracies, party discipline among Swiss MPs has been presented as 'moderate', injecting uncertainty into the relationship between the government and the Parliament (Papadopoulos 1997: 101). Factors that contribute to the relative intra-partisan fragmentation include the Federal Constitution's provision for MPs to vote without instructions;[8] the overall fragmentation of the party system across levels of government (chapter 6); the possibility for MPs to rely on non-partisan resources for their election; and the political culture within government, allowing Federal Councillors to deviate from their party line for the sake of collegiality. However, more recent trends show that, among the two largest political parties, the Swiss People's Party and the Socialist Party, party discipline has greatly increased.[9] This strengthening of party discipline among the two largest partisan competitors in Parliament does not necessarily reduce the systemic uncertainty in the relationship between the government and Parliament. However, it does strengthen partisan competition within Parliament. With this competition becoming more fervent, the overall attention of the media, the general public and the government to the parliamentary arena increases. Thus, it can be hypothesized that such developments strengthen rather

[8] Article 161.1 Federal Constitution.
[9] See the article 'Die SVP setzt sich rechts von FDP und CVP ab' by Michael Hermann and Heiri Leuthold in the newspaper *Tages-Anzeiger* of 11 October 2003, available at http://sotomo.geo.unizh.ch/papers/parlaKarte.99-03.pdf – accessed on 9 July 2007.

than weaken Parliament's position within the political system. In the light of the foregoing considerations, we would argue that – overall – a process of emancipation of Parliament can be detected. However, it is necessary to add a caveat: this emancipation process started at a very low level of parliamentary power and importance within the Swiss political system. Before one can conclude that Switzerland has a strong parliament, there is still a long way to go.

5.3 The Federal Council

The Federal Constitution of 1848 created a seven-member body, the Federal Council. It is the highest governing and executive authority of the federal state.[10] Its classification into any of the traditional categories of governmental systems is challenging and scholars situate the Swiss case somewhere between the two most common forms of democratic government, the parliamentary and the presidential systems (Lijphart 1999: 119ff.). Unlike the case of parliamentary systems, the legislative body in Switzerland cannot recall the executive and, *vice versa*, the Parliament cannot be dissolved by the Federal Council. Also, unlike the case of a presidential system, the members of the Federal Council are not elected by the people – or by a specifically elected college – but by Parliament. Other observers have therefore come to believe that the Swiss system corresponds to a distinct, third type of government: the directorial system (Lauvaux 1990; Fleiner-Gerster 1987). First put in place in the aftermath of the French Revolution, the *Directoire* lasted for only four years. It was a collegial executive body, elected by Parliament but which, once elected, remained independent from the legislative body. The formal functions of the Federal Council are enumerated in the legislation and include the function of governing the country, participating in the legislative process, leading the federal administration, implementing federal policies and, finally, communicating with and informing the public (Klöti 2007: 147).

The Swiss directorial system is characterized by two constitutional principles, the principle of *non-hierarchy* and the principle of *non-responsibility*. The principle of *non-hierarchy* assigns the same power to each one of the seven members of the Federal Council, with the exception of the President of the Confederation. This presidency, however, is assigned a purely representative and ceremonial function.

---

[10] Article 174 Federal Constitution.

Therefore, among the Federal Councillors, the President is merely a *primus inter pares*. The presidency rotates every year among the members of the Federal Council and entails no further political power. All members of government are confronted by a double task: they have to actively participate in the elaboration of governmental decisions and, at the same time, they must lead one of the seven federal ministries ('departments' in the Swiss nomenclature). These double hats worn by each member of government lead to a fusion of executive powers within the Federal Council, strengthening the latter's position in the political system. The principle of non-hierarchy also expresses itself through the collegial decision making within the Federal Council. Once a decision is taken by the government, every Federal Councillor defends this decision, even if he or she may have initially opposed it.

The second constitutionally embedded principle of the Swiss governmental system, the principle of *non-responsibility*, concerns the independence of the Federal Council with respect to Parliament. As we have seen, all members of government are elected by the Federal Assembly for the duration of an entire legislature, lasting four years. Once in office, however, Parliament has no possibility to recall the Federal Council.

A third specificity of the directorial system of government has emerged over the last decades: the principle of *concordance*. According to this principle, which is not constitutionally founded but derives from purely informal practices, the most important political parties are co-opted into government and remain in the executive on a permanent basis. While such 'oversized cabinets' or 'grand coalitions' containing one or more 'unnecessary parties' (Lijphart 1984: 60) exist elsewhere, the Swiss case represents its most radical and – simultaneously – most stable form. Since 1959, the partisan composition of the Federal Council has remained identical. Four parties, the Liberals, the Christian Democrats, the Social Democrats and the Swiss People's Party, have shared – and still share – executive responsibilities within the Federal Council. On average, these four coalition partners could (numerically) count on the support of 83 per cent of the MPs in the chamber representing the people, the National Council, and this has never fallen below 74 per cent (in 1991). Even the formula according to which the seven governmental seats are distributed among these four parties remained exactly the same between 1959 and 2003: the Liberals, the Christian Democrats and the Social Democrats had two seats each, while the Swiss People's Party was represented by one Federal

Councillor. In the literature, that specific arrangement is referred to as the 'magic formula' – magic, as Parliament did not alter the formula for forty-four years, an exceptional occurrence among modern democracies. It is only in the aftermath of the parliamentary elections of 2003 that one of the incumbent members of government, the Christian Democrat Ruth Metzler, was successfully ousted. Instead of being re-elected, Metzler had to cede her seat to Christoph Blocher, the polarizing figurehead of the Swiss People's Party. With Blocher's election to the Federal Council, a new and politically significant chapter has been written in the governmental set-up of Switzerland (chapter 6).

This partisan heterogeneity did not appear abruptly but rather arose gradually over decades. Indeed, between 1848 and 1891, the federal government was in the firm hands of the winners of the civil war, the Liberals. This movement (later a political party) took over governmental responsibilities, backed by a solid majority in Parliament. Towards the end of the nineteenth century, however, their major competitors, the Catholic Conservatives (later to become the Christian Democrats), opposed the Liberals in the arena of direct democracy. The successful launching of optional referendums and victories at the polls, particularly between 1874 and 1884 (Bolliger and Zürcher 2004: 65ff.), led to a blockage of policy making that was consequently resolved through a process of *rapprochement* between the ruling elite and their opposition. Ultimately, the formal co-optation of the latter was accomplished by the election of the Catholic Conservative MP Josef Zemp to the Federal Council. In 1919, the Christian Democrats acquired a second seat, and the predecessor of the Swiss People's Party was given a seat in 1928. In 1943, the Social Democrats obtained their first seat in the federal government, with a second seat to follow in 1959. Finally, as mentioned before, the Swiss People's Party succeeded in taking one of the Christian Democrats seats away in 2003.

According to Neidhart (1970), the governmental heterogeneity in terms of its partisan composition can be seen as a result of direct democracy. The logic behind this thesis is that all political parties capable of successfully launching a referendum have been progressively integrated into the federal government, neutralizing their systematic opposition in the direct democracy arena. Political truce, according to Neidhart, is therefore a direct result of the elite's strategy to co-opt parties into government, conferring on them responsibilities in the elaboration of governmental policies. Neidhart's mono-causal theory has been criticized by several commentators, as it cannot account for the appearance of co-optation mechanisms in countries – especially in small polities – where the referendum threat is absent, e.g. in Austria. Alternative factors have undoubtedly contributed to the establishment of pro-portional governments in several smaller European countries: Lijphart (1984 and 1999) emphasizes cultural divisions as an explanatory factor, while Katzenstein (1985) stresses the small countries' exposure to international market competition, inducing the elites to engage in co-optation processes in order to strengthen these countries' positions within world markets.

Neidhart's theory also neglects additional constraints and incentives that proved to be of importance in the progressive co-optation process of the four governmental parties in Switzerland. In particular, the integration of the Social Democrats into the Federal Council did not follow the logic of the referendum threat. In 1929, influenced by governmental experiences of Social Democrats in other countries and at the cantonal and communal levels in Switzerland, the Social Democrats officially abandoned their rigid opposition policy. They accepted and recognized the minority status of the political left and declared themselves ready to share governmental responsibilities at the federal level. When this proposed co-optation was refused by the governmental parties, the Social Democrats reverted to their strategy of opposition, particularly through the use of direct democracy. This strategy failed, however, with the refusal of a popular initiative in 1935. At the same time, the rise of fascism posed an ever growing threat to European democracies, and produced a moderating impact on the Social Democrats' party programme, thereby making their claim for integration into the federal government more acceptable. But it was not until the crucial juncture in World War II during the winter of 1942/3 – the Germans' defeat in the battle of Stalingrad – that the governing parties reassessed their perception of the Social Democrats and finally granted them a seat in the Federal Council in 1943. Notably, the governing parties' indulgence was facilitated by the fact that most of the other countries not occupied by the Axis Forces (e.g. the UK) were governed by grand coalitions, including Social Democrats. After a six-year absence from government (1953–9), the Social Democrats were finally granted two seats in the Federal Council, marking the birth of the 'magic formula'.

In short, the progressive co-optation of the main political forces into the federal government was only partly due to the referendum threat, as institutional constraints and strategic incentives played an additional major role. Thus, the grand coalition in Switzerland was not the product of an automatic institutional mechanism but above all a conscious strategy of the dominant political elite. Moreover, the *effects* of this co-optation were rather weak. Therefore, the degree of conflict at the polls did not immediately decrease after the election of the Catholic Josef Zemp to the Federal Council in 1891. As Bolliger and Zürcher (2004) show, the Catholic Conservatives were even able to increase their successes in the six years that followed their co-optation. It was only at the very end of the nineteenth century that the direct-democratic opposition of the Catholic Conservatives ebbed away, a process which was, however, only minimally affected by the 1891 co-optation. More recently, the directly democratic 'sectoral opposition' – led or backed especially by the Social Democrats and the Swiss People's Party – also puts a question mark over the grand coalition's ability to absorb political conflict (Germann 1996: 23f.). Similar findings are provided by empirically grounded studies at the cantonal level. They show that the degree of concordance neither decreases the referendum and initiative frequencies nor strengthens the governmental coalitions' success in popular votes (Trechsel 2000; Barankay *et al.* 2003).[11]

In addition to the partisan composition of the grand coalition, a number of other social and political dimensions *increase* the heterogeneity of the Federal Council. First, the Swiss government has always been a multilingual body with at least one representative coming from a French-speaking (or from the Italian-speaking) canton.[12] Second, when electing the federal government, Parliament observes an unwritten rule according to which the two major confessions, Protestantism and Catholicism, have to be represented within the Federal Council. Third, the three largest cantons have (almost) constantly held a seat in government. Finally, although the representation of women is neither a written nor a fundamental principle, it has become improbable – not to say impossible – for Parliament to elect an exclusively male government.[13]

---

[11] Note, however, that Vatter (2002) finds a more frequent use of direct democracy in cantons with lower levels of concordance.

[12] This was an unwritten rule for over 150 years. The Federal Constitution of 1999 now consecrates the Federal Council's adequate regional and linguistic representation in Article 174.4 Federal Constitution.

[13] Women are in a clear minority position in the Federal Assembly (Lüthi 2007: 137). In 2007, the voters elected 59 women (29.5 per cent) to the National

However, the heterogeneity of the Federal Council must be put in perspective. Two factors somewhat counterbalance these formal and informal mechanisms governing the selection process of Federal Councillors. First, the members of government are individually elected by the Federal Assembly, meaning that each Councillor has been given the confidence of a majority of MPs. For this to become possible, parties must find compromises in multilateral negotiations among parliamentary factions. This also means that moderate candidates tend to be more acceptable to Parliament than more polarizing ones, leading to a Federal Council that is ideologically less divided than one may expect it to be. Second, due to the low turnover of Federal Councillors,[14] coupled with the principle of collegial decision making, a mutual socialization process among Federal Councillors takes place. This process is conducive to the emergence of reciprocal respect, solidarity and loyalty among the members of government, further limiting the college's heterogeneity.

Overall, the Federal Council occupies an *important position in the Swiss political system*. As mentioned earlier, the government was designed in a way that led to a fusion of power in the hands of each Federal Councillor. Its individual and collective independence from Parliament, the strong governmental stability in partisan terms and the rather weak mechanisms for controlling its activities are features that strengthen the Federal Council's position in the political process. However, a number of factors limit the college's power. First, direct democracy severely reduces the scope of governmental autonomy. Although the Federal Council exerts a certain influence on the direct-democratic process, popular votes generate a structural uncertainty as well as, at times, (bitter) defeats of governmental policies (chapter 3). Second, the Federal Council cannot govern by decree. Similarly to the German system of administrative jurisdiction, the government's actions must rely on a legal basis, with the exception of emergency situations in which urgent decrees are permitted (Fleiner-Gerster 1987). Third, the collegial decision making limits the power of the government insofar as the political responsibility of a Federal Councillor is diluted within the college as a whole. Hence, one may argue that in a system where no one is

Council and 10 women (21.7 per cent) to the Council of States. Since December 2007, for the first time, three out of seven Federal Councillors are women.

[14] On average, the Councillors of the twentieth century who did not die in office spent 9.5 years in the Federal Council.

directly responsible for a given policy, no one effectively holds political power. Finally, and paradoxically, the fusion of executive power limits the power of the Federal Council, as it leads to a work overload for its members, preventing them from spending adequate time on substantial governmental activities. This overload therefore precludes the government from making effective use of its political power, leading to a strengthening of the federal administration.

Following up on this last point, the dependency of the government on its bureaucracy becomes visible at several points in the decision-making process (see also chapter 8). The federal administration plays an important role in the preparation of governmental projects by formulating legislative proposals, participating in expert committees, interpreting consultation procedures and writing governmental messages to Parliament. In policy implementation, the federal administration plays the predominant role as it implements and coordinates practically all federal policies.

5.4 The future of the Swiss system of government

Among modern democratic polities, the stability of the Swiss system of government is exceptionally robust. Despite its legendary stability, more recent developments have put this particular set-up under severe pressure. To start with, its *efficiency* is increasingly being questioned. As we have seen – and despite a tendency towards political emancipation – the Federal Assembly remains a weak organ, both from a resource perspective, and from the standpoint of its overall position within the political process. In the recent past, only limited reforms (particularly the structural remodelling of the parliamentary committees) have been successful. Also, the effects of these changes were merely cosmetic, leaving the pressing problems related to the lack of resources and professionalism unresolved.

The same goes for the Federal Council, whose effectiveness in dealing with the impact of internationalization and, above all, Europeanization, is criticized by numerous observers, stressing above all the work overload of the Federal Council, its resulting shift of power towards the administrative arena and its lack of a clear political vision (Germann 1996; Kriesi 1998a; Linder 1999; Klöti 2007). In addition to such overload-related criticism, structural limitations, e.g. the very short presidencies (limited to one year) of the

Federal Council and the two chambers of Parliament, can be questioned from an efficiency perspective. For instance, the presidents of Parliament and government have difficulties in establishing personal contacts at the international level, simply because their period in office is too short. In a personal communication to one of the authors, a former president of the National Council stated that at international meetings, such as the Conference of Presidents of European Parliaments,[15] for the Swiss it is not even worth exchanging business cards with their colleagues. So far, various attempts to create a modern and more efficient form of government, i.e. by introducing a two-stage executive, by increasing the number of Federal Councillors or by extending the power and mandate of the presidency of the government, have all failed: most recently, in 2004, the Federal Assembly dismissed a profound reform project, aiming at a restructuring of both the executive and the administration.

Besides external pressures, the changing face of partisan politics (chapter 6) has led to a politicization of the governmental college: open conflict within the Federal Council, coupled with a creeping personalization of Swiss politics, challenges the collegial decision-making process. As the media are revealing on an almost daily basis, the climate within the college has become increasingly frosty. After the election of the polarizing leader of the Swiss People's Party (Christoph Blocher) to the Federal Council, the traditional homogenizing mechanisms are breaking down, leading to a situation in which both the horizontal coordination efforts among the seven departments and its over fifty offices and secretaries general (Klöti 2007: 157) as well as the vertical coordination of policies across levels of the federal state (Serdült and Schenkel 2006) are becoming more difficult.

Partly due to this lack of efficiency in the system of government, its *legitimacy* is decreasing. Among all political actors, the levels of trust in Parliament, government and its administration decreased most during the 1990s (Brunner and Sgier 1997: 106). Growing distrust in parliaments and governments is not unique to Switzerland, but affects all European democracies (Schmitter and Trechsel 2004). Newer data from the Eurobarometer survey conducted in 1999 show that only 50 per cent of the population tends to trust the Federal Council; the

---

[15] Organized by the President of the Parliamentary Assembly of the Council of Europe, this conference takes place every second year.

same applies with respect to the federal administration and, in the case of the Federal Assembly, this figure even drops to 43 per cent. However, in 1999, the situation in Switzerland was still better than in the majority of the fifteen EU member states: with regard to trust in government, Switzerland comes fifth in this comparison.[16] Trust in the Swiss Parliament is nevertheless lower than in most EU countries (in 1999): it only ranks in the tenth position, although it is still above the EU fifteen mean.[17] But the process of erosion, though starting at a higher level than the EU average, is similar to the overall trend in Europe.

These shortcomings in both the efficiency and the legitimacy dimensions are not new but have been noted over decades by myriad experts. Furthermore, the political will to alter the situation has so far not been sufficiently strong. While at the time of writing profound structural changes are not likely, it is through the adaptation of informal rules that the Swiss system of government is evolving. The major risk of such a development is, however, the lack of a clear political vision that, moreover, is increasingly difficult to reach because of the growing partisan polarization in Swiss politics. In times of globalization, internationalization and Europeanization, this state of affairs may become one of the most pressing problems that the federal state is facing.

---

[16] Only Luxembourg (64 per cent), the Netherlands (63 per cent), Portugal (55 per cent) and Finland (53 per cent) had higher levels of trust in their respective governments; the EU fifteen mean was 40 per cent (source: Eurobarometer 51).

[17] Higher-ranking countries include the Netherlands (62 per cent), Luxembourg (61 per cent), Portugal (56 per cent), Finland (55 per cent), Denmark (54 per cent), Greece (51 per cent), Austria (47 per cent), Germany (45 per cent) and Spain (45 per cent); the EU fifteen mean was 41 per cent (source: Eurobarometer 51).

6 | *The party system*

6.1 Introduction

The presentation of the party system allows us to get a first idea of the political forces that determine Swiss politics. In a comparative perspective, three characteristics of the Swiss party system have long been salient – its fragmentation, its relative stability and its domination by parties of the moderate right. As Kerr (1987: 123) observed, the 'dispersion of political power finds its fullest expression in a highly fragmented party system'. The fragmentation has been typical for the system as a whole as well as for each party taken separately. It has its origin in the large number of social and cultural cleavages, in the federal structure of the Swiss state and in the effects of the electoral system. Political stability is a result of the integrative force of the institutional framework and of the consensual political culture. Switzerland has long provided one of the main examples for Lipset and Rokkan's (1967) 'freezing hypothesis', according to which contemporary party systems still reflect the cleavage structure of the European societies at the end of World War I. The traditional weakness of the Swiss left and the domination by parties from the moderate right can at least in part be explained historically by the cultural dividedness, the early industrialization and the early democratization of the country (Bartolini 2000). However, as we will show in this chapter, in the course of the 1990s, the Swiss party system started to change and its volatility increased – with profound effects on the configuration of power in Swiss politics.

6.2 The fragmentation of the Swiss party system

The Swiss party system is one of the most fragmented in Western Europe. In the 1999 and 2003 elections, members of no less than fourteen parties were elected to the National Council. As is well known, however, the absolute number of parties does not have much

84

significance; we need to take into account the number of parties that count. According to Sartori (1976), a party 'counts' if it is taken into consideration for government coalitions or if it occupies a position allowing it to veto the government's decisions. According to the first criterion, there are four parties that count at the federal level – the Radicals (the dominant branch of the Swiss liberals, called 'Free Democrats' (FDP) in the German-speaking part and 'Radicals' (PRD) in the French-speaking part of the country), the Christian Democrats (CVP/PDC), the Social Democrats (SP, called 'Socialists' (PS) in the French-speaking part) and the Swiss People's Party (SVP, known as the 'Union of the Democratic Centre' (UDC) amongst French-speaking Swiss), i.e. the four parties that have formed the grand coalition government since 1959. Sartori added to these four the Alliance of Independents (LdU/AdI) – a small centre-left party that disappeared in the 1990s. This means that, according to Sartori, the Swiss party system – at the federal level – constituted a perfect example for his category of 'moderate pluralism'. For two reasons, however, the situation in the Swiss party system is more complicated. First of all, based on the first criterion, we should also take into account the parties that count at the cantonal and local level, given that they participate in cantonal and local government coalitions. Thus, the Green Party plays a part in many cantonal and city governments. Even the Swiss Communist Party still participates in several city governments in the French-speaking part of the country and the Lega, a party of the radical right, participates in the cantonal and city government coalitions in Ticino – the Italian-speaking region. Moreover, as has been pointed out by Kerr (1987: 117), according to Sartori's second criterion, i.e. according to the criterion of the veto position, *all* parties count in Switzerland. The institutions of direct democracy allow all parties, even the small ones, to intervene in a decisive fashion in Swiss politics. In fact, small parties have often made use of these instruments and the small parties of the radical right have used them with great success (Papadopoulos 1991). Given that these small parties are ideologically far apart, we should, based on Sartori's second criterion, qualify the Swiss party system as an example of his 'polarized pluralism'.

Comparative studies frequently refer to the 'effective number of parties', a measure introduced by Laakso and Taagepera (1979). This index has the advantage that it not only takes into account the number of parties, but also their size. At the federal level, the effective number of parties reached an all time peak in the 1991 federal elections with 6.7. Since then it has declined to 5.0 in the 2003 elections. Compared to other countries, these are very high levels of fragmentation. In the post-war period (1945–96), Switzerland had the most fragmented party system in Europe (Lijphart 1999: 76). In the late 1990s, only Belgium, Italy and France had a higher effective number of parties, while the European mean was much lower and only slightly increasing after 1980 (Ladner 2001: 125).

6.3 The structuring of the party system

In general, the configuration of a party system depends on two types of factors: on the one hand, it is influenced by the structure of social and cultural cleavages; on the other hand it is determined by the political institutions. Let us first take a look at the Swiss *cleavage structure*. The relatively large number of structural conflicts that potentially serve as a basis for the formation of political parties provides a first explanatory factor for the important fragmentation of the Swiss party system. Switzerland is a country divided by the two classic cultural cleavages – religion and language – and by social class. Depending on the context, the religious cleavage takes two forms: in Protestant or religiously mixed regions, it divides Catholics from Protestants. In the predominantly Catholic regions of the former *Sonderbund*, it divides practising Catholics from the secularized parts of society. The religious conflict is articulated by two parties of uneven weight: a Catholic party – the Christian Democrats (CVP/PDC), which has been one of the key parties since the nineteenth century, and a minor Protestant party – the Evangelical Party (EVP/PEP). The Christian Democrats still have their strongholds in the predominantly Catholic cantons. Contrary to their sister parties in other European countries, they have not succeeded in attracting many Protestants and remain an almost exclusively Catholic party. Their close association with the Catholic milieu has made them very vulnerable to the secularization of Swiss society. As a matter of fact, the religious cleavage, which was still crucial for the electoral behaviour of Swiss voters in the 1970s (Lijphart 1979), lost much of its relevance by the 1990s (Trechsel 1994; Lachat 2004).

In contrast to Belgium, there are no major parties that explicitly articulate the linguistic division of the country. In Switzerland, religion has been the key divisive cultural issue, while language has always been of secondary importance. The exceptions that confirm the generally low profile of linguistic differences in Switzerland concern the canton of Berne, where the party system is divided between the dominant German-speaking region and the minority French-speaking region of the Southern Jura, and the Lega – a radical right party which articulates the dissatisfaction of the Italian-speaking minority with federal policy makers (especially in the domain of immigration and European integration). The impact of the linguistic divisions on voting behaviour has always been more apparent than real. It has been a consequence of the fact that the Swiss parties have cantonal roots and that some parties have been exclusively (e.g. the EVP) or predominantly (the small Liberal Party LPS/PLS) rooted in one language region.

As in other European countries, the class cleavage has been the most important structuring force of the Swiss party system. It divides the parties of the left and those of the right. On the left, the Swiss party system is dominated by the Social Democrats. Traditionally, they had to compete with the small Communist Party (PdA/PdT). Since the late 1960s, they were also challenged by the small parties of the new left, most of which have since disappeared. As elsewhere, the Green Party (GPS/PES) has established itself as the most important competitor of the Socialists. The Swiss left has always been one of the weakest in Western Europe. It was disadvantaged from the start by the cultural cleavages, in particular by the strong confessional loyalties among the Catholic working class and the counter-mobilization by the organizations of the Catholic pillar (Altermatt 1991; Righart 1986). Moreover, the left was also disadvantaged by the fact that, at the time of the initial mobilization of the labour movement in the latter part of the nineteenth century, the field was already occupied by its competitors – not only by Catholic organizations, but also by the Free Democrats. The Social Democrats first mobilized when the Swiss working class had already established political identities and was no longer 'available' for the socialist message (Bartolini 2000).

The Swiss right is not only divided by the religious cleavage, but also by the opposition between town and countryside. Just as in Scandinavia, the conflict between the rural interests and the interests of the cities gave rise to a farmers' party in the traditionally Protestant parts of the country (Lipset and Rokkan 1967). Thus, the precursor of the Swiss People's Party (founded in 1971) – the party of the farmers and of small businesses and tradesmen – articulated the interests of the countryside against the Free Democrats, who had their stronghold in the cities. As a result of this division, three major parties have traditionally shared the majority of the votes cast by voters on the right.

The traditional class cleavage has also weakened considerably over the past decades. With the expansion of the new middle class, the traditional conflict between labour and capital has become less relevant for the structuration of the party system. However, if we take into account the structural divisions within the new middle class, most notably the division between managers, on the one hand, and social-cultural professionals, on the other hand, we find that the reconfigured class structure is still of key importance for the structuration of the party system (Lachat 2004). As a matter of fact, compared to countries such as the United Kingdom, Germany or Sweden, the divisions within the new middle class have particularly important implications for the political choices in Switzerland (Oesch 2004, 2006). Moreover, as we shall see, there is also a new conflict shaping up in Swiss politics between the 'winners' and 'losers' of globalization – a conflict that was crucial for the restructuring of the Swiss party system during the 1990s.

As far as *political institutions* are concerned, the structure of the party system has mainly been influenced by federalism and by the electoral system. For the elections of the National Council, a majoritarian system was applied until 1919, when the proportional system was introduced as a concession to the national strike that took place one year before. As a result of the introduction of the proportional system, the predecessor of the Swiss People's Party made its entry into national politics (Gruner 1977: 153) and the configuration of power in the party system changed dramatically: the domination by the Radicals, who had always obtained a majority of the seats in the National Council, came to an end. However, the impact of the proportional system on the party system has been limited by a certain number of factors: first of all, the fact that the constituencies correspond to the cantons has served to limit the proportionality of the National Council. Since most of the cantons are quite small, i.e. since they have only a small number of seats, the electoral threshold is generally rather high. Moreover, except for the canton of Jura, the Council of States is elected according to the majoritarian system, with each constituency, i.e. each canton, returning two members. Such a two-member constituency system, which existed in many English wards of the House of Commons before the Reform Act of 1884, greatly discourages small parties (Cox 1997: 43).

Finally, Swiss federalism has profoundly marked the party system. Traditionally, the parties have positioned themselves first of all in the cantonal context. As a result, the party systems varied from one canton to the next, with the national parties hardly constituting more than federations of the cantonal parties trying to maintain a precarious unity at the federal level. According to Kerr (1987: 123), one could hardly speak of federal elections in terms of the national arena for party competition. Kerr considered it more adequate 'to speak of political contests being fought out in spatially segmented spheres of competition, defined by the relative weight of the various axes on which the partisan conflicts turn'. Schumann (1971: 125) was tempted to maintain that there was not one party system in Switzerland, but as many party systems as there were cantons. The first consequence of the fact that the parties were basically constituted at the cantonal level was the increase in the number of parties at the federal level, because, as we have already seen, some parties only exist in certain cantons and not in others. More important still is the fact that partisan federalism has traditionally contributed to the incoherence of each major party. As a consequence of federalism, the situation of one and the same party may differ considerably from one canton to another. Thus, the Christian Democrats still constitute the hegemonic party in several Catholic cantons, where they are the governing party *par excellence*. In the canton of Berne, by contrast, the Christian Democrats have always been an opposition party, a radical force that defended the rights of the Catholic and French-speaking minority in the Jura and became one of the major components of the separatist movement.

According to Klöti (1998: 49f.) and Kriesi (1998b: 6f.), we can distinguish between three types of cantonal party systems, each of which is characterized by a distinct party configuration. First of all, there is the system prevailing in Catholic cantons – a system dominated by the Christian Democrats. In these cantons, the traditional religious conflict between the Christian Democrats and their liberal opponents still predominates. The weakness of the left corresponds to the weakness of the class conflict in these cantons, where industrialization came late and never developed to the same extent as in the formerly Protestant cantons, and where the inter-classist strategy of the Christian Democrats preempted the Social Democrats. Moreover, the rural–urban conflict did not constitute a separate base for political mobilization in these cantons either, since the countryside remained mainly Catholic, while the more secularized urban regions constituted the bastions, first of the liberals and, later on, of the left. Next, there is the system of religiously mixed German-speaking cantons, where the two traditional conflicts of religion and class have been largely pacified. In these cantons, a relatively strong left is confronted with the Radicals, on the one hand, and the Swiss People's Party on the other. Third, in the religiously mixed French-speaking cantons, an even stronger left faces the two currents of the nineteenth-century liberalism represented by the (more conservative) Liberal Party and the (more progressive) Radicals. In these cantons, the traditional class conflict has long been kept alive by the competition between these two liberal currents and by the corresponding competition between the two components of the left – the Socialists and the Communists.

6.4 The parties as organizations

Swiss parties are generally rather weak organizations. Compared to parties in other western democracies and to Swiss interest associations they are underfunded, understaffed and generally lacking in resources. In Switzerland, as in France, the introduction of universal suffrage preceded the creation of party organizations. In the absence of such organizations, networks of local elites functioned as instruments for the representation of the masses. This so-called 'militia system', made up of non-professional politicians, contributed to the preservation of organizational weakness all the way to the present day. Swiss politicians work on a voluntary or part-time basis. Although the *professionalization* of the party apparatuses progresses, it does not do so at the same pace as in other countries. Although the number of staff positions in the party system doubled between the 1970s and the mid 1990s to reach about 130 full-time positions, the level of professionalization still remains below average compared to other countries. Only the United Kingdom and the Netherlands have lower rates of increase, but in absolute terms these countries reach a generally higher level of professionalization (Ladner 1998, 2001: 134f.).

Compared to parties in other countries, Swiss parties also have only limited *financial resources*, both in absolute terms and in terms of growth rates over recent years. Partly responsible for this is the almost total lack of state funding. At the national level, the state only contributes some 4.5 million francs a year to support the parliamentary groups. A parliamentary reform which would have improved the infrastructure of the parliamentarians failed to obtain a majority in a popular vote in 1992. At the cantonal level, there is hardly any direct support for the parties at all, but they benefit from indirect measures of support such as tax deductions, subsidies to cover printing and distribution costs, free poster space, etc. At the end of the 1990s, the total budget reported by the four governing parties at the federal level amounted to 9.8 million francs. In real terms, it had roughly doubled over the last three decades (Ladner 2001: 135). But compared to most of the other countries, these figures remain very small indeed. The figures are more significant when we also add in the budgets of the cantonal and local parties. Ladner (2004) estimates that the total of Swiss party budgets at all three levels amounts to 40–4 million francs in a non-election year and to about 65–75 million in an election year.

As observed above, Swiss parties have strong cantonal and local roots. Thus, Ladner (1991) found no less than 6,000 political groupings at the communal level. He found parties in more than two-thirds of the 3,000 Swiss communes, most of which are very small indeed. At the local level, parties are by far the most important political actors. Moreover, the party system proved to be quite dynamic during the 1970s and 1980s, when it went through a new phase of expansion: the number of local sections increased – even among the traditional parties. However, in a follow-up study covering the development of the party system up to the mid 1990s, Ladner could no longer confirm this expansionary trend. Instead, he now found a trend towards an erosion of the major parties, especially in the small communes. The parties tended to be replaced by local groups which do not necessarily have the character of a party (Ladner 1996).

There are other signs of a weakening of the parties: as in many other countries, party identification has been in decline over the last three decades (Nabholz 1998; Lachat 2004). Party membership is declining, too. Since the Swiss parties do not have reliable membership data, the real size of membership is difficult to estimate. Ladner (1998) has come up with an estimated 6.7 per cent of the total population, while the post-electoral survey for the 2003 federal elections reports an active membership of 5.7 per cent. These figures are still higher than the average in Western Europe (Mair and van Biezen 2001: 9). The parties also have recruitment problems. They have difficulties in filling the many positions in local assemblies and committees which are part of the

Swiss militia system. As for the parties' prestige among the general public, it is very low. Except for the press, the Swiss have less confidence in the parties than in any other political actor or institution: only 27 per cent trusted the parties in 1996, compared to 69 per cent who trusted the police, 66 per cent who trusted the courts and still 52 per cent who trusted the government (Brunner and Sgier 1997: 107). Taken together, these figures suggest that the Swiss party system as a whole has been experiencing a certain decline.

However, not all parties are suffering from such a decline. This seems to be above all a problem of the two major parties of the moderate right – the Radicals and the Christian Democrats – while the Social Democrats and the Swiss People's Party have been more fortunate over the last decades. The Swiss People's Party in particular has been making a lot of progress in recent years. Since Christoph Blocher took over the Zurich branch of the party in the late 1970s, this branch has become increasingly prominent in its own party and in the party system as a whole. Blocher gave his party a clear profile by positioning it to the right of its main competitors. Under his undisputed, charismatic leadership, the party made big strides towards the professionalization of its organization and its campaigns (Hartmann and Horvath 1995). In the course of the 1990s, the Swiss People's Party became the best-led and best-funded party in Switzerland, staffed by highly motivated people who worked hard and sponsored by some very rich businessmen. While other parties experienced a decline in their membership, by the year 2000 membership in the Swiss People's Party had increased by roughly 50 per cent. Most conspicuously, the Swiss People's Party adopted the principles of modern 'media-centred' campaigning (Swanson and Mancini 1996), characterized by:

• an increasing distance between parties and voters
• permanent campaigning
• a personalization of politics
• an increasing role for political consultants and marketing specialists
• the development of independent communication structures
• a spectator's role for the citizens

More specifically, the party adopted an aggressive style, relying on negative campaigning and systematic denigration of its direct competitors and of the 'political class' as a whole. In a populist manner, it appealed to the common sense of the ordinary voter. Its enemies included the media, board members and managers of big companies, 'social para-sites', Socialists and the left in general. Its strategy proved to be highly successful and crucial for the profound transformation of the Swiss party system that has taken place since the beginning of the 1990s (Kriesi *et al.* 2005).

6.5 The transformation of the party system

The Swiss party system had already started to change in the late 1960s. Three successive waves of opposition diminished the electoral success of the four major parties (see table A1 in the Appendix). The first wave was led by the Alliance of Independents (LdU), which mobilized above all voters without partisan attachments from among the new middle class. The next wave of opposition came from small parties on the radical right, which mobilized against the tremendous influx of foreigners. In their analysis of the 1971 federal elections, Inglehart and Sidjanski (1975: 110) had already found a first indication of what they called at the time a 'progressive-traditionalist' cleavage pitting the left and the Christian Democrats against the new radical-populist right. In the late 1970s, these parties temporarily went into decline, while a third wave of opposition led by the small parties of the new left (the Progressive organizations (POCH), Trotskyites and the Greens) took off. In the 1987 elections, these three waves cumulated for the first time and the joint success of these outsiders reached a peak in 1991. As we have seen, the result was a record fragmentation of the party system. This was, however, only the prelude to a more profound transformation of the party system under the onslaught of the mobilization by the Swiss People's Party. This party won the next three elections and increased its share of the votes for the National Council from roughly 11 per cent in the 1980s to 28.9 per cent in 2007. As is illustrated by figure 6.1, its ascent came at the expense of the moderate right and the radical right. Its clear-cut positioning on the right closed the door to the small parties of the radical right, which all but disappeared in the process. The two major parties of the moderate right – the Radicals and the Christian Democrats – were also severely beaten. The left maintained itself, but did not progress.

The victorious advance of the Swiss People's Party began with its suc-cessful mobilization against Swiss accession to the UN in 1986 and, above all, with the campaign against Swiss accession to the European

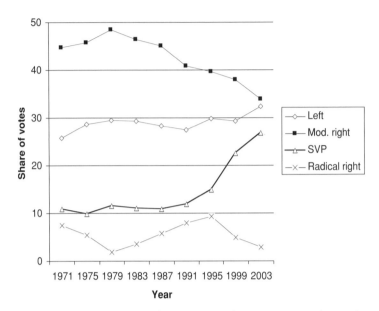

Figure 6.1 Development of party strength, 1971–2003: share of votes in National Council elections

Economic Area (EEA) in 1992. At the end of the longest and most intense direct democracy campaign ever held in Switzerland, the party won a very narrow victory against the otherwise united political elite and succeeded in putting the brakes on Swiss integration into the EU. The mobilization for the defence of a neutral and independent Switzerland first started to pay off in electoral terms in the formerly Protestant cantons in the German-speaking part of the country, most notably in the canton of Zurich. Since the 1920s, the Swiss People's Party had dominated the party system in the heavily rural and Protestant canton of Berne. In the much more urbanized canton of Zurich, it had its strongholds in the countryside, but was weak in the city and in the metropolitan area. In the course of the 1990s, the Zurich branch made great progress in the urban areas and ended up in an even stronger position than the Berne branch (see figure 6.2). After having successfully advanced on its former main turf, the party also expanded in the two types of cantonal party systems, where it had traditionally been marginal or absent. As is illustrated by figure 6.2, in 1995 the party started its ascent in the Catholic part of the country (Lucerne and Schwyz are

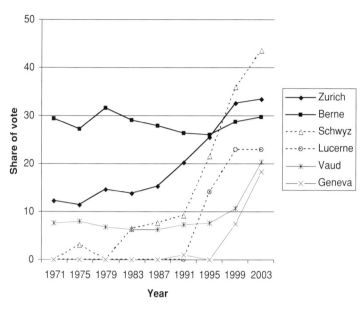

Figure 6.2 Development of party strength, 1971–2003, in selected cantons: share of votes in National Council elections

presented as typical examples), and in 1999 it started to take off in the French-speaking cantons (Vaud and Geneva serve as the examples). Beginning as a Swiss-German, rural and Protestant party, the Swiss People's Party has become a national party with a general conservative appeal.

The party mobilizes the globalization 'losers', i.e. the (unskilled) working class and the old middle class. In Switzerland, the latter has traditionally been sheltered from market pressures through public regulation. The farmers provide, of course, the typical example, but the whole sector of small businesses and tradesmen producing for the internal market (*Gewerbe*) has equally been protected in the past. With the extension of international liberalization, this sector has experienced an erosion of its politically based property rights and the related streams of income (Schwartz 2001: 44). The party's appeal, however, is not directly economic, but mainly based on its opposition to European integration and its tough stance on immigration, which have to be understood as a cultural defence of Swiss traditions. A detailed analysis of the 1999 elections (Kriesi and Sciarini 2004) has shown that, to the benefit of the SVP, the issues of EU integration and asylum had the most discriminating effects on the voting choices. In particular, the SVP's positioning on the two most important issues of the day allowed the party to reinforce its voters' initial voting intention, to win over converts from all the other three major parties and to activate undecided voters in its favour. Similarly, the left also gained from reinforcement, crystallization and conversion at the expense of the Radicals and the Christian Democrats, albeit to a lesser extent than the Conservatives. By contrast, the two intermediary party families (the Radicals and the Christian Democrats) clearly fared less well in this respect, since they could neither benefit from issue-related conversion, nor from crystallization, and hardly from reinforcement. Analyses of the 2003 election survey confirm the crucial importance of the EU-integration issue for the rise of the SVP (Kriesi *et al.* 2005). In addition, these analyses also document the key importance of the party's charismatic leader – Christoph Blocher – who became entirely identified with the party's resistance against Switzerland's participation in the European integration process.

As a result of the SVP's successful advance, the Swiss party system is now structured into three camps which can be placed in a two-dimensional space. The first dimension is the classic opposition between left and right, whereby the parties of the left which defend the welfare state and promote environmental protection oppose the parties of the right which promote economic liberalism and budgetary rigour. The second dimension, by contrast, is constituted by the cultural opposition between the promoters of an open, culturally liberal Switzerland and the defenders of Swiss traditions. As a result of the successful mobilization of the SVP, the right (which enjoys a majority in Switzerland) is now clearly divided into two camps: the moderate right, composed of the Radicals/Liberals and the Christian Democrats, who tend to be both economically and culturally liberal, and the nationalist-conservative right (SVP), which is culturally conservative and economically ambiguous – in favour of budgetary rigour but defending the privileges of its traditional middle-class clientele. These two dimensions and the three camps can be detected not only by an analysis of the parties' positioning in the electoral campaigns of the 1990s (Kriesi *et al.* 2006), but also by an analysis of the voting behaviour of the members of the National Council (Kriesi 2001) and by an analysis of the referendum votes during the two decades between 1982 and 2002 (Hermann and Leuthold 2003).

Paradoxically, it was the advance of the conservatives which has contributed to the transformation and, we should add, the modernization of the Swiss party system. The conservatives have been the main modernizers not only with respect to organizational strategies, but also with respect to the nationalization of Swiss politics. By their stepwise conquest of the three types of cantons, they have contributed to the nationalization of the Swiss party system. In addition, they have also contributed to an increase in partisan competition and to a less consensual style. Under their influence, the Swiss party system has become more polarized and has lost some of its consensual character. Finally, the conservatives have contributed to a general right-ward shift, because their competitors from the moderate right felt compelled to adjust their positions so as to limit their losses.

However, in order to get a complete picture of the transformation of the Swiss party system, we should take into account not only the elections to the National Council but also those for the second chamber – the Council of States. Given that the Swiss Parliament is characterized by a symmetrical bicameralism (see chapter 5), the party composition of the second chamber is just as important as that of the National Council. Moreover, we should also take into account the results of the cantonal parliamentary and governmental elections. We cannot go into too much detail here, but would like to point out that the transformation is less pronounced in the elections held with a majoritarian system, i.e. in cantonal governmental elections and in the elections for the Council of States. This is illustrated by figure 6.3, which compares the strength of the moderate right in the Council of States (for more details, see table A2 in the Appendix) with its electoral success in the elections for the National Council. As becomes immediately apparent from this comparison, the decline of the two parties of the moderate right in the elections for the National Council since the late 1970s contrasts sharply with their continued domination of the Council of States. This contrast points to an imbalance in the Swiss party system – an increasing tension between the territorial representation (in the Council of States) and the representation of the population (in the National Council). Given the highly unequal territorial distribution of the population and the properties of the majoritarian electoral system, the parties of the moderate right are able to maintain their domination, as long as they build electoral alliances for elections to the Council of States.

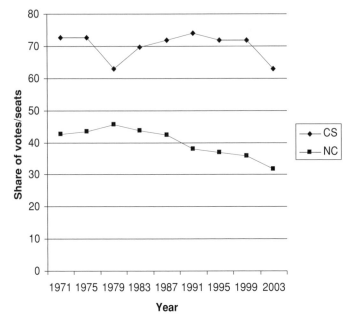

Figure 6.3 Strength of moderate right in National Council and Council of States: share of votes (NC) and share of seats (CS)

6.6 Conclusion

After the federal elections in 2003, Christoph Blocher, the charismatic leader of the Swiss People's Party, was elected to become a member of the Federal Council. With his election, the 'magic formula' came to an end after having lasted for more than forty years: Blocher became the second member of government from the SVP, at the expense of the Christian Democrats. Blocher's election to the Federal Council constitutes a strong symbol for the transformation of the Swiss party system. As the continuing and increasing tension between the composition of the two chambers of Parliament indicates, this transformation is unlikely to be complete. The realignment within the right-wing majority is likely to continue with profound consequences for Swiss politics.

7 | *Interest associations and labour relations*

7.1 Introduction

Swiss interest associations have traditionally been very important actors in Swiss politics. Their powerful position contrasts with the weakness of Swiss political parties. Interest associations have been more coherently structured and more resourceful than parties and they have traditionally played a key role in the legislative process in the pre-parliamentary arena as well as in policy implementation. Switzerland has therefore often been considered as a paradigmatic case of democratic corporatism. Thus, Peter Katzenstein (1985), who analysed how the small Western European countries met the challenge of their integration into global markets, counted Switzerland among the typical cases of 'democratic corporatism'. Three elements characterized this kind of regime: a centralized and concentrated system of interest associations; a voluntary and informal coordination of the various interests in continuous political negotiations between their associations, political parties and the various branches of public administration; and an ideology favouring social partnership. Based on the configuration of power in the system of interest intermediation, Katzenstein distinguished between two versions of 'democratic corporatism' – a liberal and a social version. In the social version, typically represented by Sweden, a strong labour movement was capable of matching the power of the business community. In the liberal version, for which Switzerland represented the typical case, power was asymmetrically distributed between a dominant business community and a rather weak labour movement. Katzenstein, however, considered that the integrative capacity of the corporatist arrangements served to reinforce the weaker partners in the political process – in the Swiss case, he believed that it was above all the labour movement and the left in general which benefited from the compensations provided by corporatist politics. Building on Katzenstein's classic interpretation of Swiss politics, Mach (2006) has arrived at a somewhat different interpretation of the Swiss version of democratic corporatism: he argues that the groups which had to be compensated for the country's integration into world markets have traditionally not only included the social partners represented by the labour unions, as Katzenstein maintained, but also farmers, small businesses and tradesmen. According to Mach, these conservative groups, which are mainly oriented towards the domestic market, had traditionally benefited from the 'liberal protectionism' of what he calls Switzerland's 'liberal-conservative' version of democratic corporatism.

In this chapter, we shall focus on the structuring of the business interest associations and trade unions (the two key elements of the neo-corporatist model and of the Swiss system of interest associations), the characteristics of their reciprocal relations in the framework of the Swiss social partnership, and their changing influence on the Swiss political process. The next chapter will then discuss in more detail the political process and the cooperative arrangements into which these associations are integrated.

7.2 The structuring of the system of business interest associations

Interest associations in general and business interest associations (BIAs) in particular are situated between their members (whose interest they represent in the political process) and the public administration, the members of Parliament and the government, whom they try to influence in the name of their members. According to their intermediary position between their members and the political process, interest associations are confronted with two kinds of logics requiring different skills and resources (Schmitter and Streeck 1981): on the one hand, they follow a 'logic of membership', i.e. they have to build up organizational capacities, to aggregate the interests of their members and to service them. On the other hand, they follow a 'logic of influence', i.e. they participate in the political process and try to influence decision makers. Both of these logics contribute to the structuring of the system of interest associations.

As far as the logic of membership is concerned, the structure of Swiss BIAs has above all been determined by the *sectoral structure of the Swiss economy*, which is characterized by a basic *dualism* between the sectors exposed to international competition and the sheltered sectors producing for domestic markets. Each of these two sectors has developed its own subsystems of BIAs. Thus, in the sheltered sectors we find two subsystems: one for the agricultural sector, dominated by the Swiss farmers' association (SBV);[1] and one for small businesses and tradesmen (SGV). Construction constitutes the most important branch of the small businesses and tradesmen, but this subsystem also includes artisans of different stripes, retailing and traditional services (such as barbers). Each branch has its own associations which, in turn, are integrated into the peak association of small businesses and tradesmen – an umbrella organization representing the whole sectoral subsystem. The sheltered sectors have traditionally been heavily cartellized and protected by state regulation. They have been among the chief beneficiaries of the compensations exchanged in the national-conservative framework of democratic corporatism. In the exposed sector, we also find two associational subsystems – the system of industrial associations (formerly Vorort, currently economiesuisse, see below) and the system of employers' associations (SAV). These two subsystems organize firms from both the industrial and service sectors. Organizing essentially the same firms, they operate a division of labour: the industrial associations represent the business community in the political process, while the employers' associations represent it in relations with the labour unions.

As for the 'logic of influence', the *federalist structure of the state* has also heavily influenced the structuration of the Swiss BIAs. Each subsystem has adapted to the requirements of both the federal state and its decentralized structure: contrary to the political parties, the BIAs have strong peak associations representing them at the federal level. At the same time, they are internally differentiated according to the requirements of both the sectoral structure of the economy and the federalist structure of the Swiss political system. The example of economiesuisse may serve to illustrate this point: economiesuisse, the main interlocutor of the federal government for all questions concerning the Swiss business community, has two types of members – sectoral associations (e.g. the association of the Swiss machine industry) and regional associations (the chambers of commerce). The chambers of

---

[1] We use the German abbreviations for these associations here, unless the association is exclusively organizing in the French-speaking part of the country. The full names of the associations can be found in the list of abbreviations on pp. xiv–xv.

commerce organize all firms of a given region independently of the sector they belong to and represent the business community at the level of the cantons. The influence of the federalist structure of the state on the structuration of the system of BIAs is also illustrated by the fact that a new chamber of commerce and new cantonal branches of sectoral associations were created following the constitution of the new canton of Jura in 1979 (Rennwald 1994). The structure of the subsystem of the small businesses and tradesmen is even more decentralized and complex than that of economiesuisse, because these sectors are particularly numerous, they include a large number of small firms, and they are highly decentralized.

While well adapted to the conditions of the traditional sectoral structure and of the federalist state, the Swiss system of BIAs has more recently been faced with profound changes in its environment which have challenged its established structure. The *process of globalization* weakens the forces associated with the logic of influence and reinforces those associated with the logic of membership: on the one hand, as the nation-state is losing some of its relevance for the business community, the BIAs – major interlocutors of the nation-state – are losing a substantial amount of their external political support which used to reinforce them with respect to their members. On the other hand, as international market competition increases, some of the BIAs' members – especially the large multinational firms operating in global markets – are increasingly unwilling to accept the constraints placed on them by national policy networks in which their BIAs are embedded and by the rules by which they have been obliged to play. In other words, globalization reduces the dependency of business, especially of large corporations, on their interest associations and reinforces the position of BIA members, especially large corporations.

As in other countries, the Swiss business community has responded to these changes by pursuing two means of restructuring its system of BIAs, one concerning the sectoral level, the other concerning the level of peak associations (Kriesi 2006). At the level of *sectoral or territorial membership associations*, the key words are 're-engineering' and 'downsizing' (Zervudacki 1999: 150). The sectoral and territorial associations are being transformed under the leadership of some key personalities of the business community – personalities who mainly come from the highly dynamic, exposed sectors, which have most directly felt the competitive pressure of globalization. In Switzerland, efforts made with respect to sectoral restructuring began in the *chemical and pharmaceutical industry*. This industry is not only a highly dynamic part of the Swiss business community, it also constitutes its most internationalized branch, and the one best organized at the international level. Moreover, it is also a highly concentrated sector, composed of only relatively few firms and controlled by the leading multinational companies (Novartis, Hoffmann-La Roche, Clariant). In the autumn of 1998, the board of the sectoral association of the chemical industry (a member of economiesuisse) cut its operational budget for 1999 by 50 per cent and announced the dismissal of more than half of its twenty-eight collaborators. At the origin of this critical step was a certain irritation and discontent on the part of member firms with their association. The members perceived the association as being too close to national politics; indeed, they had the impression that their association had become the handmaiden of the state. In their view, the association was supposed to improve the dialogue between politics and society, to close what some leading personalities perceived as an increasing gap between politics and the public on the one hand, and the business community on the other.

Not much later, the *machine industry*, together with the chemical industry, the most important branch of Swiss industry, also got involved in restructuring. In this case, the preexisting dual structure, which corresponded to the dual structure of the peak associations, was rationalized. In 1999, the two sister associations – the employers' association (ASM) and the industrial association (VSM) – created a new organization (Swissmem) and merged their boards and their office staffs, although they did not take the final step of becoming one single formal organization. In 2006, the integration of the two associations under the roof of Swissmem was almost completed, except for the fact that the ASM remains the partner of the unions for collective agreements in the machine industry. At the same time, following the example of the chemical industry, the budget (and, correspondingly, membership dues) was cut by a third and activities were focused on essentials.

'*Concentration*' and '*unification*' are the key words with regard to the restructuring of the *peak associations*. Under the pressure of the imperatives of international competition and as a result of the increasing importance of regulatory policies handed down from the supranational level, the internal pressure from the labour unions is diminishing and the dual structure of the national system of BIAs has been losing a lot of its importance. As a result, in most countries it is being replaced by a unified structure (Zervudacki 1999: 182ff.). Belatedly, the Swiss business community has joined the movement, too. The motives behind the restructuring were similar to those that had already been driving the restructuring at the sectoral level: the closer cooperation was supposed to allow the business community to speak to the public and the political authorities with a single voice, and to increase its organizational efficiency. In the year 2000, the Vorort (the traditional peak industrial association) and the originally independent organization which specialized in political campaigning for the business community merged under the new name of 'economiesuisse'. At the same time, the association of the financial sector (Schweizerische Bankiervereinigung), which had not been part of the Vorort, became a member of economiesuisse. Following the model of the merger between ASM and VSM, the staff (twenty collaborators for the Vorort and forty for the campaign organization) and the boards of the two organizations merged, but they continued to exist as formal organizations, because no common solution could be found for the financing of the merged organizations. It was also mainly for financial reasons that the employers' peak association (SAV) refused to join the movement. To complete the organizational structure, in 1999, fourteen multinational firms created a think tank for the Swiss business community – Avenir Suisse – that addresses the general public and stimulates public debates with provocative studies on hot political issues.

7.3 The structuring of the unions

Compared to the BIAs, the Swiss system of trade unions has traditionally been more fragmented and internally competitive. The religious divisions of the country, the divisions between blue- and white-collar workers, and professional and ideological divisions among workers all contributed to this fragmentation. After the dissolution of the Protestant unions in the 1970s and of the small federation of the so-called autonomous (i.e. non-socialist) unions in the 1990s, there are still three remaining union subsystems. In addition, there are several unions or employees' associations that are not aligned with any one of these three subsystems.

The most important one of the three is the *Union of Swiss Trade Unions* (SGB). It has a social-democratic orientation and is internally structured according to both the principle of industrial unions and the federalist structure of the state. Similarly to the BIAs, the SGB unions are undergoing a process of restructuring. Thus, in the course of the 1990s, a series of mergers considerably reduced the number of industrial unions within the SGB. In 2004, its two largest members – the union of engineering and watch-making (SMUV) and the union of construction and industrial workers (GBI) (itself already the product of a recent merger) – and the union of the transport and foodstuff workers (VHTL) have merged to form Unia. The resulting combination includes more than half of the SGB's membership. Until 2002, the *Catholic unions* (CNG) and the *Federation of Employees' Associations* (VSA) constituted the other two remaining subsystems. Then, the Federation of Employees' Associations split: the Association of Office Employees, its most important member, which accounted for about half its membership, left the federation. This split facilitated the merger of the rest of the VSA with the Catholic unions and the formation of a new peak association – *Travail.Suisse*. Just as in the case of the SGB, this new federation is dominated by one large member union – Syna, which is again the product of a previous merger of several Catholic unions.

Figure 7.1 shows the recent development of union membership. As we can see from this figure, unions have suffered a loss in membership – a loss that is also reflected in the degree of unionization. Between 1990 and 1999, unionization fell from 27 per cent to 24.3 per cent, which brought Switzerland closer to the bottom end of the Western European rank-order (Ebbinghaus and Visser 1999). Several factors have contributed to the unions' decline: first of all, the structural trends of tertiarization and feminization of the workforce reduced the employment share of industrial workers – the traditional core of the largest federation (SGB), which has long neglected white-collar segments dominated by women employees. The SGB's share of female members amounted to a mere 20 per cent in 1999. Second, the long economic stagnation during the 1990s that gave rise to an unusually slack labour market also contributed to the weakness of the unions. Finally, the Swiss unions are particularly vulnerable because of their fragmented structure. In fact, as has often been argued (e.g. Crouch 1982; Streeck 1981; Traxler 1982), a close link exists between the weakness of the organizational structure of a union system and the degree of unionization.

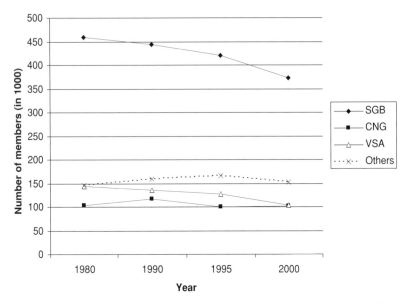

Figure 7.1 Development of union membership, 1980–2000 (in thousands of members)

7.4 Labour relations: social partnership

Swiss labour relations have traditionally been characterized by a high degree of pacification and institutionalization as well as by a pronounced autonomy with respect to the state. In the past, Swiss labour relations have not always been peaceful. Polarized class relations before and during World War I culminated in a general strike in 1918, which ended with three crucial concessions to the labour movement: the introduction of proportional representation in federal elections, the 48-hour working week in public and private corporations, and the promise to create a public pension system. During the great crisis of the early 1930s, labour relations deteriorated once again before the unions and the employers' association of the machine industry negotiated a truce: in 1937 – at about the same time as the conclusion of the treaty of Saltsjöbaden between the Swedish unions and employers (1938) – the social partners in the machine industry and in watch-making adopted the famous collective agreement which for the first time introduced an integral peace clause in Swiss labour relations. Except for a brief radicalization and a wave of strikes immediately after the end of World

War II, labour relations have been peaceful ever since in Switzerland. In addition, they have become highly institutionalized in the form of collective agreements and institutions jointly managed by the social partners. They collaborate in the administration of pension funds and especially of vocational training systems, which are organized on a sectoral basis and generally linked to sectoral collective agreements (Mach and Oesch 2003).

Autonomy with respect to the state means that the social partners determine working conditions and wages without the intervention of the state. Since the peace agreement in 1937, the social partners have always preferred a negotiated solution over a legislated one. This preference for self-organization reflects the *principle of subsidiarity* which has always played a key role in Swiss politics. According to this principle, the state or the political parties are only called upon to intervene once the actors representing civil society (the family, neighbours, churches, interest associations (BIAs and others), etc.) are no longer capable of finding a solution on their own. This principle implies that the state intervenes only if all other solutions have failed, and even then only in cooperation with the societal actors. The same principle of subsidiarity also applies at the level of the social partners. Thus, collective agreements have hardly ever been negotiated at the level of the peak associations in Switzerland. They are typically negotiated at the sectoral level, between the industrial unions and the sectoral employers' associations. Wages have always been set at either the industry or the company level (Calmfors and Drifill 1988; Fluder and Hotz-Hart 1998). It is because of this peculiarity of Swiss labour relations that the ideal-typical tripartite model of neo-corporatist cooperative arrangements between the peak associations of the social partners and the state has never applied to the case of Switzerland. This is also the reason why Switzerland has proved to be difficult to classify on comparative scales of neo-corporatism, although the structural configurations of its system of interest intermediation closely correspond to the model (see Lijphart and Crepaz 1991; Kriesi 1998a: 368–72).

The changes in the global environment in the more recent past have also left their imprint on Swiss labour relations. They have led to a general modification in the power relations between the social partners in favour of the employers' side, but also to a general decline in the capacity of both the employers' associations and trade unions to make binding commitments in the name of their members. Surprisingly, the coverage rate – the number of employees covered by collective agreements – has hardly diminished at all: it only fell from 47 per cent in 1991 to 45 per cent in 1999 (Mach and Oesch 2003). The peaceful character of labour relations has not basically changed either. However, worldwide trends towards the decentralization, deregulation and disorganization of labour relations (Crouch and Traxler 1995) have also made themselves felt in Switzerland. They have served to accentuate an already existing pattern of decentralized labour relations in a highly flexible labour market. In the second half of the 1990s, wage setting was decentralized from the sectoral to the company level in five industries – in the chemical and clothing industries, in banking, printing and, to a lesser extent, in watch-making (Mach and Oesch 2003). In these industries, sectoral agreements no longer contain any norms allowing unions to negotiate over effective wages above the company level. Similarly, collective bargaining over working time has shifted from the sectoral to the company level in the chemical industry, in engineering and printing. Inflation adjustment clauses, which had provided automatic cost-of-living compensation, more or less disappeared from collective agreements in the 1990s. In addition, decentralization also extended to intra-firm bargaining, as is illustrated by two of the largest Swiss employers (Swissair (by now defunct) and the retail chain Migros), who decentralized wage bargaining from the central company to single plants or regional branches. Moreover, the focus of wage negotiations at the company level gradually shifted from the size of wage increases to the manner of distributing them: in an exemplary case with important implications for wage negotiations in general, the management of a major pharmaceutical corporation insisted on individualized instead of general wage increases and, after a protracted battle, got its demand finally approved by the arbitration court.

Mach and Oesch (2003) insist, however, that we should differentiate between sectors: the deterioration of the negotiating power of the unions has been most pronounced in low-skilled branches of the exposed sector (e.g. the textile industry), whereas collective bargaining at the sectoral level remained relatively intact in highly skilled branches of the sheltered sector (e.g. the construction industry). Even between otherwise structurally rather similar sectors such as watch-making and the engineering and chemical industries (all belonging to the highly skilled part of the exposed sector), important differences may be observed with regard to decentralization, which is much less important in watch-making than in the engineering or chemical industries. For Mach and Oesch these differences can be explained by the political moderation of the employers' associations and the stronger position of the trade unions in watch-making, as well as by the absence of employees' associations competing with the trade unions for members and influence in this sector. As Mach (1999c) has observed, the division between white-collar workers' associations and blue-collar workers' unions allows for the emergence of the type of 'cross-class flexibility coalitions between firms producing high-quality goods for fragmented and volatile international markets and groups of highly skilled workers enjoying favourable market positions', which have played such an important role in Scandinavia (Iversen 1996). In the 1990s, when the major white-collar workers' associations obtained a pivotal position in the negotiations of collective agreements, the traditional division between white-collar employees and workers acquired a new significance.

Diminished in their role as social partners in industrial relations, the unions responded by increasingly turning to procedures of direct democracy and to the legislative process in order to defend workers' demands. It is in this way that they obtained some important successes since the 1990s. Thus, the unions scored two substantial victories in direct democratic votes: by way of a referendum, they succeeded in blocking a number of projects, among them the first version of the revised labour law in 1996, a modification of the unemployment insurance system in 1997, the liberalization of the electricity market in 2002, and the pension reform in 2004. More generally, as Bonoli (1999) argues convincingly and as we shall see in more detail in chapter 10, the institution of the referendum makes policies of welfare state retrenchment quite difficult in Switzerland. But it is in the legislative arena that the unions scored their most important victory: in 1999, they made their support for the bilateral treaty with the EU – a treaty which the Swiss business community badly wanted – dependent on the adoption of compensatory domestic measures. In other words, they used the leverage they got thanks to European regulation policies for important pieces of labour legislation to strengthen their position in the Swiss labour market. This success is rather ironic given that one usually expects the representatives of capital, i.e. of the mobile factor, to benefit from the opening up of markets (Fischer 2003).

7.5 Other associations and actors

There are, of course, other types of interest associations beyond the BIAs and trade unions, which defend specific interests in particular policy domains. The institutions of Swiss direct democracy provide many different interest associations with the opportunity to veto legislation, or at least to credibly threaten to block it with a veto (see chapter 4). As a result, all interest associations that are capable of making a credible threat through the referendum are likely to be integrated into the pre-parliamentary political process. A well-known example is provided by the associations of the medical professions and of health insurance providers, which have decisively shaped Swiss health policy (see Immergut 1992a, 1992b). Other examples include the various powerful associations representing the interests of car drivers (TCS, ACS), truck owners (ASTAG) and environmentalists (VCS) in transport policy, and the Association for a Neutral and Independent Switzerland (AUNS), which is closely linked to the Swiss People's Party and has powerfully mobilized against the participation of Switzerland in the UN, the EU and NATO.

The openness of the political institutions has provided many types of challengers with easy access to the political decision-making process. Therefore, not only established interest associations but also social movement organizations tend to have a considerable impact in Swiss politics. As a comparative study of new social movements in Western Europe has shown, mobilization by these movements (which include, among others, movements concerning the ecology, peace and solidarity, as well as the rights of women, squatters and consumers, and basic human rights) has been particularly strong in Switzerland. Given the openness of the system, however, their mobilization was relatively moderate and did not give rise to the same amount of radical confrontations as it did in France, Germany and the Netherlands (Kriesi *et al.* 1995). A famous example is the GSOA – an organization of the peace movement that successfully launched an initiative for the abolition, purely and simply, of the Swiss army. This initiative was voted down in 1989, in a ballot with record participation, but indirectly it succeeded in triggering far-reaching reforms of the Swiss army.

Although these movements no longer mobilize to the same extent as they did in the 1970s and 1980s, they left a legacy of organizations which today participate in the political process in a more or less institutionalized way. As a result, the number of veto players in Swiss politics has multiplied and the position of the traditionally dominant economic interest associations has become more difficult. Ecologists' organizations in particular have developed into important actors in transport, research and energy policy as well as in territorial planning – domains of great interest to the business community. Thus, with the adoption of the initiative of the Alps in 1994, the ecologists scored a resounding success, which forced the government to adapt its transport policy to ecological constraints. The initiative against genetic engineering, which posed a major threat to the chemical and pharmaceutical industry, was voted down after a protracted and (for the business community) exceptionally expensive campaign in 1998. Still, the issue has not been settled and the ecologists continue to influence the legislation concerned. In energy policy, the configuration of power has been shifting in favour of a 'pro-ecology coalition' and against the business-dominated 'pro-growth coalition' (see Kriesi and Jegen 2000, 2001). The adoption of the initiative imposing a moratorium on nuclear energy in 1990 demonstrated the increasing political clout of the ecologists. More recently, however, the ecologists suffered several setbacks in popular votes: after an intensive campaign led by the major BIAs, an energy policy reform which included an ecological component was voted down at the polls in 2000, and, in 2003, the initiatives of the anti-nuclear movement for a prolongation of the moratorium and a phasing out of nuclear energy were also rejected.

These new challengers are not the only ones who increasingly constrain the manoeuvring space of the traditionally dominant BIAs. The number of relevant actors in the domain of economic policy has also increased for other reasons (Mach 1999b: 429ff.). As we shall see in the next chapter, although Switzerland is not a member of the European Union, the latter's legislation plays an increasing role in Swiss national economic policy making, as do the regulations of such international institutions as the OECD, the World Trade Organization (WTO) and the International Monetary Fund (IMF). Moreover, certain economists at Swiss universities and private consulting firms also have an increasing influence on the public decision-making process as a result of their applied research, publications and direct recommendations.

7.6 Conclusion

The present chapter has put the emphasis on those interest associations – BIAs and trade unions – which constitute the key players in Swiss economic and social policy making. Although these policy domains are of course not the only ones, they are easily the most important ones in policy making at the federal level in Switzerland. As we have pointed out, relative to the BIAs, the trade unions' influence has declined in labour relations, but not necessarily with respect to legislation. As we have also pointed out, the rise of new types of actors – associations and other kinds of participants in the political process – have tended to constrain the action space of both the BIAs and the trade unions over the last decades.

To complete this brief presentation of Swiss interest associations, we would add that the formerly dominant position of the BIAs in Swiss politics has not only been put into question by the rise of new challengers from the outside but also by internal dissent. An indication of the increasing heterogeneity of interests in the business community is the increasing division between the associations representing the 'exposed' sectors and those representing the 'sheltered' sectors with regard to the issues of liberalization and deregulation of the domestic markets. A case in point is cartel legislation (Mach 2006), where the SGV opposed a reform which was supported by economiesuisse. Transport policy provides other illustrative examples: in 1998, economiesuisse sided with the supporters of new railway tunnels through the Alps and of a new ecological tax on trucks, while the peak associations of the sheltered sectors (SBV and SGV) strongly mobilized against the latter and remained undecided (SGV) or did not take a stance (SBV) with regard to the former. The battle over the ecological tax on trucks between economiesuisse and the truckers' association gave rise to one of the most intense campaigns in the history of Swiss direct democracy. The voters finally decided in favour of the exposed sector. Overall, the sheltered sectors – both agriculture and small and medium-sized artisan and industrial firms – have lost much of their traditionally very strong position in Swiss politics. While back in the 1970s, the SGV was capable of mobilizing a majority of Swiss voters against major reforms – such as fiscal reform (including the introduction of VAT), territorial planning, and the introduction of macro-economic policy instruments – nowadays it has much less political clout. The farmers' peak association SBV is even more weakened – not only by external opposition but also by internal dissent: the division between the interests of different categories of farmers has led to the creation of oppositional associations – the VKMB, the German-speaking Swiss association for the defence of small and medium-sized farmers, and its French-speaking equivalent, the UPS (Union des producteurs suisses). Agricultural reforms have been imposed against the resistance of the SBV by a coalition of the federal administration and the export sector (Sciarini 1994) and a series of popular votes on agricultural policies throughout the 1990s indicated that the voters no longer habitually accept the policy propositions of the farmers' associations.

In addition, the concentration and unification of the associations in the Swiss business community gave rise to considerable frictions, especially between the financial sector and the traditional branches of Swiss industry (Swissmem), and between the exposed and non-exposed sectors (SGV, the peak association of the construction industry), which came to a head in summer 2006, when the two associations threatened to leave economiesuisse. Financial issues (in the case of Swissmem) and issues of interest representation (in both cases) played a key role in these tensions.

Moreover, the associations of the exposed sector have had to face internal dissent. In their ranks, irritation and discontent of leading figures with their peak associations led not only to the restructuring efforts described above but also to a spectacular lobbying initiative which bypassed the usual associational channel. At the beginning of the 1990s, a group of CEOs from key corporations of the exposed sector and of influential academic economists, preoccupied with Swiss competitiveness on the world markets, launched a campaign for the liberalization of the Swiss domestic market. Instead of passing through the Vorort – the predecessor of economiesuisse – they published a 'white book' formulating a programme for a neo-liberal reform of the Swiss economic and social policy, which included three aspects (Leutwiler *et al.* 1991): liberalization of the domestic markets, integration into the EU, and reform of fiscal and social policies. This reform programme was directly addressed to the federal government and to the general public, because the group felt that it was no longer adequately represented by the Vorort. This is not to say that the large firms have chosen to dispense with the lobbying efforts of their BIAs altogether. In fact, the creation of an informal pressure group was quite an exceptional step and, as we have also observed, to speak with a single voice is still considered to be very important by the central figures of the Swiss business community.

Let us note finally that the transformation of the party system has had its repercussions on the interest representation of the business community, too. Traditionally, the relationship between the three major parties on the right and the business community has been a rather cosy one (Kriesi 1980, 1998a): the members of Parliament representing these parties have always held large numbers of seats on the boards of major and minor Swiss corporations. Moreover, some staff members of important BIAs and employees of major corporations have always held seats in the national Parliament for these parties and major corporations have always relied on their members in the Parliament to represent their interests. The increasing divisions between the moderate and the nationalist-conservative camps on the right (see chapter 6) with regard to key questions of Switzerland's relationship with the EU and supranational organizations have, however, tended to complicate these relations and to exacerbate the divisions between the associations representing the interests of the sheltered sectors, on the one hand, and those of the exposed sectors on the other.

8 | *The decision-making process*

8.1 Introduction

As we have seen, Swiss 'consensus democracy' is characterized by a high degree of power sharing between different institutions and political actors, and by a large number of veto points, where policy proposals can be blocked by coalitions of opposing actors. Following Neidhart's (1970) well-known argument, we have already pointed out that the direct-democratic opening of the Swiss political system has led to the transformation of a 'plebiscitary democracy' into a 'negotiation democracy' (chapter 4). In other words, all actors capable of making a credible referendum threat have been integrated into the decision-making process. This includes not only the major political parties that have all been integrated into a stable, grand coalition (see chapter 5), but also major interest groups, the cantons and even social movement organizations, which are usually integrated from the start into elaborate pre-parliamentary consultation and negotiation procedures.

As a result of its inclusive and complex character, the political decision-making process in Switzerland has traditionally been *reactive, slow* and *incremental* (Kriesi 1998a: 293–7). Thus, decision making with regard to major societal problems is usually only taken up under immense external pressure – either from the international environment, or from exogenous domestic sources such as the economy or the citizens. Moreover, the decision-making process usually takes a very long time. Poitry (1989) calculated the average duration of such a process for all the proposals adopted by Parliament during the legislative period 1971–6. According to his calculations, the average process took about five years from its initiation to the final vote in Parliament! The median was situated at close to three years, which means that half of these processes lasted longer than three years. There has been no significant change since the 1970s (Sciarini 2007: 475). However, while decision making takes a long time, it usually does not result in major reforms. It only leads to incremental solutions, i.e. short-term compromises which have to be reconsidered after a relatively short lapse of time. Together with a chronic lack of resources, this incremental nature of decision making contributes to the overload of the whole process.

In this chapter, we follow the different stages of the decision-making process at the federal level before we turn to the more recent transformations which have occurred under the joint impact of increasing internationalization, polarization (chapter 6), diversity of interests (chapter 7) and the increasing role of the media in the political process. Following the heuristic framework of the 'stages approach' to the policy process (Deleon 1999; Héritier 1994), the Swiss legislative process can be broken down into the following phases:

- agenda-setting or initiation
- preparatory, pre-parliamentary phase
- parliamentary phase
- direct-democratic phase
- implementation phase

We shall take up these stages one by one, starting with the pre-parliamentary phase. With regard to agenda-setting, let us just note an important shift that has taken place over the last decades. In the 1970s, the Parliament was still the main agenda-setter and Poitry (1989: 180) concluded that the classical parliamentary initiation function was still very much alive in Switzerland. In the meantime, however, the Parliament lost a lot of its agenda-setting influence to the federal administration (Sciarini *et al.* 2002: 11): while it initiated 46 per cent of the legislative processes in the early 1970s, it only did so in 26 per cent of the cases by the late 1990s. Conversely, the corresponding share of the federal administration increased from 26 per cent to 41 per cent. This result is in line with a general trend towards increasing executive power at the expense of parliaments that can be observed across liberal democracies (Mény 1992: 358), and in Swiss politics in particular (Kriesi 1998a: 194). By the late 1990s, the executive seems to have taken the place of the Parliament as the organ most responsive to the pressure from the international environment and from below. Let us add that, in the second half of the 1990s, unmediated direct pressure from below – mainly from the citizens by way of initiatives – got the decision-making process going in 15 per cent of the cases, while direct pressure from the international environment accounted for 17 per cent of the initiations. The share of popular pressure was unchanged since the 1970s, whereas that of international pressure was up by 4 per cent.

8.2 The pre-parliamentary phase

The pre-parliamentary procedure is the main factor contributing to the long duration of the Swiss decision-making process. In the early 1970s, it accounted for no less than three-quarters of the average time it took to make decisions, and in the late 1990s it was still responsible for two-thirds of the total response time. It is not so much the difficulty of reaching a consensus which accounts for the slowness of the process, but rather the time it takes the administration to get its part of the work done (Poitry 1989: 358). More specifically, Sciarini (2004: 531) shows that the length of the process mainly depends on whether or not a formal consultation procedure is implemented. It is the evaluation of the answers to such a procedure by the responsible branch of the administration which takes so much time.

The manuals concerning Swiss politics usually break down the pre-parliamentary procedures into a series of veto points which include:

• elaboration of a pre-proposal
• committee(s) of experts
• formal consultation procedure(s)
• administrative consultation procedures
• decision by the government

According to this ideal-typical sequencing, the process starts with the elaboration of a pre-proposal by a public official, an independent expert or a working group including both types of actors. At this stage, the goal is to analyse the problem, collect the necessary information and to sketch a legislative text. Next, a proposal for a text is elaborated by a committee of experts which includes both experts with specialized knowledge and representatives of special interests, cantons and political parties. Sometimes, more than one committee is constituted to work on the proposal. Such committees are composed according to a skilful proportioning taking into account political, cultural and regional factors (Morand 1987). Germann (1985: 184) concludes that the composition of expert committees reflects a compromise between a 'purely technocratic' (knowledge-based) and a 'representative' (special interest-based) logic. Expert committees serve to forge the kernel of a compromise solution capable of avoiding a referendum at the end of the procedure. The result of the committees' work is submitted to the different services of the federal administration that are concerned by the issue in question and to the relevant political actors outside the administration. The new Constitution adopted in 2000 grants the cantons, the political parties and the specialized interests the right to be consulted in the preparatory stages of important legislative acts and other important projects (article 147). The traditional formal consultation procedure took a written form and basically included the same organizations that had already been represented in the expert committees. Since the early 1990s, the written procedure can be replaced by oral forms of consultation (conferences, hearings, etc.). Finally, before the final proposal is adopted by the government, it is again circulated in a consultation procedure internal to the administration.

In reality, a new proposal does not always pass through all these steps. There is a general tendency to streamline the process. Thus, the share of legislative acts that were prepared by a committee of experts was cut in half between the 1970s and the late 1990s (from 37 per cent to 18 per cent). Moreover, while the number of legislative acts that were submitted to a consultation procedure slightly increased (from 42 per cent to 45 per cent) over the same period of time (Sciarini *et al.* 2002: 16), the government sought to reduce the number of these procedures: according to the new law on consultation procedures, only the government (and no longer individual departments and offices) and parliamentary committees are entitled to launch such a procedure. In addition, they are restricted to genuinely important legislative acts.[1]

The overall degree of pre-parliamentary consultation varies with the juridical nature of the act, its importance, the degree of conflict involved and the department responsible for preparing the legislation (Sciarini *et al.* 2002: 16–19). The degree of consultation is higher for constitutional acts and federal laws than for urgent decrees or popular initiatives. If decisions need to be taken urgently, there is no time for elaborate preparatory consultation. For popular initiatives, the response time is limited by law and initiatives usually are in any case rejected by large

---

[1] See Bundesgesetz über das Vernehmlassungsverfahren (Vernehmlassungsgesetz VIG), 18 March 2005.

majorities of the political elite. It is also highly plausible that the more important and initially more divisive proposals give rise to particularly elaborate consultation procedures. The variation across departments suggests that there are different departmental 'traditions'.

Surprisingly, and contrary to the common wisdom of observers of Swiss politics, the pre-parliamentary procedures do not seem to contribute to the reduction of the level of conflict in the subsequent parliamentary phase. This unexpected result had already been found for the early 1970s (Poitry 1989; Kriesi 1998a: 202), and it has been confirmed by a more recent, and more adequate, analysis of the legislation in the late 1990s (Sciarini *et al.* 2002). This is to suggest that when a proposal is highly controversial at the outset of the process, it is very likely to remain so in the parliamentary arena, regardless of whether or not committees of experts and consultation procedures have tried to find a preliminary compromise solution.

8.3 The parliamentary phase

Once a proposal reaches the parliamentary phase, it is prepared in each chamber by one of a dozen permanent committees. As a result of the parliamentary reform of 1991, these committees replaced the large number of committees that had traditionally been created on an *ad hoc* basis for the preparation of specific legislative acts. This change tended to strengthen the position of the parliamentary committees in Parliament, but also with respect to the government (Lüthi 1996). In a system of symmetrical bicameralism, the capacity of the Parliament to reach a decision depends on the ability of the two chambers to reach a compromise. Given the discrepancy in the composition of the two chambers (see chapter 6), the capacity to find compromise solutions has traditionally been surprisingly high: until the 1980s, no less than 90 per cent of the draft proposals were adopted after a maximum of two deliberations in each chamber (Riklin and Ochsner 1984: 90). Recent results show a slight decrease in convergence between the two chambers (Nicolet *et al.* 2003). A particularly ominous sign is the increasing need to resort to a conference of conciliation – the ultimate attempt to find a compromise between the two chambers – in the 1995–9 legislative period. In these four years, fifteen conferences were requested, as many as in the entire period from 1905 to 1989. Overall, however, the degree of consensus reached in the final votes in Parliament remains very high. Sciarini and Trechsel (1996) have evaluated the consensus for all the legislative acts which were adopted between 1947 and 1995 and submitted to one of the three main direct-democratic instruments. Their results show that, for acts submitted to the optional or compulsory referendum, the rate of support in the final vote has never been lower than 90 or 80 per cent respectively. Indeed, 64 per cent of the former and 27 per cent of the latter have even been accepted unanimously. However, with regard to the popular initiatives, there are signs of an increasing level of polarization since the early 1980s.

Compared to the pre-parliamentary phase, the legislative activity in Parliament has traditionally been considered to be less important in Switzerland. Thus, the members of the political elite of the 1970s who were interviewed by Kriesi (1980) concurred that the veto points situated at the early stages of the process were much more important than parliamentary decision making. Moreover, according to an analysis of the legislative activities of Parliament in the early 1970s by Riklin and Zehnder (cited in Linder 1987: 41), Parliament only modified a minority of the government proposals, and its modifications generally concerned only minor points. Substantial changes were only introduced in a small number of cases.

8.4 The direct-democratic phase

As has been argued by Barry (1975), the direct-democratic institutions introduce a strong 'majoritarian' element into political decision making in Switzerland, an element which is at first sight incompatible with its consensus-oriented character. Criticizing this argument, Papadopoulos (1991: 9) draws our attention to the fact that the final vote in Parliament is also a majority vote. In his view, the consensus does not result from a suppression of majoritarian procedures but from their mutual neutralization. Accordingly, it is not the majoritarian character of the direct-democratic procedures that poses a problem for the model of consensus democracy but rather the fact that they constitute the final step in the decision-making procedure and that they put an end to the interplay of successive veto points.

As we have seen, the Swiss political system has developed a series of mechanisms allowing the political elites to reduce the uncertainty introduced into the decision-making process by the direct-democratic opening at its very end. These mechanisms make it possible to reduce the chances that an optional referendum will in the end be launched against a legislative act adopted by Parliament. Indeed, of the more than 2,000 acts submitted to the optional referendum during the period 1848 to 1997, only about 7 per cent have ultimately been attacked by such a referendum. This share has been relatively stable over the period covered, although the absolute number of successful attacks has increased in the more recent past (Sciarini and Trechsel 1996). The likelihood of an optional referendum is not at all affected by the degree of pre-parliamentary consultation: whether a consultation procedure or an expert committee is held or not has no effect on the likelihood of such a referendum (Scarini *et al.* 2002: 26). However, the degree of support a legislative act obtains in the final vote in Parliament has a direct relation with the likelihood of a referendum: the smaller the parliamentary majority adopting a government proposal, the higher the probability of a referendum (Lehner 1984: 38f.; Sciarini and Trechsel 1996; Trechsel and Sciarini 1998).

Once a vote becomes unavoidable, the political elite still has the possibility of controlling the process and reducing the uncertainty of its outcome. This applies both to the optional referendums that have been launched successfully and to the compulsory votes (referendums and initiatives). Democracy, as defined by Schattschneider (1960, 1988: 135), is 'a competitive political system in which competing leaders and organizations define the alternatives of public policy in such a way that the public can participate in the decision-making process . . . Conflict, competition, organization, leadership, and responsibility are the ingredients of a working definition of democracy.' This definition also applies to the direct-democratic process. Not only do the political elites define the choices that are presented to the public in direct-democratic voting procedures, but the competing elites also provide the crucial cues for the vote and they mobilize the citizens during the campaign. This does not mean that the elite as a whole is in complete control of the direct-democratic process. Only when the elite as a whole reaches a *consensus* are the citizens left with no other choice but to follow their lead (Zaller 1992) – in the absence of conflict, there is no real choice. This happens in a few cases of uncontested modifications of the Constitution by compulsory referendums. In the usual cases with *divided elites*, however, the citizens' choice becomes unpredictable, as Papadopoulos (1991, 1994b, 1995, 1996, 1997, 1998) has pointed out repeatedly. Even if the elites play a key role in the final choice, the

Swiss direct-democratic vote is not simply a ritual exercise in 'democratic gymnastics' (Papadopoulos 1995: 441).

An analysis of some 150 direct-democratic votes at the federal level during the period 1981–99 shows that the size and the composition of the coalitions that form in the course of the campaign in support of the government's position are absolutely crucial for the eventual fate of a legislative proposal (Kriesi 2005). The coalitions are basically defined by the alignment of the partisan forces. Their additional members, especially interest associations of various stripes, are embedded in the partisan alignments. While interest associations are important suppliers of resources for the partisan coalitions during the campaign, they usually do not add anything to the explanatory power of the configurations of coalitions defined by the partisan alignments. It is sufficient to know the configuration of the partisan forces in order to predict the outcome of the vote.

This general pattern varies somewhat according to the type of instrument. Initiatives generally have little success at the polls. The government virtually always rejects initiatives and it almost always has its way in the popular vote. This does not mean, however, that the government's success is always guaranteed in advance. Initiatives often pose a serious threat to the government. But if the government's camp anticipates a close vote, it is capable of investing large sums in the campaign, heavily outspending the initiative's supporters. On average, initiative campaigns are much more intensive than campaigns for referendums. Only in exceptional cases can a promising initiative impose itself against the barrage of publicity opposing it during the campaign. On the other hand, even if the initiative's supporters are capable of outspending the government's camp – as is typically the case for the few initiatives launched from the right – their chances are quite slim. Here we find confirmation of the difficulties faced by 'direct modifying campaigns' Gerber (1999) observed in the United States. Still, some recent initiatives were accepted in the popular vote: in 1981, an initiative in favour of consumer protection passed; three ecological initiatives obtained popular support in 1987, 1990 and 1994; and two initiatives from the right were also adopted – one in favour of the introduction of a work-free national holiday in 1993 and one in favour of the perpetual incarceration of dangerous sexual offenders in 2004. Moreover, many initiatives have an indirect influence on legislation, even if they are not adopted outright (Werder 1978).

Referendums are more dangerous for the government. This applies in particular to optional referendums. Roughly half of the legislative acts that were ever attacked by an optional referendum ultimately failed at the polls. However, more recently the rate of government success has increased somewhat. The weapon of the referendum tends to wear itself out over time: the multiplication of optional referendums launched since the 1970s was accompanied by a decline in the success rate of the challengers, especially since the 1990s. Still, challengers who launch a referendum not only benefit from the institutional logic – a referendum gives rise to a 'direct preserving campaign' – but a successfully launched referendum also often contributes to a fragmentation of the right. A referendum often provokes a 'redistribution of the cards' within the elite (Trechsel and Sciarini 1998). Given that the right constitutes the 'natural' majority in Swiss politics, and given that it is much more resourceful than the left, a lack of cohesion on the right becomes particularly dangerous for the government's position. If the right is fragmented, the balance of the campaign tips against the government and the more intense the campaign becomes in such a situation, the greater the chances are that the camp that outspends its adversary will win the vote. For compulsory referendums, as in the case of initiatives, the intensity of the campaign, in turn, depends on the anticipated closeness of the vote. However, in the case of optional referendums, the intense minorities who launch them tend to invest in the defence of their cause, whether they anticipate a close vote or not. In addition to the general failure of initiatives, this is an important reason why the overall relationship between the direction of the campaign and the outcome of the vote is not as strong as has often been maintained.

8.5 The implementation phase

Once a new policy proposal has been adopted, the political decision-making process has not yet come to an end. The decisions adopted by Parliament and by the popular votes have to be implemented and, given the trend towards framework laws, many details have to be specified before the legislation can be enacted. In Switzerland, implementation is often treated as synonymous with 'executive federalism', that is the delegation of implementation of federal programmes to the cantons, the subnational levels of government. However, implementation can also follow different patterns. Kissling-Näf and Wälti

(2007: 503–7) distinguish between three models of implementation: in addition to implementation by federal delegation, they refer to 'para-governmental' and 'new subsidiary' implementation. *Federal delegation* has always been the predominant model. According to this model, the federal government is responsible for framework legislation, the implementation of which is delegated to the cantons. This type of implementation is accompanied by intense negotiations between the federal government and the cantons. Currently, the logic of implementation by federal delegation not only strengthens the cantons' position in the implementation process, but it also allows them to play a key role at the policy formulation stage. Their growing role during implementation weighs against the centralization of policy-making powers at the federal level.

Para-governmental implementation involves the delegation of implementation to para-governmental and private organizations such as interest associations rather than to the cantons. This pattern is in line with the subsidiarity principle (see chapter 7), according to which the federal government only intervenes when the self-organization of private actors proves inadequate for problem-solving. Typical of the neo-corporatist arrangements in Switzerland is that, in many areas, powerful peak associations also play a decisive role in the implementation process. The distribution of power between public and private actors as well as the instruments of regulation vary a great deal from one policy domain to another. Graphic examples of what Streeck and Schmitter (1985) have called 'private interest governments' can be found in the field of agriculture, where the public sector is integrated in many different ways with the associative agents (see Linder 1987: 119).

With the third model of implementation, the set of relevant actors is extended beyond administrative offices and classic interest associations and constitutes an open, pluralistic network of public and private actors. The state attempts to make use of non-governmental organizations and harness the knowledge and experience of target groups by involving them directly. Examples of this *new subsidiary implementation* are provided by the environmental policy domain, where environmental organizations obtained formal rights to appeal in impact assessment procedures (Kissling-Näf 1997; Wälti 2001), and in the domain of AIDS prevention, where the state not only delegates the implementation to private organizations, but creates them in the first place for this very purpose (Bütschi and Cattacin 1994; Kübler 2001).

8.6 The transformation of the decision-making process: internationalization

Swiss political decision making is not taking place in a vacuum, but is increasingly affected by policies adopted in the international context. Although Switzerland is not a member of the EU and although it has only recently joined the UN (see chapter 2), its policy-making process is increasingly 'internationalized'. By reference to the work of Sciarini and his collaborators (Fischer 2003; Sciarini and Nicolet 2005), we can distinguish between 'direct' and 'indirect' forms of internationalization. 'Direct' internationalization includes international treaties and related legislative adaptations. A case in point would be the Bilateral Treaty I (1999). 'Indirect' internationalization, by contrast, refers to the 'autonomous adaptation' of Swiss legislative acts to European legislation. An illustrative example of this form of internationalization is provided by the liberalization of the Swiss telecommunications sector, which closely followed the legislation previously adopted by the EU, although the EU did not by any means require such an adaptation of Swiss regulations. As a result of the increasing influence of the international context on Swiss policy making, at least four changes in political decision-making procedures have been observed: a modification of the consultation procedures, a reduction in the level of conflict, a shift in the distribution of power and the rise of new actors.

As we have seen, the formal Swiss consultation procedures are very time-consuming. Their slowness does not fit with the rapid and discontinuous rhythm of international negotiations. Moreover, international negotiations do not allow for the formal inclusion of a great many domestic actors. Given the strong 'take it or leave it' character of an agreement negotiated at the international level, there is even very little room for consultation and modification at the ratification stage (Fischer *et al.* 2002: 148). However, given the need to include in the decision-making process all those groups who, if neglected, might endanger the agreement in the domestic ratification phase, the Swiss authorities cannot simply dispense with consultation procedures. *Informal* consultations are increasingly introduced to provide a solution to this dilemma. For acts of 'direct' internationalization, Sciarini and Nicolet (2005) find less frequent and less important formal consultations, compensated by an increased importance of informal consultations. Instances of autonomous adaptation are also characterized by a high degree of informal consultation, in addition to a (still) high degree of formal consultation. Similarly, in relation to three measures of economic liberalization which have been implemented under international pressure – the reform of the cartel law, the telecoms reform and the internal market law – Mach *et al.* (2003) observe that these measures were not prepared by the traditional expert committees. In these cases, the traditional expertise of interest associations has been replaced by independent experts – consultants, economists or lawyers. Moreover, Parliament had to discuss these measures under heavy time pressure in order to keep up with the rhythm of international calendars (of the General Agreement on Tariffs and Trade (GATT) and of the EU).

As Katzenstein (1984, 1985) has pointed out, economic openness and vulnerability favours the emergence of domestic consensus. Accordingly, we may expect the *level of conflict* to be lower for internationalized forms of legislation. Sciarini and Nicolet (2005) confirm this expectation. Although there have been some spectacularly divisive internationalized proposals such as the Treaty on the European Economic Area (EEA) in 1992 and the creation of a Swiss UN 'Blue Helmet' corps in 1994, most of the (directly and indirectly) internationalized acts do not lead to much conflict on the domestic front.

Börzel and Risse (2002) distinguish between two more ways in which internationalization affects domestic policy making: first, it modifies the opportunity structure in which actors evolve, which leads to a *redistribution of power among domestic actors*. Actors who have direct access to international arenas (such as European institutions and the World Trade Organization (WTO)) are strengthened domestically. As many authors have argued, this mechanism reinforces the position of the state *executive* in domestic policy making. The executive benefits from an increased autonomy with regard to domestic actors, since it is the only actor involved at both the international and domestic levels. In addition, internationalization reinforces those actors whose *preferences are in line with international policy developments*, because they can legitimize domestic reforms by reference to external changes. This general analysis of the international impact on domestic power relations is also relevant for Switzerland. Thus, Sciarini's (1994, 1995) analysis of the negotiations in the Uruguay round of the GATT documents the reinforcement of the Swiss actors who were directly involved in the negotiations – the government and the OFEA – in domestic agricultural policy making, at the expense of the Parliament, the Office of Agriculture and the traditionally all-powerful farmers' associations. The analysis of the negotiations of the Bilateral Treaty I by Sciarini and Nicolet (2005) also provides strong evidence for the reinforcement of the executive relative to private actors and the Parliament. Finally, Mach *et al.* (2003: 310) argue that the major initiators of the economic regulatory reforms of the 1990s were all actors whose preferences were in line with regulatory reforms at the international level.

Among the private actors, the political and economic preferences of the exposed sectors and of mobile capital more generally are most clearly in line with international market liberalization. Their position is strengthened because they can credibly threaten an 'exit option', whereas labour and sectors depending on the domestic market are weakened (Keohane and Milner 1996). Moreover, the business community is generally reinforced, because it has more competences at the international level and more channels of access to European institutions, given that it has been able to organize itself internationally much earlier than unions. The analysis of the negotiations of the Bilateral Treaty and its accompanying measures shows, however, that the generally expected asymmetrical empowerment of business interests is not an inevitable result of internationalization. As Fischer *et al.* (2002) and Fischer (2003) show, much depends on the strategic use that the different actors make of the available domestic veto points. Their analysis of the domestic measures accompanying the Bilateral Treaty I (1999) indicates that, in this case, the process of Europeanization did not significantly reinforce the business community. Their analysis also confirms the reinforcement of the executive as a consequence of Europeanization. But neither the government nor the business community was in complete control of the ratification process. Aware of the importance of the ratification of the agreement for both the government and for the business sector, the unions used the opportunity to issue a referendum threat, which allowed them to pressure their opponents into offering major side-payments compensating them for the losses they faced as a result of the agreement (see p. 109). As Fischer *et al.* (2002: 164) point out, this case illustrates the importance of the strategic use of veto points by veto players and the extent to which such a strategy is credible.

According to the second mechanism discussed by Börzel and Risse, internationalization initiates learning processes among domestic elites and gives rise to the emergence of *new 'norm entrepreneurs'* who will

promote domestic reforms. Mach *et al.* (2003: 310f.) find confirmation
for this general proposition in their analysis of Swiss economic regulatory reforms. By appointing them to draft the initial bills of the reforms,
the government empowered new 'norm entrepreneurs' (new administrative actors or independent experts) who had previously not, or only
marginally, been involved in the policy domains under consideration:
the OFEA for all three reforms in question, and the Office of
Telecommunications (OFCOM), created in 1992, for the 1997 telecoms reform.

8.7 The transformation of the decision-making process: the changing national context

For various reasons, the context of political decision making is also
changing at the national level. With respect to social policy making in
particular, Häusermann *et al.* (2004) suggest that the relevance of corporatist concertation in the pre-parliamentary phase is declining. They
argue that three factors contribute to this decline. First of all, faced with
economic recession, budget deficits and socio-demographic pressures
on the pension systems, the policy objectives of business and labour
unions tend to become increasingly polarized. As a result, agreement
between the social partners becomes less likely even though they may
continue to negotiate. Second, the increasing heterogeneity of interests
among the members of employers' associations and trade unions and
the decreasing representativeness of these organizations due to a declining membership undermine the legitimacy of their peak associations
(see chapter 7). Third, the increasing importance of media coverage
is also likely to render compromises in corporatist bargaining more
difficult. Increasing media coverage contributes to the tension between
the 'logic of influence', which requires a relatively protected and secre-
tive sphere of negotiation to build mutual confidence, and the 'logic of
membership', which stresses loyalty to the objectives of membership
of the respective negotiators.

Comparing the major pension and unemployment insurance
reforms of the 1970s with those adopted in 1995, Häusermann
et al. (2004) show that these factors contributed to the declining
importance of corporatist negotiations between the social partners.
Whereas, in the 1970s, inclusive negotiations between the social partners in the pre-parliamentary arena resulted in broad agreements,

compromise-seeking in similar negotiations largely failed in the 1990s. This led to the increasing importance of the parliamentary arena for social reforms, as not only the social partners but also the government failed to produce viable proposals for reform. Under the pressure of the referendum threat, the parliamentary committees relaunched the negotiations and were able to completely reformulate the government bills. The parties – most notably the Social Democrats and the Radicals – proved to be more open than the social partners were to new, value-based social demands such as gender equality (especially important in the case of the pension reform). In a similar vein, Jegher (1999) shows that the Parliament has become more active with regard to social policy making: from 1995 to 1997, it amended two-thirds of the social policy proposals, almost twice as many as the average. Häusermann *et al.* (2004: 51) point out that a similar weakening of the traditionally predominant social partners has been observed in Austria, the Netherlands and Denmark. In these countries, however, it was not the Parliament but the government which became the key actor for reform.

Fischer (2003), who analysed the most recent pension reform, the eleventh such reform following on the tenth, which was the object of the analysis of Häusermann *et al.*, confirms the declining importance of the traditional pre-parliamentary arenas and the increasing importance of the search for parliamentary majorities in social policy making. However, according to Fischer (2003), in spite of the declining importance of their traditional turf in the pre-parliamentary arena, the peak associations of the social partners have not become less influential in the decision-making process. Fischer argues that this is to be explained by shifting power relations *within* the major parties: while the new values-based wing of the Social Democrats got the upper hand in the tenth pension reform, the trade union wing regained a key position in the eleventh reform. The unions regained some of their former strength more generally – a development which Fischer attributes to their capacity to block welfare retrenchment measures in the referendum phase. As we have seen in chapter 4, it is much easier to defend the *status quo* with the referendum than to pass a new reform. In chapter 10, we shall see that, given the changing context in social policy – in which welfare state expansion is being replaced by welfare state retrenchment – the referendum has become a crucial weapon for the left in general, and for the trade unions, which are the primary organizations on the left with the required resources to mobilize a successful referendum campaign.

As a result of social change and the mobilization by new political actors, power relations are also in flux in other policy domains. The energy policy, which has been studied by Jegen (2003) and Kriesi and Jegen (2001), may serve as an example. Analysing the structure of the coalitions at the organizational level, Jegen (2003) uncovers a large amount of continuity in the configuration of power. In the domain of energy policy, the 'electricity consensus' of the 1990s largely reproduces the predominance by a coalition of the political right with the business peak associations that Kriesi (1980) had found for the federal political system of the 1970s more generally. At the level of the individual representatives, however, there are more signs of change than at the organizational level. Although Kriesi and Jegen (2001) found the same structure of coalitions at the level of the individual representatives – a 'pro-growth coalition' challenged by a 'pro-ecology' coalition – the power relationship appeared to be more symmetrical at the level of the individual members of the energy policy elite than at the organizational level. The importance of the individual representatives of the 'pro-ecology' coalition surpasses that of the entire coalition – the sum is smaller than its parts. The reasons why this is so are not entirely clear, but we suspect that the pro-ecology coalition lacks the coherence of its adversaries and that, in the final analysis, individual resources such as innovative ideas and mediation capacities are becoming secondary to the organizational power of mobilization.

8.8 Conclusion

In spite of the changing context, political decision making in Switzerland has not fundamentally changed. The key characteristic of the political process – its slow, reactive and incremental character – remains the same. The changing international context has contributed to a reinforcement of the government and of those offices of the federal administration that are in direct contact with the international and supranational system. Both the changing international and national contexts have contributed to the slow but continuous decline of the traditional pre-parliamentary mechanisms of compromise-seeking. These mechanisms are too slow in a rapidly changing world where the rhythm of decision making is dictated by supranational organizations, intergovernmental arrangements and international markets. These mechanisms also prove too demanding with respect to the capacity to make concessions in an increasingly polarizing political system that is under increasingly close public scrutiny. As a result, pre-parliamentary consultation is becoming more informal. Moreover, lobbying is no longer limited to direct interventions with public authorities, but increasingly includes attempts to influence public opinion and to instrumentalize it in order to put pressure on public authorities (Kollman 1998; Zervudacki 1999: 162, 175ff.).

Political influence increasingly takes an indirect route, passing via the public space and the public's reactions measured by opinion surveys. Thus, the director of the peak employers' association (SAV) pointed out in an interview with one of the authors that he spends about half of his time on public relations (working for and with the media). Using the example of a recent debate on security policy, he maintains that the point of view of the employers' association has been much more effectively defended by an article in the Sunday press than by his lobbying efforts in Berne. From the point of view of the associations, interventions in the media have the additional advantage that they are highly visible to their own members, who get the impression that the association is doing something on their behalf. But attempts to instrumentalize the media are not without pitfalls of their own. The media are no longer the ready servants of politicians. They move from the periphery to the centre stage of the political process and submit the politicians to the journalists' criteria of success. Following their own rationality, the media prefer reporting on stars and spectacular events and they do not hesitate to stage the political process accordingly. The politicians and those who wish to influence them have to adapt to this logic and those who cannot adapt face a loss of influence. In German-speaking Switzerland, the TV-show *ARENA* has come to provide the crucial stage for the public debate of national politics. Late each Friday evening, the hottest issue of the week is debated by the political stars of the day. The resonance and success of this show is unparalleled by anything Swiss politics has known in the past, and to be 'fit-for-*ARENA*' has become a crucial asset for a politician's career.

The slow, but irreversible demise of traditional forms of pre-parliamentary negotiations should, however, not be deplored too much. As the empirical analyses of their implications have shown, their impact on the level of conflict was already limited in the 1970s, and has been still less effective in the more recent past.

9 | Economic policy: liberalization under constraints

9.1 Introduction

Switzerland has a longstanding global reputation as an economic success story, but also as a special case (OECD 2006: 20). The reasons for this success are not obvious, but they are usually attributed to a combination of factors including openness to international trade and investment, a flexible labour market (see chapter 7), a sound monetary policy, a highly developed financial sector, a strong record of innovation, a high level of human capital development, and a unique system of government which we have described in the previous chapters. However, since the 1990s, economic liberalization on a worldwide scale has put the traditional Swiss model of adjustment under pressure. Unleashed by a series of changes in the American economy, Western Europe in general and Switzerland in particular have been put under increasing pressure. Liberalization means the introduction or reinforcement of market competition which goes hand in hand with an often dramatic erosion of different forms of traditional privileges. According to Schwartz (2001), 'liberalization' means, above all, the erosion of politically guaranteed property rights and the income streams associated with them. Liberalization therefore especially concerns individuals and firms in the sectors that have been protected against competition by state intervention since the 1920s. While liberalization implies the introduction of greater market competition, it does not necessarily imply deregulation, i.e. the reduction or elimination of regulation; in fact, in most cases, liberalization goes together with *re*-regulation, i.e. the reformulation of old rules or the introduction of new ones. The result often consists not only in an increasing competition, but also in more rules (Vogel 1996).

The 'neo-liberal turn' has been characterized by a reorientation of economic and social policy in Western democracies more generally (Keohane and Milner 1996; Kurzer 1993; Jobert 1994;

Esping-Andersen 1996; Mach 1999a). This turn has favoured the abandoning of Keynesian recipes for neo-classic solutions in order to react to the challenge of the transformed nature of world markets. With the decline of Keynesianism, the international competitiveness of national products has replaced the growth of aggregate demand as the main goal of economic policy (Schmitter and Grote 1997). Since the 1990s, the notion that the Swiss economy needed better conditions in order to improve its competitiveness on the world market has gained increasing acceptance among the Swiss political elite and the improvement of these conditions has become the main objective of the economic policy reforms of the 1990s.

Although the goal has been the same in all countries, its implementation has been influenced by many national specificities (Berger and Dore 1996; Crouch and Streeck 1996). And while it has become commonplace to take into account external factors in the analysis of the Swiss policies, internal factors still filter and modify the impact of the external context. Without any doubt, the increasing weight of international institutions such as the WTO and the EU restricts the available options for economic policy making at the national level. But in order to determine how national policy makers choose among this more restricted set of options, one has to take into account the national configurations of power and the strategies of the different actors at the national level.

As we have seen in chapter 7, Katzenstein (1984, 1985) stressed the capacity of small European countries such as Switzerland to adapt to the vicissitudes of the world markets. He pointed out the great success of Swiss economic policy, which, he claimed, has mastered the challenges of the world markets by combining a liberal foreign economic policy with compensations for those groups who were disadvantaged due to their exposure to such markets. But Katzenstein was mainly interested in the restructuring of certain branches of the economy (most notably the textile and watch-making industries) which were heavily exposed to international competition (Mach 1999a). Focusing his analysis on the exposed sector, he concluded that the small countries, and Switzerland in particular, were able to reconcile economic flexibility and political stability. Moreover, by concentrating on the compensations in favour of the left, Katzenstein overlooked the fact that the Swiss version of democratic corporatism was rather a 'liberal-conservative' one that compensated not only the left but above all conservative groups such as the farmers, small businesses and tradesmen. Had he paid more attention to the non-exposed sector and the 'selective protectionism' that served to compensate the conservative forces attached to it, he might have arrived at somewhat less sanguine conclusions with regard to the small open economies' capacity to face the world markets. This, at least, is implied by the much less benevolent interpretation of some Swiss economists who pushed for a 'neo-liberal turn' in Swiss economic policy (Borner *et al.* 1990, 1994; Wittman 1992).

As is pointed out by Krugmann (1996), the debate about international competitiveness is nothing but a debate about productivity. Accordingly, the gross national product per capita, corrected for purchasing power, constitutes a simple indicator of the relative competitiveness of a given country. It provides a summary measure for the level and quality of the production of a country, the firms' capacity to innovate and the policies' support for the economy. Measured by this indicator, Switzerland has experienced a relative decline over the past thirty years (see figure 9.1). The Swiss economy has grown more slowly than its main competitors. Switzerland is still among the richest countries in the world, and it is still richer than the average member of the EU or the OECD, but its relative advance over other OECD countries has declined considerably over the past twenty years. It was overtaken by the United States at the beginning of the 1990s and, at the beginning of the present century, after Norway and Luxembourg, Ireland too caught up with the Swiss. Although the Swiss are still privileged, their way of life is no longer much different from that of their European neighbours or, for that matter, from that of the population of any other country with a highly developed economy. The Swiss economy has proved as vulnerable as any other to the ups and downs of the business cycle, and it is not as uniformly efficient as the Swiss themselves like to believe.

This lacklustre performance has been attributed to different causal factors. On the one hand, it has been attributed to supply-side factors (Federal Department of Economic Affairs 2002; OECD 2004, 2006). According to this reasoning, there are only two possibilities of improving the production of goods and services – one has to increase either the number of hours worked or the product per hour worked, i.e. the labour productivity. Since the number of hours worked per head of the population in Switzerland (together with Japan) is markedly higher than in all the other OECD countries, the problem must lie with lagging

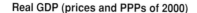

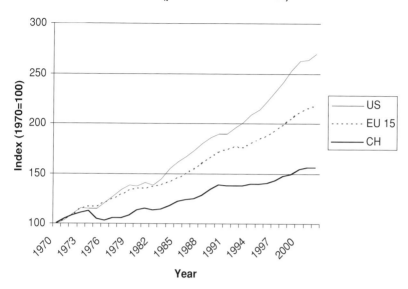

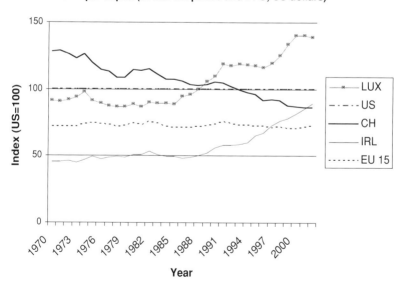

Figure 9.1 Growth of the Swiss economy in comparison with the US, EU fifteen and other countries
Source: OECD.

productivity. And indeed, labour productivity has grown at a declining rate in Switzerland over the past decades, which can be explained by insufficient, albeit urgent, structural reforms. On the other hand, the unimpressive economic performance may also be attributed to other factors, such as the unanticipated consequences of immigration policies, the deficient management of the business cycle and, possibly, the relocation abroad of production activities by major Swiss corporations. In this chapter, we discuss the different ways to account for the relative decline in Swiss economic performance and the measures taken to redress this negative trend.

9.2 Structural reforms

As Mach *et al.* (2003: 302) observe, in many respects, 'the 1990s can be seen as a turning point for economic policies in Switzerland. They stand in sharp contrast to previous decades which were characterized by slow, incremental, and generally limited policy changes. During the 1990s, substantial reforms took place in various fields.' Some years earlier, Mach (1999a) had concluded his assessment of the structural economic reforms by observing that there had never been as many structural reforms and innovations in economic and social policy as there were in the 1990s, and he suggested that future historians who were going to study the 1990s would emphasize the wide scope and the number of changes that had been adopted in such a short lapse of time. Although this assessment is far too sweeping, it certainly points to a renewed vigour in Swiss economic policy making.

Three factors contributed to the shift in this domain: the recession and the sharp increase in unemployment in the early 1990s, the international pressure exerted by the Uruguay round of the GATT (the predecessor organization of the WTO) and by the European integration process, and the pressures exerted by the most internationalized sectors of the Swiss business community. In fact, the campaign for structural economic reform was launched, at the beginning of the 1990s, by a group of CEOs from key corporations operating in the exposed sector and by influential economists from academia, who were concerned by the decline of Swiss competitiveness on the world markets. As we have observed in the conclusion to chapter 7, instead of passing through their peak associations, this group published a 'white book' formulating a programme for a neo-liberal reform of the Swiss economic and social policy, which amounted to a three-pronged strategy (Leutwiler *et al.* 1991): liberalization of the domestic markets, integration into the EU, and reform of fiscal and social policies. This reform programme was directly addressed to the federal government and to the general public, as the group felt that it was no longer adequately represented by the peak association of the business community.

The programme was rapidly implemented. Early in 1992, before the vote on Switzerland's accession to the European Economic Area (EEA) in December of that year, a working group initiated by the Federal Ministry of the Economy and headed by David de Pury, one of the authors of the 'white book', presented thirty-three specific proposals for the liberalization of the Swiss economy. Inspired by this programme, four motions were adopted by Parliament in the summer of 1992 which proposed a series of measures for the 'revitalization' of the Swiss economy. Immediately after the rejection of the EEA Treaty by the voters in December 1992, the government launched a 'revitalization programme' that took up several of these propositions and also reintroduced some measures that had been part and parcel of the domestic adjustment programme required by the EEA Treaty. Parliament started to implement elements of this programme in an extraordinary session devoted to it in the spring of 1993. Two years later, the same group that had launched the structural reform process published a second 'white book' assessing the state of the implementation of the reforms and proposing a second 'programme of revitalization'. In this chapter, we consider in more detail how the internal liberalization and the reform of fiscal policies fared in the political process. The reform of social policy will be treated in chapter 10, while the integration of Switzerland into the EU will be discussed in chapter 11.

Internal liberalization

One of the most promising sets of measures for improving the productivity of the Swiss economy attempts to increase competition in the internal Swiss markets. International comparisons always reveal the massively higher prices in Switzerland, which is, for example, illustrated by *The Economist*'s Big Mac Index. In 2007, a Big Mac cost roughly 53 per cent more in Switzerland than in the USA.[1] On average,

---

[1] *The Economist*, 7 July 2007, p. 74.

Swiss price levels are 40 per cent above EU levels, with particularly important differences for housing, health, public transportation and food. Such international price comparisons suggest that competition is still rather weak in many parts of the non-exposed economy. Accordingly, the liberalization programme included reforms of three major laws designed to increase internal competition – the law on cartels, the law on the domestic market and the public procurement law, all adopted in 1995 – as well as the liberalization of basic infrastructures, i.e. telecommunications, electricity and postal services.

The *law on cartels* constitutes the legal basis for the reinforcement of the competition in Switzerland. Representatives of the exposed sector, together with scientific experts and the Federal Office of Foreign Economic Affairs (a new player in this policy domain – see chapter 8), pushed through a reinforcement of the anti-cartel measures, with the support of the left, but against the resistance of the peak association of small businesses and tradesmen. The revised version of the law still did not declare cartels unlawful *per se*, but only prohibited abusive practices. Mach (2006) stresses the continuity with past practices: he qualifies the new legislation as a 'qualitative jump', but not a decisive break with the past. The new law proved, however, quite toothless when it was tested by the merger of the two biggest Swiss banks in 1998 and by the discovery of the vitamins cartel in 2001. In the first case, the Swiss competition commission only imposed symbolic constraints on the two banks, and in the second case, whereas Roche, the Swiss multinational which had been part of the vitamins cartel, was fined a record 675 million Swiss francs by the EU, the Swiss commission had no power to impose any direct sanctions. This led to another revision of the cartel law which was adopted in 2004. The principal innovation of this new version of the law is the introduction of direct sanctions for violations of the law, which can rise to 10 per cent of the turnover obtained in Switzerland during the last three years.

The *law on the domestic market* attempts to suppress the commercial barriers within Switzerland by applying the EU's principle of mutual recognition (established in the 'Cassis-de-Dijon' judgment of the European Court of Justice) to cantonal norms and regulations, i.e. to the domestic Swiss market. Specifically, the law intended to allow practitioners in different professions (such as teachers, barbers, architects, taxi drivers, therapists) who are accredited in one canton to exercise their profession in other cantons as well. The adoption of the principle

of mutual recognition avoided the introduction of a new federal competence (which would have required a modification of the Constitution),
but it also proved to be quite ineffectual. A revision of the law designed
to improve its effectiveness was adopted in 2005. In addition, the government made an attempt to introduce the Cassis-de-Dijon principle
unilaterally in its relations with the EU to eliminate technical barriers
to trade – an attempt that predictably met with great resistance from
the small businesses and tradesmen.

The opening up of the *public procurement markets* was imposed
by the conclusion of the Uruguay round (GATT) and the creation of
the WTO. Public procurements were traditionally hardly subject to
competition by outsiders but rather belonged to the preserve of local or
cantonal suppliers, and the local construction industry was thus greatly
privileged in the competition for public contracts. The new treaties of
the WTO imposed new competition rules in this traditionally highly
protected domain.

The *liberalization of basic infrastructures* began with *telecommunications*. Under pressure from the liberalization process within the EU,
the government proposed a revision of the law on telecommunications
in summer 1996 and, in record time, the new law was adopted in spring
1997 and implemented in 1998. It separated the post and telecoms services into two distinct companies (Post and Swisscom) and introduced
a far-reaching liberalization of the telecoms sector with the removal
of the public monopoly and the creation of an independent regulatory
agency – the Communications Commission (ComCom) – which could
guarantee free access to the telecoms market in collaboration with the
newly created Federal Office of Communications (OFCOM). The liberalization did not go all the way, however, since it did not include
the 'last mile' (i.e. the 'local loop'), which means that the competitors of Swisscom – the successor of the federal monopoly – do not
have equal access to local connections. In 2005, Parliament adopted
a compromise solution for the 'last mile', partly taking into account
the interests of Swisscom, and partly those of its competitors. Finally,
the federal infrastructure – post, telecommunications and railways –
was completely reorganized: Post, Swisscom and the federal railways
became independent corporations directed by their boards and their
CEOs, just like privately held companies.

The *liberalization of public services* met with considerable resistance from the unions and citizens at large. Thus, the closing down of

numerous local post offices prompted unions and consumers' associations to launch an initiative for the preservation of 'postal services for everybody', which was only barely rejected by the voters in autumn 2004. The liberalization of the electricity market foundered on the resistance of the voters in autumn 2002. Against the background of the widely publicized negative consequences of the liberalization of the energy market in California and of the railway system in the United Kingdom, the 'grounding' of Swissair (October 2001) and additional scandals in the Swiss business community, as well as the mobilization for the maintenance of the 'public service', a majority of the voters rejected this proposal, because it was correctly perceived as favouring only large, industrial consumers of electricity and providing no direct advantages for the average consumer (Federal Office of Energy 2003). It was only in spring 2007 that Parliament adopted a more cautious, stepwise liberalization of the electricity market.

Under the pressure of the Uruguay round (GATT), the deregulation of *agriculture*, the most protected sector of the Swiss economy, also became the object of structural reforms (Sciarini 1994). In 1992, a new approach was introduced in agricultural policy which increasingly emphasized ecologically friendly production and started to replace subsidies for products by direct payments for the maintenance of agricultural land and ecological production. However, these adjustments did not imply a fundamental restructuring of agricultural policy (Kappel and Landmann 1997: 131). The direct payments served to replace the loss of income due to GATT regulations. Economists keep recommending a profound reform to improve the productivity of the sector. But the resistance of the agricultural community has been formidable. For decades, the voters have supported its demands, although they prove to be extremely costly for consumers. It is only more recently that their support has become less unconditional, as is illustrated by the voters' refusal to accept the superficial agricultural reform submitted to them in spring 1995. Instead of the reform proposed by the government, the voters asked for a more fundamental reform of agricultural policy.

In 2006, the OECD presented a review of regulatory reforms in Switzerland. This report still mainly attributed the slow growth of the Swiss economy to 'the inadequate functioning of the product and services markets, reflecting a lack of competition, together with the high cost of services supplied by the public sector or financed through compulsory contributions' (OECD 2006: 11). The report recommended the whole panoply of internal liberalization measures that the neo-liberals have tried to introduce and that we have just reviewed: the promotion of internal market competition; a further strengthening of competition policy; the adoption of the 'Cassis-de-Dijon' principle to enhance foreign competition, allowing parallel imports; promoting a more efficient and effective public sector; improving the performance of the infrastructure sectors; and the reform of the agricultural sector. While these reforms have been assiduously pursued by Swiss economic policy makers, they met with more resistance than the economic experts and the neo-liberal politicians expected.

Fiscal reform

According to the Swiss business community and its representatives, the Swiss state is the main culprit responsible for the relative decline of the country. The 'white book' not only claimed that the state intervened too much in the economy but also heavily criticized its unbridled growth, which increasingly aggravated the competitiveness of the Swiss economy. This claim is debatable, in the first place because the very size of the Swiss state is controversial. Because of the complexity of the institutional arrangements in a mixed economy like that of Switzerland, it is particularly difficult to separate the private from the public realm in this country (Lane 2002: 56). Depending on the way the Swiss public sector is calculated, its size varies considerably. According to OECD criteria, Switzerland still has a relatively limited public sector; according to more appropriate Swiss data, its size appears to be considerably larger, putting Switzerland among the countries with an above-average public sector. Given the difficulties of establishing the exact size of the public sector, the debate has become focused on its increase over the past decades: expenditures, taxes and deficits have substantially increased over the past decade. Indeed, over this period, the Swiss public sector has grown at a faster pace than the public sectors of comparable OECD countries.

With the economic stagnation of the 1990s, the federal budget above all, but also the cantonal and local budgets, slipped into the red. While some observers argued that these deficits functioned as automatic stabilizers of the economy, the neo-liberal challengers insisted on their structural nature and asked for substantial fiscal reforms. Accordingly, several reforms in this domain were adopted in the course of the 1990s.

Switzerland reacted more quickly and with more rigid measures than other countries to the deterioration of its public finances. We concentrate here on the reform of the federal fiscal policies.

First of all, a *new fiscal regime* was introduced at the federal level in June 1993. The most important innovation concerned the replacement of the old indirect tax regime by a value-added tax (VAT). After three aborted attempts in 1977, 1979 and 1991 respectively, the voters accepted the introduction of value-added tax. The left finally gave in because it obtained a major concession – the possibility of subsequently increasing the rate of VAT in order to guarantee the financing of the old-age pension. The current rate of the Swiss VAT (7.6 per cent) is quite low, and does not even amount to half of the average rate in the EU. The right of the federal government to levy direct taxes was extended, but only for a limited period of time (until 2006), which required another popular vote for yet another limited extension in 2004. The introduction of VAT was accompanied by the increase of other indirect taxes – such as the taxes on petrol and on tobacco – and the introduction of a tax on the use of national highways and a tax on trucks (1994). Overall, indirect taxes provide the bulk of the income of the federal government, while direct taxes only make up about one-fourth (26 per cent in 2003) of its income. At the same time, the system for equalizing fiscal charges between rich and poor cantons has been reformed (see also chapter 3). This reform, which was in preparation for more than a decade and which included a new distribution of tasks between the federal government and the cantons, was adopted in a popular vote in autumn 2004.

Second, a series of *programmes for the stabilization of the federal finances* was adopted. The first measures included linear cuts in subsidies in 1992 and more specific cuts in 1993. Next, a procedural measure – the 'expenditure break', according to which legislation on additional expenditures (above a certain threshold) requires qualified majorities in Parliament – was adopted in 1995. In another step, the government proposed a new plan for the gradual reduction of the structural budget deficits – the 'budget objective 2001'. According to this measure, the federal budget deficit had to be reduced by 1 billion Swiss francs by 2001. In case the reduction was not achieved, propositions for new cuts were required. The measure was adopted in a popular vote in 1998. In order to meet this objective, the political parties agreed to spending cuts of 2 billion Swiss francs for the budget of 2001. Finally, in 2001 the voters accepted a new 'expenditure break' which replaced the 'budget objective 2001' and stipulated that the federal government had to balance the budget in the medium to long run. Against all expectations, this objective was already attained by 2000, but the surprising success proved to be the result of exceptional circumstances. In the following year, diminishing fiscal returns due to the bursting of the stock-market bubble and the stagnation of the economy revealed the structural nature of the deficit once again. The government reacted rapidly and Parliament adopted two separate programmes – one in 2003 and one in 2004 – to alleviate the federal budget. These programmes were to be accompanied by renewed efforts to streamline the federal administration. In autumn 2005, the government announced plans to reduce the federal expenditures by no less than 20 per cent in the medium term.

Third, the federal government proceeded to *alleviate the fiscal charges* for particularly sensitive parts of the economy, i.e. the mobile production factors. In order to increase the attractiveness of the Swiss financial marketplace, duties on the emission of foreign bonds and foreign shares, on participations in investment funds and on life insurance were abolished by a popular vote in 1992. This measure cost the federal coffers half a billion Swiss francs. In 1997, the legislation on the taxation of firms was adapted to the new international context, which relieved the treasury of another 400 million Swiss francs. As a result, Switzerland continues to offer very favourable fiscal conditions for private firms. In the OECD, only Iceland, Ireland and the new Eastern European members offered better conditions in 2004.[2] More recently, to keep up with measures adopted in other countries, a new revision of the tax code for firms has been adopted that is still more favourable for the business community. The new code reduces the tax on dividends for large shareholders by half. It has been attacked by a referendum from the left, but was narrowly accepted in a popular vote in 2008.

In addition, a proposal for a more comprehensive tax reform was introduced in Parliament. This proposal ended up as a package with three components: an undisputed alleviation of additional duties on financial transactions, an alleviation for families – the disadvantage for married couples compared with unmarried partners was to be suppressed and families with children received important tax breaks – and

---

[2] See *Neue Zürcher Zeitung*, no. 69, 23 March 2004, p. 23.

the introduction of a new system for the taxation of real estate. The whole package proved to be very controversial in Parliament and it was attacked both by a referendum from the left (the Social Democrats, Greens, unions and the tenants' association) and by a referendum launched by the cantons in the name of fiscal federalism. It was the first time in the history of the Swiss federal state that eleven cantons decided to launch a referendum against a federal piece of legislation. Another nine cantons asked their citizens to oppose the fiscal package in the vote in spring 2004. The cantons argued that the package was unconstitutional, since it unilaterally imposed massive reductions in cantonal and local revenues. They mainly turned against the reform of the tax on real estate, which they considered to be unfair. The left argued that the whole package disproportionately benefited the wealthy. The average citizen would hardly stand to gain in terms of taxes, but would lose in terms of higher charges for public services. Although the package was supported by the business community and the three major bourgeois parties, it had no chance at the polls and was voted down by two-thirds of the voters. On the same date, a proposal to raise the rate of VAT by 1 per cent to cover the impending deficit of the old-age pension and by 0.8 per cent to cover the current deficit of the disabled insurance was also rejected by an equally large majority of the voters. This proposal had been supported by the left and the Christian Democrats, while it was opposed by the Radicals, the SVP and the business community.

The question of fiscal reform has become a major battle ground for the neo-liberal camp. As this brief summary of the vicissitudes of the reform indicates, with the exception of the final fiscal package, the voters have generally followed the neo-liberals' proposals. The neo-liberals' claim that rising shares of public expenditure reduce the competitiveness of the Swiss economy resonates well with the Swiss public, although it is not as plausible as it appears at first sight. First, one should not forget that the share of public expenditure is, to a large extent, a matter of definition. Thus, minor changes in the organizational status of some social insurance scheme may lead to major changes in the share of the public sector – for example, when a given social insurance scheme, which has already reached almost complete coverage in a given population, becomes formally compulsory, as happened with the Swiss health insurance in 1994 (Kriesi 1999). Second, one should not forget that, to a considerable extent, the rising share of the public sector has been the result of the stagnation of the Swiss economy: since the Swiss economy as a whole has grown more slowly than the economy of the other OECD countries, the share of the Swiss public sector in the whole economy appears to have grown more rapidly than the corresponding share of the public sectors in those other countries (Armingeon 2007: 667). Finally, it is not possible to determine the optimal size of the public sector, and one should keep in mind that large public sectors are not necessarily detrimental to a nation's international competitiveness, as is illustrated by the Scandinavian countries, which are highly competitive despite the fact that they have much larger public sectors than Switzerland.

In narrowly fiscal terms, the efforts undertaken to alleviate the federal budget and to prevent Parliament from adopting new expenditures proved to be successful. With a little help from the improving economic situation, the federal budget deficit vanished earlier than expected and sound public finances have been restored – at least at the federal level: in 2006, the federal budget closed with a surplus, and fiscal planning counts on continued surpluses for the years to come.

9.3 Other factors

As we have pointed out above, there are other factors which may also have contributed to the comparatively slow growth of the Swiss economy. We shall take up these factors one by one, first those related to the labour market, next macro-economic policies and, finally, factors related to private investment strategies.

The labour market

In spite of its low level of growth, Switzerland used to have an exceptionally low level of unemployment. Thus, in the crisis of the 1970s, the unemployment rate remained very low, although the country lost an extraordinary number of jobs. As Schmidt (1985, 1995) has shown, the solution to the unemployment problem of the 1970s can be characterized as a 'national-liberal' one: on the one hand, the labour market was largely left to its own devices, while on the other hand, Swiss immigration policy largely favoured the preservation of the employment of indigenous employees to the detriment of foreign workers. At the time, most of the unemployment was 'exported', given that the foreign workforce was reduced by about 250,000 persons. In addition, a

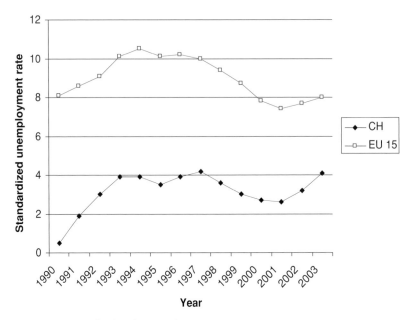

Figure 9.2 Standardized unemployment rate

sizable percentage of women retired from the labour market. Further more, the employers contributed to the stabilization of employment by having massive recourse to schemes of 'reduced working hours'. Finally, part of the unemployment rate did not show up in the statistics because unemployment insurance was not compulsory at the time and most Swiss employees were thus not insured against unemployment.

By the 1990s, however, the weak growth for the first time man-ifested itself in increasing unemployment levels. As is shown in figure 9.2, Swiss unemployment rose rapidly at the beginning of the 1990s, although it did not reach the much higher levels of the EU countries. Schmidt (1995) explains this increase mainly by the fact that the two most important factors, which were at the origin of the exceptional situation characterizing Switzerland in the 1970s, had dis-appeared by the 1990s. First, the immigration policy no longer worked as it did in the 1970s. On the one hand, this policy was better than its reputation, given that the share of immigrants with permanent res-idence status increased from 16 per cent to 58 per cent between 1960 and 1992. On the other hand, this policy had unanticipated negative consequences for the problem of unemployment. Because of its system of four classes of foreign workers – seasonal workers, workers with annual permits, workers with permanent residence permits and frontier workers – a large number of immigrants first came to Switzerland as seasonal workers before they obtained permanent residence status. But those who first arrived in Switzerland as seasonal workers mainly found their first employment in unskilled jobs in tourism, construction and agriculture. As they succeeded in stabilizing their status later on, these workers changed sectors for better-paying jobs. In other words, the low-paying sectors looking for a cheap, unskilled labour force served as gatekeepers for the immigrants coming to the Swiss labour market, which resulted in serious structural distortions (Dhima 1991): while the demand for low-skilled workers was satisfied, the more advanced sectors suffered from shortages. According to Arvanitis *et al.* (1992), the shortage of qualified personnel was the most important factor impeding innovation in the Swiss economy at the beginning of the 1990s. Similarly, the firms interviewed by Borner *et al.* (1997: 49) attributed a very high priority to the availability of highly qualified personnel. As a result of this policy, the unemployment rate was much higher among foreign employees (8.8 per cent) than among indigenous ones (2.8 per cent) in 1997. In 1993, about 40 per cent of the unemployed were low-skilled workers, i.e. precisely those kinds of workers who are disproportionately represented among the foreign labour force (Kappel and Landmann 1997: 159).

Second, a compulsory and generous unemployment insurance scheme had been created in the meantime, which meant that the economic crisis became visible. The existence of this insurance not only implied that the foreigners who lost their jobs now continued to stay in the country, but it also contributed to a change in the behaviour of the employers. They no longer hoarded their workforce by way of reduced working hours, as they had done in the 1970s, in the hope of the return of better times. Instead, as is observed by Flückiger (1997), they proceeded to structural reforms and massively reduced the number of jobs at the beginning of the 1990s. In sum, according to this reasoning, increasing unemployment is to a large extent attributable to the implications of social and economic policy – the creation of a generous unemployment insurance scheme and the unexpected consequences of past immigration policies.

However, even if the Swiss unemployment rate has increased since the beginning of the 1990s, it has never reached the levels of the surrounding countries in Western Europe. Bonoli and Mach (2001) highlight the original combination of different policy elements, which seems to be particularly conducive to favourable labour market performance. On the one hand, like Anglo-Saxon countries, Switzerland has a liberal and flexible labour market and a low tax wedge for low-skilled employment (i.e. a small difference between what the employee gets and what the employer pays for one's work), which favours employment creation in the low-skilled service sectors. On the other hand, contrary to Anglo-Saxon countries, generous unemployment benefits with tight entitlement conditions (see chapter 10), sector-specific industrial relations, embedded in sectoral social partnership institutions (see chapter 7), and an efficient vocational training system, combine to provide highly skilled workers with sector-specific skills, who are much in demand in the Swiss labour market.

Macro-economic policy

While the neo-liberal challengers emphasize the structural distortions on the supply side, economists close to the left maintain that the economic difficulties of the 1990s were the result of an insufficient demand in the home market, which they attribute to erroneous macro-economic policy making. Early in the 1990s, consumption stagnated, investments declined substantially and, as we have just seen, unemployment rose. The economists close to the left interpret these trends as clear signs of an insufficient domestic demand. Macro-economic policies are called upon to solve such a problem – expansive monetary and fiscal policies and wage restraint are the corresponding instruments. There was wage restraint – real wages stagnated throughout most of the 1990s. But the structural fiscal reforms did not leave any room for anti-cyclical fiscal stimulation, and monetary policy was much too restrictive for far too long a period. The restrictive monetary policy was designed to come to terms with the very high inflation that characterized the beginning of the 1990s. However, this policy was maintained far too long and gave rise to a 15 per cent appreciation of the Swiss franc from 1993 to 1995.[3] After 1995, the monetary policy became more pragmatic in the

---

[3] The successor of the Swiss National Bank's president, who had been responsible for this policy, admitted publicly that this policy had been too restrictive. The IMF qualified it as 'too prudent' and the *Neue Zürcher Zeitung* talked about an

sense that it no longer only targeted the monetary mass, but also took into account the exchange rate and limited the fluctuation of short-term interest rates. Ettlin and Gaillard (2001) estimate the effects of the interest rate and the exchange rate on the yearly rate of growth with an econometric model and arrive at average yearly estimates of -1.25 per cent for the period 1991–6, and of $+2$ per cent for the period 1997–2001.[4] They explain the restrictive policies by reference to, among other things, a 'monetarist consensus' among Swiss policy makers and an erroneous interpretation of the events in the 1970s: the very restrictive monetary policy of the seventies had contributed to rapid structural reforms, but did not have the negative consequences on the labour market and the public purse for the reasons we have discussed in the previous section. As the situation on the labour market had drastically changed by the 1990s, the consequences of the restrictive monetary policy were to be much more serious. Ettlin and Gaillard (2001) argue that the rigid monetarist policy, which was implemented in the name of structural reforms, had detrimental long-term structural consequences of its own: it involved high costs for the social insurance schemes, contributed to the public debt and reduced the manoeuvring space of the fiscal policy, reduced the investment rate and the innovative capacity of the economy, and raised resistance in the population against necessary structural reforms.

Investment

Economists unanimously maintain that, in the final analysis, economic growth is determined by the volume of investments. Traditionally, Switzerland has had a very high level of investments, financed by a very high savings rate among the Swiss population (Cusack 1995: 11), and has always benefited from very low real interest rates. Investments in equipment grew rapidly during the 1980s and then declined at the beginning of the 1990s (as discussed in the previous section) before increasing again beginning in 1994. These investments were accompanied by an important restructuring in the exposed sector of the Swiss

---

'evident mistake'. Beat Kappeler, 'Banque nationale: le prix des erreurs', *L'Hebdo*, 28 November 1996, p. 53.

[4] The effect of the change in monetary policy was reinforced by the 'investment programme 1997' of the federal government, which launched investments to the order of 2 billion Swiss francs by 1999.

economy, which gave rise to large mergers: for example, Ciba and Sandoz became Novartis, UBS merged with SBS and Winterthur Insurance merged with Crédit Suisse, to mention but the most important ones (Bonoli and Mach 2000). Such restructurings contributed to the reduction of jobs and put pressure on the domestic sector of the economy.

These large corporations are less and less concerned by the social and economic situation in their home market. They have become 'global players' for whom the Swiss business community loses its importance. The following observations of the president of the board of the Crédit Suisse Group, Rainer E. Gut, illustrate this tendency.[5]

The president and three members of the board are Swiss, but two Americans, an Australian and a German are also part of this team. Its composition is symptomatic of our corporation. Our home institution is in Zurich, but we are at home all over the world. In Switzerland, we employ 28,000 persons, but 55 per cent of our collaborators work abroad and come from all corners of the world. In 1997, our operations in Switzerland generated 55 per cent of our revenue compared to 45 per cent for the rest of the world.

And Gut went on to pose the critical question, i.e. whether this was still a Swiss corporation. As the leaders of these corporations are less and less concerned with Switzerland, they may make their investment decisions with less and less consideration for the well-being of the Swiss economy. Accordingly, the high investment rate of the Swiss corporations may not necessarily contribute to the growth of the Swiss economy.

An important part of the investments of Swiss corporations is not made in Switzerland. Swiss *direct investments* abroad have always been very important. They have always been part of the offensive private strategy characterizing the adjustment to economic openness of the liberal version of democratic corporatism (Katzenstein 1985). Thus, already before the 1990s, Switzerland occupied first place in the world in terms of foreign investments per head of the population, followed by the Netherlands – another example of the liberal model of democratic corporatism (Bairoch 1990). In the 1990s, we note another substantial increase in Swiss direct investments abroad. They tripled between 1990 and 1998, and more than doubled again to reach a record peak in 2000

---

[5] Rainer E. Gut, 'Plaidoyer pour une Suisse autocritique, sûre d'elle et solidaire', *Le Temps*, 28 January 1999, p. 10.

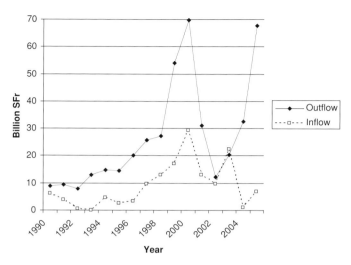

Figure 9.3 Foreign direct investments

and once again in 2005 (figure 9.3). In sectoral terms, the chemical industry and the banks and insurance companies are the largest direct investors abroad.

However, direct investments abroad are not necessarily detrimental to the growth of the Swiss economy. It is possible that they do not compete with but complement the business activities in the country of origin: they are not only motivated by considerations of production costs, but may also be part of a strategy to move closer to the clients and improve the sales and distribution of Swiss products in the country of destination. Such investments may also create new markets for products coming from Swiss production sites. Moreover, investment projects abroad are often supported by the mother corporation only in the first phases, while later on investments are financed by retained earnings and third sources. Indeed, several studies suggest that direct investments abroad do not substitute activities in Switzerland, but rather serve to complement them (see Arvanitis *et al.* 2001; Henneberger and Ziegler 2001; Hollenstein 2005). Thus, the research and development activities, which Swiss corporations increasingly locate abroad, tend to augment the knowledge basis of the production site in Switzerland, and not to substitute for corresponding activities in Switzerland (Arvanitis *et al.* 2005: 176–83). In other words, the lacklustre performance of the Swiss economy may hardly be attributed to the high rate of direct investments abroad. In fact, the

high returns produced by these foreign investments make a major contribution to the GNP (but not to the GDP). As a result, Switzerland
is the only OECD country where the GNP is considerable larger than
the GDP. Moreover, the growth rate of the GNP in the period 1997–
2003 was much higher than that of the GDP, which suggests once
more that the main source of the Swiss lack of growth is homemade
(Rich 2005).

Finally, Switzerland is not only the country with the largest capital stock abroad. Compared to its GDP, it is also among the largest
receivers of foreign direct investments. As figure 9.3 indicates, the
inflowing direct investments have increased parallel to the outflows,
although at a lower level and with greater variability over time. This
is due to the fact that a large number of foreign corporations put up
their (European) headquarters in Switzerland. Google is a conspicuous
example, although most of the inflowing investments are made in the
domain of financial services.

9.4 Conclusion

Sciarini (1994) had already pointed out that Katzenstein's formula –
external flexibility combined with internal stability – was no longer
valid in the 1990s: the political stability guaranteed by concertation
mechanisms had become problematic given the transformation of the
international context. The slowness and the inefficiency of these mechanisms constituted a predicament rather than an asset for the economic
flexibility on the international markets. Sciarini had concluded that
Switzerland needed to find a new internal flexibility in order to be
able to meet the new challenges of the world market. In this chapter,
we have seen that Swiss economic and fiscal policy has been making
important attempts to regain a certain flexibility under the pressure of
political actors who succeeded in bypassing the rigid channels of traditional politics. The list of structural reforms is impressive and indicates
that Swiss politics has been capable of putting through major reforms,
even if direct-democratic and federalist institutions combined with the
polarizing configuration of power have set certain limits to the implementation of the neo-liberal reform programme.

As we shall see in the next chapters, the welfare state has been hard
to retrench, given the mobilization of the left, and the opening to the

European integration process has been blocked by the mobilization of the national-conservatives. In this chapter, we have seen that the deregulation programme of the neo-liberals met with resistance from the cantons and from the representatives of the domestic sector of the economy, and encountered non-cooperation on the part of certain large multinational corporations (such as UBS and Roche). Even without having recourse to direct-democratic interventions, the inertia of the domestic sector of the Swiss economy and the slowness of the implementation of public policies in general have not allowed the neo-liberals to go all the way with their programme of deregulation and liberalization.

The results are mixed and, in the end, not too far removed from the Swiss tradition in economic and social policy making. As it turns out, the impact of the deregulation programme has been weaker in Switzerland than in any other OECD country (Federal Department of Economic Affairs 2002: 39). By contrast, sound public finances have been restored, the labour market functions well, monetary policy has been greatly improved, and foreign direct investments appear to contribute to the welfare of the country as well. Assessing the competitiveness of the Swiss economy in the early 2000s, Arvanitis *et al.* (2005) arrive at the conclusion that, in comparative terms, Swiss labour productivity is above average, with large sector-specific disparities: it is generally higher in exposed sectors than in sectors oriented towards the domestic market, it is higher in industry than in services, and it turns out to be rather poor in highly regulated sectors (such as agriculture, energy, transportation and telecommunications, or health care). And, finally, the Swiss economy has again been growing at a rate of 2 or more per cent since 2004.

Swiss economic and social policy has traditionally been characterized by a pragmatic mix of divergent elements. The liberal elements of these policies have always been important. Given the liberal heritage and given the constraints we have just pointed out, the 'neo-liberal turn' has not fundamentally modified economic policy making in this country. However, having stated the path-dependence of the measures taken, we should not belittle their impact: on the one hand, they imposed new limits on the domestic compensations for the economic openness of the country. These limits concern both social security and the domestic sector of the Swiss economy (i.e. the farmers, small businesses and tradesmen). On the other hand, they reduced the regulations by the state, restricted its manoeuvring space, rendered the public administration less attractive as an employer and made public services less viable. In a word, the renewed flexibility made the Swiss model a little less comfortable and a little tougher on the domestic front: this seems to be the price to be paid for competitiveness at the international level.

10 | *Social policy: the Swiss welfare state*

10.1 Introduction

In his classic study, Esping-Andersen (1990) distinguishes between three ideal-typical worlds of welfare – a social-democratic, a liberal and a conservative welfare state. The *social-democratic welfare state*, typically represented by Scandinavian countries, is a generous, universalistic one that provides social security to all irrespective of gender, former employment status or nationality. Moreover, social services are provided by the state itself, which implies a large amount of public employment. The *liberal welfare state*, exemplified by the United States, is a residual welfare state of limited size which essentially constitutes the last resort for people in need, providing not much more than a minimal level of benefit. Social security over and above the basic safety net is left to individual initiative. Like the social-democratic model, the *conservative* or *Christian-democratic welfare state*, exemplified by the 'Bismarckian' or German model, is an onerous one. But it implies less public employment than the social-democratic model and mainly provides massive transfer payments with the aim of maintaining the social status which the beneficiaries have acquired during the period of active employment. Moreover, the conservative welfare state is oriented towards the maintenance of the family with one (typically male) breadwinner.

The Swiss welfare state has proved *notoriously difficult to classify* by reference to this threefold classification. Esping-Andersen himself considers it a liberal regime, while others refer to it as a Christian-democratic welfare state (Scharpf and Schmidt 2001; Huber and Stephens 2001), a 'Western European welfare state with a liberal face' (Armingeon 2001: 162), a mixed regime (Obinger 1998) or as a case of a welfare state 'disciplined by Protestantism' (Manow 2002). The difficulty of classification is, first of all, a result of the fact that we deal with *a moving target*. As all observers agree, the Swiss welfare state developed *belatedly*. For a long time, it was less generous than most of the other welfare states in Western Europe and shared many of the characteristics of the liberal model. The expansion of the Swiss welfare state only took off after World War II with the introduction of the basic old-age insurance (AHV/AVS) in 1948, but it continued to lag behind other rich countries in Western Europe until well into the post-war period. For a long time, there was little pressure for reforming the minimalist social insurance schemes. Unlike the situation in other European countries, budgetary deficits, unemployment and poverty remained very low in Switzerland throughout the 1980s. However, since the 1970s and certainly since the 1980s, the Swiss welfare state has started to catch up and to become more generous and universalistic. Transfer payments grew massively in the period 1980–95, almost twice as much as the OECD average (Armingeon 2001: 146–7). Public sector employment, by contrast, has grown at a less than average pace and, in this regard, Switzerland remains a lean state. The situation changed even more dramatically in the early 1990s, when the recession arrived and unemployment rose to unprecedented levels in post-war history, although the Swiss unemployment rate remained well below the usual European standards (see chapter 9). As observed by Merrien and Bonoli (2000: 134), the recession of the 1990s marked a watershed in the development of the Swiss welfare state.

In addition, the difficulty of classifying the Swiss welfare state is a result of its complexity, which, in turn, is linked to the *specific institutional conditions* of its development – Swiss federalism and direct democracy structured social policies in quite specific ways. As a result of these conditions, the characteristics of the welfare state vary from one insurance scheme to another. Armingeon *et al.* (2004) even find evidence of large intercantonal variations in welfare state policies, given that cantons retain substantial room for manoeuvring in several important areas of social policy. In this chapter, we shall begin by accounting for the origin of the specificities of the Swiss welfare state before we turn to an analysis of its recent convergence towards a more general continental European model.

10.2 The origins of the specificities of the Swiss welfare state

Armingeon (2001: 153–7) reviews a number of factors that account for the belated development of the Swiss welfare state. First of all, he refers to several *functional arguments* that explain the limited need for its expansion: as he observes, the oldest democracy in Europe – contrary to the German empire under Bismarck, for example – did not need social policy measures to stabilize the political order against the challenge of a politically mobilized population. He also points out that Swiss industrialization was not accompanied by massive urbanization and impoverishment, which limited the social problems linked to industrialization elsewhere in Europe. Moreover, as already observed, after World War II, Switzerland enjoyed a long period of full employment, which served as a functional equivalent to the expansion of social security. Second, Armingeon refers to the traditional weakness of those *political forces* – Social Democrats and Christian Democrats – who have typically been the driving forces behind welfare state expansion in Western Europe. Third, he also invokes the *political institutions*, which have been particularly important for the specific path along which the welfare state has developed in Switzerland. As is argued most notably by Obinger (1998) and Wagschal and Obinger (2000), the institutions of federalism and direct democracy (and, one could add, the specific form of social partnership in Switzerland) have left their mark on the Swiss welfare state in at least three ways: they determined its overall structure, its level of expenditure and the rhythm of its expansion. Finally, Manow (2002) makes a *cultural argument* which attributes the belated development of the Swiss welfare state, a characteristic that it shares with the Dutch and the British welfare states, to the specific *Reformed Protestant culture* we find in all three countries. We shall first discuss this cultural argument in somewhat more detail and then elaborate the impact of the institutional factors.

The impact of a Reformed Protestant culture

Manow observes that, geographically, the expansion of the welfare state in Western Europe followed a pattern of 'westward spread': the welfare state developed first in the countries with a Lutheran state church (Germany and Scandinavia) and only later on in the countries with many Protestant sects, evangelical, Calvinist or Reformed Protestant churches (the UK, the Netherlands and Switzerland, as well as the other Anglo-Saxon countries overseas). Contrary to the Lutheran church, which associated closely with the state authorities, these Protestant currents emphasized communal self-help, individual asceticism and private initiative. Manow argues that the anti-state orientation of these Protestant currents tended to have a retarding effect on the development of the welfare state. He distinguishes two ways in which this orientation influenced the formation of the welfare state: on the one hand, the religious divide cross-cut the class divide and reduced its impact; on the other hand, it had a general impact on 'societal symbol management'. In Switzerland, not only the religious divide cutting across the class cleavage, but also the fact that democratization and the accompanying political identity formation among the mass population preceded the rise of the labour movement, considerably weakened the political mobilization of the left (Bartolini 2000). Accordingly, the 'window of opportunity' for the Radicals was wide open for a long time and it was the Radicals, a Protestant party imbued with the ethos Manow describes, who dominated democratic national politics throughout the first seventy years of the new federal state. The Radicals' hegemony throughout the period up to World War I and their continued domination until the most recent past had a profound impact on the general orientation of the Swiss welfare state.

We find a *strong liberal element* above all in those insurance schemes, such as *health insurance*, which got underway rather early. A first version of the law on health insurance, presented to Parliament in 1899, was brought down by referendum by a coalition composed of the medical profession, conservative liberals and existing mutual societies. In 1910, a minimalist compromise was adopted, which still constitutes the basis of the current health insurance scheme: membership was optional; the law prescribed a minimal level of basic coverage in terms of reimbursed treatments and drugs, which had to be granted by the already existing mutual societies; premiums paid by the insured persons were the main source of funding and the premiums were uniform, unrelated to income. Basic coverage could be complemented by additional private contracts. Until 1994, when the law was finally adapted to changing circumstances, this system essentially remained unchanged. The 1994 reform made membership compulsory, which did not change much, since almost everybody was insured anyway by the early 1990s. Otherwise it hardly modified the basic elements of the system.

The other main elements of social insurance of the current Swiss welfare state were introduced much later – the basic old-age pension scheme was introduced in 1948, the 'second pillar' of occupational pensions became compulsory with the implementation of the corresponding law in 1985, and unemployment insurance, first introduced in 1947, was put on a solid foundation only in 1984. These more recent forms of insurance combine conservative and social-democratic elements with the original liberal ones. Thus, the pension scheme combines a universal ('Beveridge'-like) basic old-age pension allowing for some amount of redistribution with an income-dependent occupational pension scheme providing for the maintenance of one's status. The unemployment insurance scheme also combines social-democratic (generous, universal coverage) and conservative features (status preservation). It is currently amongst the most generous within the OECD countries.

Still, the impact of Reformed Protestantism makes itself felt in social policies until the present day. As Manow argues, the early solutions to social problems *pre-structure* the further development of the welfare state in decisive ways: where the voluntary collectivization of provision had preceded state interventions by decades, and mutual societies or unions had built up extensive institutional networks of their own, they tended to resist any takeover by the state and to oppose compulsory arrangements (de Swaan 1988: 157). This is an example of what Dutch historian Jan Romein has called the 'law of arresting advance'. Thus, as Manow (2002: 220) demonstrates in a comparative analysis, current levels of social expenditure are generally lower in Reformed Protestant welfare states. Moreover, the combination of universalistic basic pensions with occupational pensions is typical for the latecomers among the welfare states that are 'disciplined by Protestantism' (Manow 2002: 218). In Switzerland, in particular, the general liberal orientation was all the more consequential, since it was strongly reinforced by the effects of the institutions of federalism and direct democracy.

The impact of federalism

The structural effect of federalism results from the distribution of competences in the social policy domain adopted by the Federal Constitution of 1848 (and its revision of 1874). Since the federal government did not have any competence in this domain, it was up to private institutions, municipalities and cantons to react to the social problems created by the early industrialization. According to the *principle of subsidiarity* (see chapters 3, 7 and 8), decentralized social security systems were organized by mutual aid societies, private corporations, municipalities and cantons. Certain programmes – family policy, social assistance and education – are still today mainly operated by cantons and municipalities (Armingeon *et al.* 2004). Several important programmes, however, were transferred to the federal level later on, when the decentralized solutions ran into difficulties. But even in those instances, where the federal government was called upon to intervene in a given policy area, its legislation had to take into account the already existing structures which the early initiatives had established. The subsequent stepwise transfer of tasks from a lower level to the Confederation implied that the federal government had to build on the pre-established organizational structures when it became responsible for the corresponding tasks. It had to be acceptable to the defenders of the already established programmes and institutions, since they could threaten with the weapon of the referendum, which proved to be very powerful in legislative conflicts concerning social policy (see below).

With respect to *finances*, Swiss federalism imposed spending limits on social policy. This is a result of the reticence among cantons to transfer any competence in fiscal matters to the federal level. The interdependence between the Confederation and the cantons in fiscal matters has created strong barriers to the expansion of expenditure in such domains as social policy. However, federalism has not given rise to a 'race to the bottom' as a result of fiscal competition between the cantons. On the contrary, the constraints of federalism led to the *externalization of the fiscal burden*: as far as its financial sources are concerned, the Swiss welfare state relies heavily on joint contributions of the social partners. More specifically, given the weakness of the labour movement, the brunt of the contributions is borne by employees: while old-age pensions have always been jointly financed, employers were exempted from contributions to the unemployment insurance scheme until 1977 and they still are exempted from contributions to health insurance. This strategy of externalizing the fiscal burden made it possible to avoid conflicts in fiscal matters and, by relying mainly on contributory schemes that establish a direct link between contributions and benefits, it limited the resistance of privileged groups against social insurance.

Federalism's *delaying effect* mainly results from the *two-phased legislative process* that it imposes. Since the introduction of each new insurance scheme implied the transfer of some competences to the federal level, it involved the modification of the Constitution – as we have seen in chapter 3, all tasks not explicitly attributed to the federal level by default belong to the domain of the cantons. The legislative process was therefore always divided into two phases – a constitutional phase and a legislative phase proper, which offered the cantons and the defenders of specific interests ample opportunities to delay the process. Obinger (1998: 136) adds that, sometimes, federalism had innovative effects as well, but the examples he gives all date from the nineteenth century and concern the first steps in the construction of the welfare state, i.e. a period when the cantons were still the only responsible organs for social policy making.

The impact of direct democracy

The *structural* effect of direct democracy also contributed to the liberal character of the Swiss welfare state. The example of health insurance serves to illustrate this point. Instead of following the example of Bismarck, as was the intention of the government at the time, the Confederation had to content itself with a liberal solution, since, as we have already seen, its original proposal was defeated by a referendum in 1900. Later on, in spite of a series of attempts to reform the law, it was not possible to change its liberal conception, because of referendum threats by the medical profession and by the mutual societies, and because of defeats in popular votes (Immergut 1992a). As already observed, it was only in 1994 that a reform introducing compulsory insurance but maintaining many of the original liberal elements succeeded.

The *financial* effect of direct democracy is documented in a detailed study of the votes on legislative proposals with budgetary consequences. Wagschal and Obinger (2000: 479–80) have analysed all proposals of this type and found that, among the proposals that were adopted in federal votes, those with a *restrictive* budgetary effect largely dominated those with an *expansive* effect. In other words, direct democracy limits the expansion of state activities in general. In their comparative study of the impact of direct democracy at the cantonal and local level, Kirchgässner *et al.* (1999) arrive at the same conclusion: direct democracy puts the brakes on public expenditure and on public debt. The citizens appear to be generally (and not only in social policy) more frugal with public resources than their political elites.

The *delaying effect* of direct democracy is a consequence of the legislation in two phases. The constitutional phase implies a compulsory referendum, and the legislative phase proper allows for an optional referendum, which gives the opponents of the new legislation two occasions to mobilize against the reform. In the social policy domain, the opponents have often made use of this opportunity, which contributed to the belated expansion of the Swiss welfare state (Wagschal and Obinger 2000: 479; Armingeon 2001: 149). The optional referendum alone is responsible for delaying the introduction of new social insurance schemes by an average of fifteen years. The most telling example of this delaying effect is provided by maternity insurance, which failed three times in a referendum vote (in 1984, 1987 and 1999), before it was finally accepted in 2004.

10.3 Factors behind the catching-up

Originally a liberal latecomer, the Swiss welfare state has expanded enormously in the more recent past. In the process of expansion, as we have already argued in the introduction, it has acquired some elements of the conservative and social-democratic models. We shall first discuss the factors behind the quantitative expansion of the welfare state and then turn to the factors contributing to its structural transformation.

Autodynamic processes

The first factor contributing to the expansion of the Swiss welfare state concerns the autodynamics of the social insurance schemes adopted in the past (Obinger 1998: 228–9). Thus, the general *ageing of the population* and the *increase in unemployment* in the 1990s strongly contributed to the expansion of the welfare state. The ageing of the population contributes to the expenses of the basic old-age pension and disability insurance and to the costs of health insurance. Not only has the number of retired citizens continuously increased, but the belated introduction of the basic insurance scheme has contributed to the increasing financial burden created by an ageing population. The transitional generations received pensions rights over and above the entitlements they had acquired based on their contributions alone. Moreover, the indexation of the basic pensions (introduced by the ninth revision of the AHV/AVS in 1978) proved to be an additional onerous modification of the basic pension scheme. Finally, the number of persons entitled to a disability pension doubled between 1975 and 1995 and has continued to increase at an explosive rate ever since. As far as unemployment is concerned, we have seen in the previous chapter that it started to increase rapidly in the early 1990s, which put increasing pressure on the very generous insurance scheme that was adopted in the early 1980s, at a time when the level of unemployment was still very low.

Institutional factors

In addition to autodynamic processes, institutional factors have also contributed to the expansion of the welfare state (Obinger 1998: 229–30). The same institutions which had originally slowed down the implementation of social insurance schemes prevented timely reactions once the pressure rose to adapt them to changing circumstances such as, in particular, the cost explosion in the domain of health care. Although the debate about the limitation of costs in the health system has been going on in Switzerland since the 1960s, it has not been possible to impose the required measures. Between 1964 and 1994 a series of attempts to reform the health insurance system failed in federal votes. Because of these multiple non-decisions, the cost explosion in the health system could not be contained and the result was that the state increasingly externalized these costs to private households, which had to assume ever increasing premiums. In a desperate attempt to do something, the federal government enacted emergency legislation aimed at containing health-care costs in 1991 and 1992. Finally, in 1994 a new law was adopted. The most remarkable innovation of the new law was the attempt to create a competitive market between mutual societies – an attempt which, for various reasons, has largely failed (Merrien and Bonoli 2000: 134–5). A second important change concerned the targeting of subsidies for those most in need. This measure was not as effective as planned either, given that the cantons which were supposed to receive matching funds for the sums they spent for the persons in need did not all contribute their part to the scheme.

The attempts to reduce the costs find their limits above all in the *federalist structure* of the country which contributes to waste (such as an abundant supply of hospital beds and luxurious hospital equipment) and a lack of coordination. Moreover, as Armingeon (2001: 160) observes, the multiplication of decision arenas in a federalist system implies a high probability that a majority in at least one of these arenas refuses to accept measures of retrenchment concerning some group of clients of the welfare state. Accordingly, federalist countries generally have the most expensive health-care systems (Schmidt 1998). The study by Schmidt also shows that the countries with a national health-care service, or countries where the state is heavily involved in the financing of the health-care system, have been most successful in limiting the costs of health care.

Similarly, *direct democracy* not only has retarding effects on the welfare state, but it also contributes to its expansion (Armingeon 2001: 160–1; Wagschal and Obinger 2000: 480ff.). First of all, by way of *popular initiatives*, the left has exerted pressure on the political elites to proceed to the introduction of new social rights. In spite of the fact that no initiative has so far been accepted in the domain of social policy, several initiatives have led to the adoption of *direct* (at the level of the Constitution) or *indirect* (at the level of specific legislation) *counterproposals*. Thus, in two cases, the counterproposals of the federal government have been imposed directly against popular initiatives – the project for 'the three pillars' of old-age pensions in 1972 and the project in favour of public housing support, also in 1972. Moreover, four counterproposals have been accepted in compulsory referendums after the withdrawal of the corresponding initiatives – equal rights for men and women (1981), and the protection of families (1945), consumers (1981) and tenants (1982). It was mainly during the 'golden age' from the 1960s up to the early 1970s that social policy initiatives launched by the left developed an important *instigating effect*. These initiatives contributed to the expansion of the basic old-age pension (eighth AHV/AVS revision in 1972), to the lowering of the retirement age and to the introduction of disability insurance (Werder 1978). Important impulses have also been given by initiatives in the domains of housing policy and tenants' rights. Since the 1970s, these effects have, however, been weakened. With the exception of the initiative promoting equal rights for men and women, which had a considerable effect on the modernization of several key laws concerning social policy (Senti 1994), all other initiatives of the left aimed at reforming old-age pensions or the health-care system have failed.

Finally, direct democracy also exerts a *protective effect* with respect to established social rights. Although the conservative orientation of the Swiss citizens has delayed the expansion of the Swiss welfare state on several occasions, it has also contributed to the preservation of established rights in a period of retrenchment, as is shown by Bonoli (1999) in his analysis of the reforms of the 1990s. Under the pressure of increasing deficits in most forms of important social insurance and under the assault of the neo-liberals (see chapter 9), in the 1990s the phase of expansion had also come to a halt in Switzerland. However, as Bonoli (1999) observes, while retrenchment measures in social policy meet with great resistance in all countries, because of the referendum resistance is particularly effective in Switzerland. Based on a discussion of the tenth revision of the AHV/AVS, Bonoli shows that measures designed to reduce the level of social protection pass the threshold of the referendum only when they are coupled with concessions in other respects. Thus, the tenth revision of the AHV/AVS increased the retirement age for women from 62 to 64, but at the same time created more gender-equal conditions for the splitting of pensions as well as compensatory measures for housewives with children. The unions launched the referendum against this reform, but were not followed by the Social Democrats, who considered the advantage of equal treatment of men and women to be more important than the increase in the retirement age. In order to allow the adherents of the left to vote in favour of the tenth revision and to express themselves separately on the principle of the retirement age, even before the vote on the tenth revision, the Social Democrats launched a 'compensatory' initiative whose only goal was to keep the retirement age for women at 62. In the vote in 1995, the tenth revision was adopted, but the 'compensatory' initiative was rejected by a rather narrow margin in 1998.

Similarly, the reform of *unemployment insurance* in 1995, which was adopted after a series of urgent decrees had been taken to adapt the legislation to the dramatic increase in unemployment, was accompanied by measures incorporating concessions on the part of both social partners. On the one hand, in line with the demands of the business community, the reform reduced the duration for entitlements, which used to be unlimited, to a maximum of two years. At the end of this period, unemployed persons came to depend on local social assistance, which is less generous and more stigmatizing than unemployment benefits. On the other hand, the reform constituted a turning point from a rather passive labour market policy to an active one. In line with the demands of the left, active labour market policy measures were introduced for the first time. Moreover, the reform reinforced the financial basis of the insurance by increasing the contributions from 2 to 3 per cent of salaries (1.5 per cent each for employers and employees). In 1997, the Federal Council tried to reduce the level of benefits of the unemployment insurance without any measure of compensation. Against this unilateral proposal, the referendum was launched by a group of unemployed persons in La Chaux-de-Fonds who found support on the left. The proposal was narrowly defeated in a popular vote in 1997, indicating once again that one-sided measures of retrenchment do not pass the hurdle of the popular vote. The case of the *reform of the labour law* and of the eleventh *revision of the AHV/AVS* (see below), both of which failed in the popular vote (in 1997 and 2004 respectively), confirm the importance of this argument.

10.4 Factors contributing to the structural transformation

Obinger (1998: 231–5) mentions three factors which contributed to the structural transformation of the Swiss welfare state. First of all, the *introduction of female suffrage* in 1971 provided an impulse for taking into account questions concerning gender equality, especially in the field of social insurance. Second, the establishment of the '*magic formula*' in 1959 attributed a majority in the Federal Council to the combination of Social Democrats and Christian Democrats – two parties in favour of expanding the welfare state. From 1960 to 2002, the Department of the Interior, which is responsible for social insurance in Switzerland, was always in the hands of a Social Democrat or a Christian Democrat. Most significantly, in 1960, it was taken over by the Social Democrat Hanspeter Tschudi who introduced an accelerated rhythm into the process of social reform – the famous 'speed of Tschudi'. Third, Obinger stresses the *external and internal pressure* which rendered the reforms inevitable and forced the policy makers to react – by urgent measures at first, by more far-reaching reforms later on. In line with this argument, Armingeon (2001: 157–8) stresses the importance of so-called '*critical junctures*' for social policy. He identifies a first critical juncture during the 1930s. Under the impact of the double threat of fascism and the economic crisis, the government succeeded in introducing the basic old-age pension (although, delayed by the war, it was only adopted in 1947). The breakdown of the labour market in 1975/6, when 10 per cent of the employment was lost, constituted, according to Armingeon, another critical juncture. It provided a 'window of opportunity' for the reform of the unemployment insurance scheme. In 1972, a proposal for such a reform had already been submitted to the consultation procedure by the Federal Council, but had failed at the time because of the opposition by the peak associations of both the business community and the unions. While the unions defended their own mutual societies, the employers' associations saw no need to introduce a compulsory unemployment insurance scheme in the midst of an overheated economy! When the crisis struck unexpectedly in 1974/5, only 22 per cent of the Swiss labour force was insured against unemployment and the government had to adopt an urgent decree in 1975 to introduce first improvements. One year later, the people adopted the constitutional basis for a compulsory insurance scheme, which was first introduced by a temporary decree in 1977 and finally by the promulgation of the law in 1984. Although the regime reacted with unusual speed under the pressure of the crisis of the mid 1970s, it still took almost ten years to definitively implement the new insurance scheme.

More recently, like all the other developed welfare states, the Swiss welfare state has been facing a double challenge (see Bertozzi *et al.* 2005: 105–8). On the one hand, demographic ageing of the population is causing an automatic increase in the traditional benefits, and the desire to maintain the achievements of the 'golden age' of the post-war period, especially among the older generations. On the other hand, the transformations of the economy and society, of the labour market and family structures, create new social risks and, accordingly, new needs for support, especially among the younger generations and families. Confronted with this double challenge, Bertozzi *et al.* (2005: 105) suggest that welfare state reform increasingly has to turn to '*investment-oriented*' *social policies*, i.e. to policies favouring employment while allowing everybody to reconcile work and family. The Scandinavian welfare states have progressed most in the direction of such investment-oriented social policies. Thus, Denmark invests roughly 2 per cent of its GDP in services for families (such as child-care centres) and another 1.7 per cent in active labour-market policies – 15 and 2.5 times more than Switzerland in the respective domains.

In other words, an investment-oriented social policy requires additional funds. The question is, of course, where to find more money in a period of fiscal retrenchment. As Bertozzi *et al.* (2005: 107) point out, one possibility for financing such a social policy would be to use value-added tax (VAT). As we have seen in the previous chapter, its

Swiss rate of 7.6 per cent is still much lower than in the rest of Western Europe, where the corresponding rates are at least twice as high. By European standards, an increase of VAT by 7 or 8 percentage points would, therefore, be nothing unusual and supply additional funds to the tune of 21 to 24 billion Swiss francs per year. Of course, everybody has his or her own idea of how such additional funds should be used. For some, like the business community and the Radicals, an increase in VAT would only be acceptable if it did not supply additional funds and if it was to be compensated by a corresponding reduction of the direct taxes.

10.5 Conclusion

In their comparison between welfare state reforms in France and Switzerland in the 1990s, Merrien and Bonoli (2000: 142) come to the conclusion that, whereas France, a strong state, was unable to implement such a reform, Switzerland, a weak state, managed to transform its welfare system incrementally. According to the authors, this differential capacity can be explained by the 'political culture embedded in political regimes, the different policy styles as well as the institutionalization of relationship patterns between the state and civil society'. In Switzerland, a 'culture of consensualism', reinforced by the 'fear of referendums', encouraged the search for compromise solutions. By contrast, the top-down approach to policy making in France led to extremely powerful counter-mobilizations which eventually caused the reform-minded government to back down.

Comparing pension reform processes in Switzerland, Germany and France between the 1970s and early 2000s, Häusermann (2007) arrives at the conclusion that, in the final analysis, transformative institutional change in continental European welfare states – among which she counts the Swiss welfare state – is a result of structural societal change. However, as she keeps underlining, structural change does not automatically lead to political reform. Power resources, strategy and political institutions intervene to determine when and how structural change is translated into policy change. With regard to pension reform in particular, she notes that in all three countries, reform agendas have become differentiated. Under the impact of the rise of the new social risks and the new needs for support, pension reforms have to take into account not only questions of cost control, financing mechanisms and established insurance rights, but also new aspects, which go beyond the issues of the 'golden age' – such as questions concerning the eligibility to pension benefits of persons with precarious and atypical employment status, or of persons who have not been active in the labour market. The differentiation of issues corresponds to a differentiation of conflict lines, actors' configurations and alliances. Häusermann's empirical analysis turns up multiple cross-cutting cleavage lines in all three countries. In the Swiss case, the new issues have given rise to a new division on the right of the party system, with the Radicals becoming an ally of the parties of the new left for the implementation of policies enforcing labour-market outsider interests and gender equality (such as in the case of the tenth revision of the AHV/AVS mentioned above). In all three countries, all major reforms since the 1990s combined cutbacks in insurance rights with expansive reforms in the domain of the new needs, and all these reform packages split the actors along several independent dimensions. As Häusermann points out, the coalitional flexibility in the party system and the fragmentation of the union system have been beneficial for the Swiss reform capacity.

In the meantime, however, it appears that the Swiss 'culture of consensualism' has weakened under the onslaught of the mobilization by the nationalist-conservative right (see chapter 6), and the 'threat of referendums' no longer seems to discipline policy makers to the same extent as in the past. The result is a weakening of the Swiss policy makers' capacity to make necessary adjustments to the welfare state. As we have argued in chapter 8, in the 1990s the corporatist negotiations between social partners had already lost a great deal of their capacity to find compromise solutions. Instead, it was Parliament which increasingly became the decisive arena for the formulation of packages capable of avoiding the popular veto. However, while Parliament succeeded in finding such solutions for the welfare reforms in the 1990s, it has appeared less and less capable of arriving at such solutions in the more recent past. Despite mounting demographic pressure on the old-age insurance and despite the exploding costs of the health-care system, Parliament has adopted legislation either lacking the necessary concessions to avoid a defeat at the polls or stopping short of a structural solution to the problem, or it has simply been unable to take any decision at all.

Thus, the *eleventh revision of the basic old-age pension scheme* adopted by a centre-right majority only included cutbacks to the detriment of women – above all a further increase of the retirement age for women up to 65 and cuts for certain categories of widows – and did not make any concessions to the left, which had asked for certain measures to facilitate early retirement. As a result, the united left – unions and Social Democrats – launched a referendum and the reform was massively rejected at the polls in spring 2004. On the same occasion, the voters also massively rejected a proposal to increase VAT by 0.8 per cent to finance the ever increasing deficit of the disability insurance scheme and to allow for the possibility of increasing VAT by another 1 per cent to avoid future deficits in the basic old-age pension scheme. While all parties agreed on the need to raise additional money to finance the deficit of the disability insurance scheme, the peak associations of the economy, the conservatives and the Radicals (against their own member of government, who defended this measure) argued that it was premature to attribute additional funds to the basic pension scheme – in spite of the fact that they had been complaining for years that the demographic pressure on pension schemes was not being taken seriously enough by policy makers.

In the domain of pensions, Parliament only succeeded in a first reform of the second pillar – the *occupational pensions* – where it introduced more transparency and increased the circle of beneficiaries by lowering the income thresholds for eligibility, but failed to address the problems of the weak performance of Swiss pension funds and the lack of competition in the system. In the domain of *the disability insurance*, Parliament proceeded to revise the corresponding law. It made access to the disability pension more difficult, and strengthened the early detection and reinsertion of the disabled into the labour market, but it did not resolve the problem of the structural lack of resources – the estimated economies of 300 million Swiss francs provided by the proposed measures fall far short of the insurance scheme's yearly deficit of 1.5 billion Swiss francs, and do not help to reduce its accumulated debt of 10 billion Swiss francs. The revised law was duly attacked by some associations of the disabled and by the left, who argued that the reinsertion measures proposed by the law remained an empty promise as long as the employers were not ready to make corresponding efforts, and that the new measures were mainly designed to make life for the disabled more difficult. In spite of this resistance, the revised law passed in a popular vote in June 2007.

With respect to the *reform of health insurance*, as we have already seen, the 1994 reform of the system failed to attain its basic goal – the limitation of costs. Instead of reducing costs, the system led to a transfer of such costs from the state to the insured persons: by the early part of this millennium, the state accounted for no more than 15 per cent of the costs of health care, whereas it had contributed 45 per cent twenty-five years earlier. As a result, the premiums increased by 70 per cent between 1990 and 1997 (and continued to increase beyond that date), while expenditure of the mutual societies only increased by 45 per cent over the same period. Faced with alarming reactions among the population, the reform proposals multiplied. Basically, three ways to improve the situation were discussed: (a) cost reductions by interventions on the supply side (e.g. price regulations for pharmaceuticals and medical services or restrictions concerning the supply of medical services by limiting the physicians' access to refunding by mutual societies); (b) cost reductions by interventions on the demand side (e.g. by providing stronger incentives for systems of 'managed care', by increasing the patients' participation in covering their bills, or by limiting the set of services in the basic insurance scheme); and (c) redistributive measures to improve the sharing of burdens (e.g. the reduction or even elimination of premiums for children, the creation of a common pool for the insurance of high risks, or the increase of the federal subsidies for alleviating the premiums of those who need it most). Early in 2002, the Federal Council refused to accept propositions made by Ms Dreifuss, the Social-Democratic head of the Department of the Interior responsible for health care. After Dreifuss stepped down in 2003, a member of the Radicals became the new head of this department. In spring 2003, the initiative of the Social Democrats, who proposed, among other things, the introduction of income-related premiums, was rejected by a vast margin in a popular vote. In spring 2007, a related initiative of the Social Democrats proposing to consolidate the multitude of competing insurance schemes in a unified health insurance system was also voted down by a large majority in a popular vote. The new proposals by the Federal Council did not fare any better either. After elaborate deliberations in both chambers, Parliament simply took a non-decision and decided not to pursue any of the reform proposals. In the meantime, individual premiums keep rising. To conclude, social policy is the domain where the increasing polarization of the Swiss political system is clearly leading to an impasse.

11 | *Foreign policy: Switzerland and the EU*

11.1 Introduction

Although Switzerland is at the heart of Europe, the country resembles a tiny island on the political map of Europe, surrounded by the twenty-seven member states of the European Union. In chapter 2 we argued that recent domestic and international developments have altered Switzerland's renowned political-island status. However, its outsider position in EU politics, due to its formal non-membership, prevents the country from full political integration. As we shall see in this chapter, solutions have nonetheless been found that allow Switzerland to deal with the challenges imposed by European integration.

We commence this chapter by providing a historical overview of the relations between the European Union and Switzerland. Structured in four stages, this overview is followed by a discussion of the prospects for eventual EU accession. We will conclude this chapter by arguing that Switzerland's current and probable future relationship with the EU can best be characterized as a 'customized quasi-membership'.

11.2 Historical overview

The historical outline of Switzerland's relationship with the European Community (EC), and later with the EU, can be structured in four, consecutive stages: initial multilateral failures, stagnation, further multilateral failure and enhanced unilateral and bilateral integration.

Stage one: initial multilateral failures (1955–72)

The developments leading to the Treaties of Rome, which created the European Economic Community (EEC; now known simply as the European Community or EC) and the European Atomic Energy Community (EURATOM) in 1957, demanded a Swiss reaction in order to avoid the country's isolation. From among several policy options available to Switzerland, the federal government chose to push for the establishment of a multilateral free-trade agreement within the Organization of European Economic Cooperation (OEEC), excluding closer association with – let alone accession to – the EC. Had it been successful, such a free-trade agreement would have maximized economic benefits, particularly for the export-oriented branch of the Swiss economy. At the same time, its political costs would have remained minimal. However, as Dupont and Sciarini (2001: 216) stress, this option was highly dependent on the outcome of the multilateral negotiations that eventually failed, due to the withdrawal of France from the OEEC in November 1958. Therefore, the Swiss government's initial strategy to deal with institutionalized economic cooperation at the European level failed miserably.

The Swiss failure was also a failure for the other six non-EC member states of the OEEC who, in the immediate aftermath of the French withdrawal, met for a first round of talks in Geneva.[1] These talks culminated in the signing of the Stockholm Convention, which established the European Free Trade Association (EFTA) in January 1960. The original aim of EFTA was twofold: the removal of trade barriers among its members and closer economic cooperation with the other members of the OEEC, including the members of the EC. Already by 1961, however, and following the EC's informal invitation to EFTA member countries to seek accession or association solutions, Denmark and the UK were willing to leave EFTA and join the EC. This pointed to a weakening of EFTA's ability to create a credible 'antipole' to the EC. Considering its earlier *passive* integration strategy, the Swiss government made a bold move in conjunction with the other two neutral EFTA member countries, Sweden and Austria: in December 1961, the three neutral states asked for the initiation of negotiations with a view to an association with the EC. The association attempt was a radical change in the Swiss strategy, as it was based on a broad and positive integration strategy that aimed at the establishment of an integrated European market (Zbinden 1992: 229). But this strategy also ran up against a series of technical and political problems that proved to be, as it were, tough nuts to crack. At the domestic level, the pre-negotiation

---

[1] These six countries were Austria, Denmark, Sweden, Norway, Portugal and the UK.

preparations took over a year and a half before they abruptly became futile as a result of de Gaulle's veto against UK membership in January 1963. This veto effectively sealed the fate of the attempt at an association with the EC by Switzerland and its fellow neutral states.

The initial failures of multilateral solutions and the aborted association attempt made the Swiss government revert back to its passive conception of integration. In 1967, however, three EFTA member countries (Denmark, the UK and Norway) as well as Ireland took up negotiations with a view towards a future EC accession. After de Gaulle's resignation in April 1969, his successor, Georges Pompidou, decided to add the support of France to the other EC member states' willingness for enlargement. These new developments provoked a reaction by the Swiss government, which became willing to move towards the creation of a Western European free-trade zone that was ultimately consecrated by a free-trade agreement on industrial goods between the EC and the individual EFTA member countries in 1972 (Dupont and Sciarini 2001: 219f.). In a mandatory referendum that took place on 3 December 1972, 72.5 per cent of the voters and all cantons voted in favour of the free-trade agreement. The agreement entered into force in 1973, the year that saw the EC's first enlargement with the accession of Denmark, Ireland and the UK.[2]

Stage two: stagnation (1972–86)

This second stage in Switzerland's European integration process is both the longest and the most uneventful. For fourteen years, Switzerland's involvement with the EC remained narrow (based on the free-trade agreement that exclusively covered industrial goods) and rather stagnant. The stagnation in Swiss–EC relations was, of course, a corollary to the EC's own stagnation, or 'eurosclerosis', during this period when no major integration effort saw the light of day (for a classic account, see Moravcsik 1998). It was not until the Schengen agreement in 1985 and, above all, the Single European Act (SEA) in 1986 that the process of European integration was relaunched.

[2] On 25 September 1972, 53.5 per cent of Norwegian voters rejected their country's accession to the EC.

Stage three: further multilateral failure (1986–92)

The remaining EFTA member countries were compelled to react to the prospects of a single European market. They did so in two steps: first, by defining their responses independently of one another (until 1988) and, after 1989, by defining them jointly (Dupont and Sciarini 2001: 220f.). Switzerland's first step encompassed an intermediate strategy – somewhere between inaction and accession – aimed at the establishment of bilateral, sector-specific agreements with the EC. This strategy had to be abandoned in 1989, when Jacques Delors, then-President of the European Commission, proposed to relaunch the dormant 'Luxembourg process', initiated in a ministerial meeting between the EC and EFTA in 1984. This process aimed at a multilateral dialogue leading to the establishment of a European Economic Area (EEA) (Sidjanski 1987: 141).

Delors' proposal was well received by the EFTA members. The prospects of an EEA Treaty promised access to the common market, based on the four fundamental freedoms guaranteed by the EC treaties (free movement of goods, services, people and capital) but without forcing them to adopt a number of EC policies, such as the (relatively costly) Common Agricultural Policy (CAP). However, the end of the Cold War strengthened the EC's position in the EEA negotiations and it rapidly became clear that EFTA-member-state-specific derogations from the *acquis communautaire* would not be tolerated by the EC. Also, the overall power within the newly established EEA Council, the EFTA Court and the EEA Joint Committee was dominated by the EC and its member states. The negotiations leading to the EEA Treaty had such a disillusioning effect on EFTA members that five of them (Austria already in 1989, Sweden in 1991, Finland, Norway and Switzerland in 1992)[3] asked to initiate accession negotiations with the EC. In the case of Switzerland, the federal government hinted at a future change of tack in May 1991, before making its strategic goal of EC membership official on 19 October of the same year. Within eighteen days of the signing of the EEA Treaty on 2 May 1992, the Federal Council had already submitted a formal demand for opening negotiations with a view towards EC membership.

---

[3] Austria, Finland and Sweden joined the EU in 1995. On 28 November 1994, 52.2 per cent of the Norwegian voters rejected EU membership (for the second time – see the previous footnote) in a referendum.

Most observers agree that this abrupt *volte face* regarding EC accession had devastating effects on the credibility of the federal government
during the EEA Treaty referendum campaign. While stressing the EEA
Treaty's substantial advantages over the *status quo*, the federal government also acknowledged the institutional shortcomings of the treaty
and in particular the lack of co-decisional power of Switzerland within
the EEA framework (Federal Council 1992a: 47ff.). At the same time,
the Federal Council declared that the EEA Treaty should be considered
within the larger context of EC membership and that this would be
the ultimate goal of Switzerland's integration policy (Federal Council
1992a: 52ff.). The EEA Treaty therefore became a simple stage on the
road towards membership (see also Federal Council 1992b). During
the referendum campaign, the Federal Council's attempt to separate
the EEA Treaty from the question of EC membership opened up new
and successful angles for the opponents of the treaty (Kriesi *et al.* 1993;
Goetschel 1994, 1995: 85).

The campaign leading to the vote on the EEA Treaty on 6 December
1992 was to be the longest and most intense referendum campaign
ever held in Switzerland (chapter 6). It actually started in July 1992
when the Zurich section of the Swiss People's Party, led by Christoph
Blocher, took all the other parties (including its own federal umbrella
organization), interest organizations, Parliament and the government
by surprise by announcing its opposition to the EEA Treaty (Schneider
and Hess 1995: 102). The opponents gained support from the powerful association for a neutral and independent Switzerland (AUNS – see
chapter 7) and a number of extreme right-wing and left-wing parties,
green parties and movements. Overall, however, the EEA Treaty was
preferred to the *status quo* by the greater part of the political elite.
The agreement received a considerable approval rating in Parliament
(67.6 per cent) and was backed by a large majority of political parties and peak associations. On the other hand, under conditions of
direct democracy, the clear preponderance of the 'yes' position among
the elite did not constitute a guarantee of success at the polls. The
opponents were well organized and coordinated their efforts efficiently.
Studies have shown that the 'no' camp managed to cover roughly the
same surface of ads in the newspapers as the EEA supporters (Schneider and Hess 1995: 104; Marquis and Sciarini 1999: 463). In addition, the opponents' argumentative arsenal was much larger than that

of their adversaries; finally, their campaign not only started earlier, it also persisted until the very last moment preceding the vote, contrary to the strategy of the 'yes' camp (Schneider and Hess 1995: 103f.). On 6 December 1992, the EEA Treaty was rejected at the polls by a thin majority (50.3 per cent) of the voters and a comfortable cantonal majority (18 of 26 cantons). Furthermore, turnout reached its highest level since 1947, with 78.8 per cent of the electorate casting a vote.

The outcome of the vote was a shock for the political and economic establishment in Switzerland, as it dealt a major blow to the Federal Council's European integration policy. Equally, if not more, traumatizing was the sharpness with which the referendum split Switzerland along its internal linguistic borders. While the voters of all French-speaking cantons accepted the EEA Treaty, with majorities of up to 79 per cent (Neuchâtel), all German-speaking Swiss cantons (with the exceptions of Basle-City and Basle-Country) as well as the only Italian-speaking canton (Ticino) rejected it, with majorities of up to 74 per cent (Uri). As we saw in chapter 1, European integration strongly nourishes the linguistic cleavage in Swiss society. In the wake of the cataclysmic referendum on the EEA Treaty, analyses of the cleavage structure and the cleavages' individual salience have presented further evidence of the importance of the linguistic cleavage in Switzerland's integration efforts (Kriesi *et al.* 1993, 1996). As we saw in chapter 4, the 1990s also witnessed the emergence of a new openness-tradition cleavage. Although the survey conducted in the aftermath of the EEA referendum does not provide measurements of this cleavage, the data reveal strong cultural and identity effects on the voters' decision at the polls (Kriesi *et al.* 1993; Christin *et al.* 2002: 250).

The EEA-induced trauma marked a turning point in the federal government's integration policy, as it became clear that the deep-rooted identity antagonisms in Swiss society, in conjunction with the institutionalized veto mechanisms of direct democracy (and in particular of the double majority – see chapters 3 and 4), would constitute a formidable obstacle to accession. The federal government did not wait long: in its message to Parliament of 24 February 1993, it announced its willingness to 'freeze' Switzerland's request to open accession negotiations with the EC, to refrain from preparing subsequent EEA membership and to privilege a deepening of EC–Swiss bilateral relations.

*Stage four: enhanced unilateral and bilateral integration
(1993–2007)*

In the EEA referendum ballot pamphlet, the Federal Council (1992c:
3) had stressed that, if Switzerland were to choose not to participate
in the EEA, then bilateral agreements would be much more difficult
to negotiate in the future. The government's prediction came true –
at least in the immediate aftermath of the EEA rejection. Already on
5 February 1993, the Federal Council proposed to the EC Council a list
of fifteen topics on which Switzerland desired to take up bilateral negotiations. In November of the same year, the EC Council agreed to open
negotiations on seven topics that covered ten of the topics mentioned by
the federal government (Federal Council 1999c: 9). In addition to not
accepting the full panoply proposed by the Swiss, the EC also included
two domains not mentioned by the Federal Council, namely freedom
of movement of persons and agriculture. Having agreed on the topics
both sides started to prepare for the opening of the negotiations. In
the middle of these preparations, however, the process was struck by a
direct-democratic thunderbolt: on 20 February 1994, a majority of the
Swiss voters and cantons accepted a popular initiative – the so called
'initiative of the Alps' (see chapter 7) – whose content was potentially
incompatible with the bilateral transit agreement concluded between
Switzerland and the EC in May 1992 (Germann 1995: 42). The immediate reaction of the European Union (which it was by then called,
following the coming into force of the Maastricht Treaty) was to put
its preparations for negotiations on hold. It took the Federal Council
nine months to unblock the situation by clarifying Switzerland's non-
discriminatory strategy for implementing the initiative's goals. On 12
December 1994, the bilateral, sector-specific negotiations were finally
able to commence.

The ensuing negotiations were as cumbersome and tedious as
their preparations had been. They lasted over four years before
the seven dossiers – bundled into a single, 800-page long agreement – could be politically settled and signed in Luxembourg on 21
June 1999. Over the course of the negotiations, two subjects stood
out as particularly difficult: the free movement of persons and the
dossier on road transportation.[4] Also, the negotiations were tough

---

[4] The five other areas concerned research, air transportation, public procurement,
technical barriers to trade and agriculture.

from the outset, as the EU insisted on the concept of 'parallelism', i.e. that the seven issues had to be treated as an indivisible package. This complicated the Swiss position, as a multitude of referendum threats against individual aspects of the agreements were omnipresent throughout the negotiations, endangering the overall success of the bilateral treaties. Therefore, the Federal Council decided from early on to consult widely all relevant political actors, a strategy that was clearly different from the previous approach (Oberer 2001: 56). In these consultations it became clear that concessions to various organizations – in the form of compensatory measures – were unavoidable in order to forestall their opposition by way of referendums. As we saw in chapter 7, this led to an important victory of the Swiss unions in the legislative arena, as they were able to obtain from the Swiss business community a number of important concessions, above all in the field of anti-dumping measures for wages. Actors concerned with the protection of the environment were also able to obtain successes, albeit to a somewhat lesser extent than the unions did in the field of labour regulations (Oberer 2001: 77).

Overall, the seven bilateral agreements were a success for (almost) all political actors. As Oberer (2001: 56) remarks, in the end, everybody somehow felt like a 'winner'. Only two parties (the Swiss Democrats and the Lega dei Ticinesi) and a number of rather insignificant associations opposed the agreements. Although they succeeded in collecting the necessary signatures for the referendum, they could not bring down the treaties at the polls. On 21 May 2000, 67.2 per cent of the voters (turnout was 48.3 per cent) accepted the bilateral agreements, which came into force on 1 June 2002. Note that due to the 2004 EU enlargement, the Swiss government agreed to extend the agreement covering the freedom of movement of persons to the ten new EU member states. At the same time, the accompanying measures to the agreements were revised. In the spring of 2004, several eurosceptic organizations collected 92,901 valid signatures against the extension of this agreement. On 25 September 2005, a clear majority of 56 per cent of the voters (turnout was 53.8 per cent) accepted the proposal at the polls (see also Dupont and Sciarini 2007).

However, even before the seven treaties of the bilateral agreements were ratified, the Swiss government gently knocked on the doors of the EU Commission in order to sound out the possibility of a *new* round of agreements. A number of areas for follow-up negotiations had already been outlined by the EU and Switzerland in the final act of the bilateral agreements of 21 June 1999. To these areas, the Swiss – unilaterally – added their willingness to intensify the cooperation in the domains of internal security and asylum policy, respectively covered by the Schengen and Dublin agreements. Initially, the areas of mutual interest were mainly 'leftovers' from the first round of bilateral agreements. Although reluctant from the outset, the EU gave the opening of the 'Bilaterals II' the green light in June 2001, mostly due to the EU's own interest in two additional domains: Switzerland's integration into the planned system of cross-border taxation of savings and an increased cooperation with the Swiss regarding the fight against fraud in the area of indirect taxes. The federal government reacted positively to these demands, though it formulated three conditions for its compliance with the opening of negotiations: first, Switzerland insisted on the need to safeguard the interests of the country as a platform for financial trade and services, in particular the protection of Swiss banking secrecy; second, it desired negotiations on the catalogue of areas that had been put forward earlier to no avail; and third, it wanted to negotiate on these dossiers in parallel (Federal Council 2004b: 5989ff.). Consequently, both sides formulated their respective negotiating mandates and opened the negotiations, first partially in July 2001, and then fully, in relation to a total of ten domains, in June 2002.[5]

In certain areas – e.g. in the domain of processed agricultural food – a breakthrough was achieved in a very short time. However, in other areas it was more difficult to get to an agreement, above all in the fields of taxation on savings, combating fraud, internal security (Schengen), asylum (Dublin) and the liberalization of services. The latter domain proved to be so complex that both sides rapidly agreed to suspend the process and to take up negotiations at a later date. Overall, however, by making use of a rather tough negotiation strategy, the Swiss were able to secure their initially formulated goals of obtaining a global package of nine agreements covering all the domains – other than services – in which they perceived an interest (and in particular in the area of Schengen/Dublin), as well as the permanent protection of Switzerland as a financial platform (especially the safeguarding of banking secrecy).

---

[5] The ten domains were the following: internal security (Schengen); asylum (Dublin); taxation on savings; combating fraud; processed agricultural products; the environment; statistics; media; pensions; and services.

After only two years of negotiations, a political agreement was finalized in May 2004, and in October of that year the 'Bilaterals II' were signed in Luxembourg.

The domestic ratification process differed from the 'Bilaterals I' in two important respects: first, following the pre-parliamentary consultation procedure there was no need for the adoption of compensatory mechanisms.[6] Only Switzerland's participation in Schengen and Dublin encountered a clear opposition (by the Swiss People's Party, the AUNS and EDU). Second, since the nine negotiation outcomes were not bundled together, they were submitted to Parliament (and, in seven cases, to the optional referendum process) individually.[7] Therefore, a single, negative referendum would not have endangered the coming into force of the successful dossiers. The sole 'guillotine clause' concerned the agreements on Schengen and Dublin, which had to be agreed upon (or rejected) *in corpore*. During the first months of 2005, the opponents of Schengen/Dublin managed to collect 86,732 valid signatures, thus forcing the agreement to be voted upon by the Swiss electorate on 5 June 2005. After an intensive campaign, a majority of 54.6 per cent of the electorate voted in favour of Switzerland's entry into the Schengen/Dublin area (turnout was 56 per cent, over the recent past an above-average figure – see also Alfonso and Maggett 2007: 227). Although this optional referendum did not require a double majority to be reached, it is notable that a majority of the cantons rejected the treaty at the polls.[8] Overall, the success of the government and the parliamentary majority in this referendum is significant, and it has confirmed Switzerland's successful bilateral approach.

The enhanced and successful integration efforts of Switzerland since the EEA debacle were not only bilateral in form. Stage four of our

---

[6] Several associations of owners of firearms, hunters and shooting enthusiasts opposed a number of changes of the federal legislation on firearms linked to the Schengen agreement. The Federal Council took this opposition into account and amended the draft legislation accordingly (see Federal Council 2004b: 6026ff.).

[7] To be precise, there were nine negotiation outcomes, eight of which are agreements (processed agricultural products, statistics, pensions, the environment, media, Schengen/Dublin, the fight against fraud and taxation on savings) that needed parliamentary approval. In one case (education/vocational training/youth), the EU and Switzerland agreed on a declaration of intent which was not submitted to Parliament.

[8] Fourteen of the 26 cantons (totalling 12 cantonal votes out of 23) rejected the agreement.

historical overview also contains a strong *unilateral* component, both legislative and financial in form. In 1988, the Federal Council decided to include in its messages to Parliament a chapter on the compatibility of legislative acts with EC law and policies. Ever since, by means of an institutionalized and standardized procedure, changes to federal law are systematically checked for their 'eurocompatibility', a process that leads to a unilateral adaptation of federal law to EU norms. At times, this 'Europeanization through the back door' even contained whole packages of legislative adaptations, such as EUROLEX, a package of revisions of federal laws which was contained in the EEA agreement and which, despite the refusal of the treaty at the polls, was in large part adopted in 1993 under the name SWISSLEX. This institutionalized procedure of incorporating EU norms into federal law, also known as 'autonomous implementation' (*autonomer Nachvollzug*), can be compared to the transposition of secondary EU legislation into national law by EU member states (Kux 1998: 9). Indeed, it is hard to estimate the extent to which Swiss and EU legislation overlap. Kux estimated in 1998 that about 85 per cent of all economic legislation in Switzerland was eurocompatible (Kux 1998: 10). Another indicator is provided by a study of over 300 legislative acts that were submitted to the mandatory and the optional referendum process between 1993 and 1998: only about 20 per cent of these acts contained EU-incompatible rules (Federal Council 1999a: 333ff.). In addition, these inconsistencies between EU and Swiss law were in most cases rather limited. A study covering the same period but focusing on the cantonal level found similar results: only a small minority of cantonal legislation adopted in this period would have stood in conflict with EU law (Federal Council 1999a: 336ff.). Overall, it is safe to consider the large majority of Swiss legislation to be eurocompatible.[9]

Switzerland's unilateral 'participation' in the EU also concerns voluntary financial subsidies. Recently, on 12 May 2004, the federal government agreed to participate in the EU's Cohesion Fund. Over a ten-year period, Switzerland will contribute to the Fund an overall amount of one billion Swiss francs (at an even rate of 100 million Swiss francs per year). The Swiss contribution will be administered autonomously and

---

[9] Karine Siegwart, legal adviser of the Federal Integration Office in Berne confirmed this statement to the authors in a telephone interview on 12 May 2005.

will need to have a neutral impact on the federal budget. When the EU requested a Swiss contribution to the Cohesion Fund, announced in May 2003, the federal government explicitly stated that this could neither be included within the framework of the 'Bilaterals I' nor be added to the 'Bilaterals II' (which were still in the negotiation stage). Furthermore, the Federal Council made clear that it would also be inconceivable for *substantive* reasons to link the contributions to the Cohesion Fund to the 'Bilaterals I and II'. However, a year later, Switzerland announced its willingness to contribute to the fund only seven days prior to the political agreement on the 'Bilaterals II'. This time, the federal government's press release explicitly stated that the discussion with the EU on this topic would not start before solutions could be found in the negotiations on the 'Bilaterals II'. One could interpret this move as a clever strategy on the part of the Swiss to get a breakthrough in the negotiations. Yet a competing and equally sound hypothesis would be that the EU delayed the political agreement on the 'Bilaterals II' in order to assure Switzerland's contribution. While analyses of this bargaining process are still to be produced, it may be assumed that the financial contributions of Switzerland to ongoing EU policies are intrinsically linked to the outcome of past and future bilateral negotiations.

In March 2006, Parliament adopted the federal law which serves as the legal basis for Switzerland's participation to the EU's Cohesion Fund. At the beginning of August of the same year, 82,664 valid signatures were deposited at the Federal Chancellery in Berne, forcing the law to be decided upon at the polls. The popular vote took place on 26 November 2006 and a majority of 53.4 per cent of the voters accepted the 'cohesion billion'.

11.3 Prospects for accession

As we have seen, in May 1992 the Federal Council asked the EU to take up negotiations with a view to Switzerland's accession. The request was frozen – but not abandoned – following the rejection of the EEA Treaty by both the people and the cantons in 1992. This triggered a reaction by EU-hostile actors of the radical right (i.e. the Swiss Democrats and the Lega dei Ticinesi) to launch a popular initiative in 1994. The initiative asked for the introduction of a new form of referendum on the opening of accession negotiations with the EU (see chapter 4).

If successful, the initiative would have forced the Federal Council to immediately retract its frozen accession request. Furthermore, any future demand for accession would have had to be submitted to the agreement of the people and the cantons. In Parliament, the initiative did not stand a chance and was vigorously rejected by both chambers[10] and the government. Except for some small organizations on the far right of the political spectrum, the initiative was opposed by all major parties and, on 8 June 1997, it was rejected by a majority of the voters (74.1 per cent) and all cantons. The rejection of the initiative was, however, not the result of a sudden 'europhile' sentiment among the Swiss, but rather caused by institutional motives (voters rejected the introduction of new direct-democratic institutions; see also Delgrande and Linder 1997).

The second popular initiative directly related to the 1992 accession demand was launched by a number of pro-EU movements and organizations in 1996. The initiative asked for an immediate revitalization of the accession request. Although the federal government opposed the initiative, it proposed an indirect counterproposal in which the executive agreed to *prepare* for the opening negotiations in view of EU accession. However, both proposals were refused by the two chambers of the Federal Parliament.[11] The ensuing campaign doubly split the political elite, *among* and *within* parties and organizations. At the federal level, Social Democrats, Christian Democrats, the Green Party and most unions recommended the acceptance of the initiative, while the Liberals, the Swiss People's Party, radical right parties and most peak associations recommended its rejection at the polls. Furthermore, a large number of cantonal sections of federal parties, especially among Christian Democrats and Liberals, adopted recommendations deviating from their respective federal parties. Finally, on 4 March 2001, a clear majority of the voters (76.8 per cent) and all cantons rejected the initiative at the polls.

---

[10] The National Council refused the initiative by 174 votes to 10, while the Council of States did so unanimously, with 37 votes.
[11] The initiative was rejected in the National Council by 94 votes to 69, and in the Council of States by 33 votes to 9. The indirect counterproposal was initially accepted by the National Council (with 97 votes to 83), but twice refused by the Council of States (with 29 votes to 15, and, the second time, with 26 votes to 16), whereupon the counterproposal was dropped.

The outcomes of the two post-EEA initiatives on Switzerland's EU accession show that the political elite predominantly preferred the bilateral negotiation approach to the 'de-freezing' of the 1992 accession request. Ever since the EEA debacle, the Federal Council's evaluations of a possible EU accession have consistently stressed that such a move, while desirable in the long-term, was suboptimal in the short- and medium-term. So far, majorities in Parliament, most political parties and large parts of the economy agree with this policy. Coupled with the rise of the Swiss People's Party and the accession of Christoph Blocher to the Federal Council (see chapter 6), one may assume that pro-accession sentiments will be swimming against the current of public opinion for some time to come.

From a bottom-up perspective, the results of the popular initiatives at the polls are equally indicative of insufficient levels of 'europhilia' to support a successful accession referendum – at least for the near future. Also, public opinion on EU accession is rather stable over time, slightly oscillating around the 50-per cent mark between favouring and rejecting EU membership (figure 11.1).

Even if a future trend showing a clear majority of voters favouring EU accession were discerned, one would have to take into account the unequal distribution of europhiles and europhobes across the cantons. As we have seen, most German-speaking cantons clearly oppose EU membership while urban centres, as well as the French-speaking cantons, support further integration. This is highly relevant because the double-majority mechanism (see chapters 3 and 4) – applicable to any mandatory referendum on EU accession – requires a cantonal majority. For the time being, this institutional hurdle is clearly too high to be cleared.

Regarding public opinion towards EU accession, Christin and Trechsel (2002) have shown the citizens' profound sensitivity to the perception of threats to national interests and the electorate's attachment to fundamental Swiss institutions. More particularly, the perceptions of the effects of EU accession on the national economy as well as (to a lesser extent) the attachment to neutrality are strong predictors of attitudes towards future membership. National identity and the image of Switzerland's neighbouring EU member states only weakly contribute to the explanation of Swiss public opinion with regard to EU membership. As Christin and Trechsel (2002: 432) stress, these findings show that significant shifts in public opinion on the question of

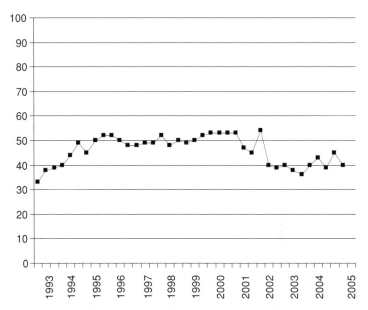

Figure 11.1 Public opinion in favour of Switzerland's EU accession, 1993–2005 (percentages)
Source: gfs.Berne, Europa-Barometer, November 2005 (N = 700–1,000 per wave, two waves per year)

EU membership are not to be expected unless the perceptions of future gains (or losses) for the national economy and for political institutions – and in particular neutrality – are altered.

In sum, the prospects for EU membership appear rather dismal, both from a top–down (elite) and bottom–up (voters) perspective. Within the current institutional framework, and in particular under the present rules of direct democracy, Switzerland is quite far from full membership of the European Union. The question therefore arises: unless and until accession becomes feasible, what alternative European future can Switzerland realistically achieve?

11.4 Switzerland's European future: customized quasi-membership

We argue that Switzerland is currently integrated in the great majority of policy fields that are of interest to the country. In some areas,

Switzerland is even *more* integrated than a number of EU member states, e.g. with regard to the Schengen/Dublin agreements. Also, in the fields where Switzerland has synchronized its policies with the EU it has done so quite to its advantage. Over the past decade, the Swiss have been able to achieve a 'customized quasi-membership' by creating their own *Europe à la carte*. In the Swiss–EU relationship, and for the time being, there is not much left that the Swiss authorities, the great majority of political actors or the private sector would wish to push forward in order to take further integration steps.

How did this occur? In our historical overview, we have seen that multilateral attempts to deepen Switzerland's relationship with the EU have failed. Conversely, the bilateral, sector-specific and incremental approaches have been successful.[12] One may refine this observation even further and argue that the failure of the (multilaterally negotiated) EEA Treaty was actually *beneficial* to Switzerland's integration efforts. In the aftermath of the 1992 referendum, the Swiss were able to negotiate some dossiers bilaterally that the government probably could not have negotiated as straightforwardly in a multilateral framework. One may even draw a parallel to the failed association attempt of 1961–3, where, according to Röthlisberger (1969, cited in Zbinden 1992: 222), the Swiss government may have had reasons to be happy about this failure after the preparatory efforts had revealed numerous problems.

Let us add that the 'autonomous implementation' of secondary EU law has gone very far. In some areas, the Swiss possess a more 'European' corpus of legislation than some of the EU member states. One may argue, however, that this autonomous implementation is not so much autonomous as *heteronomous* (Freiburghaus 2004), for the simple reason that Switzerland has no other choice than to adapt its legislative developments to those of the EU. So how does such a situation differ from membership? Besides the complete absorption of the *acquis communautaire*, membership would first and foremost signify that Switzerland would acquire formal decision-making power at the EU level. While the potential inclusion of the Swiss in Brussels' daily policy-making processes should not be underestimated, Switzerland's

---

[12] Note that since 1992, every EU-integration-related popular vote – with the possible exception of the 1994 initiative of the Alps – was won by the government and the majority in Parliament (Trechsel 2007b: 47).

overall power within the EU would probably remain quite limited and comparable to other small member states. For example, it is not very realistic to imagine Switzerland using a veto (in policy areas where unanimity is the rule, or in cases of treaty amendments) to prevent twenty-seven or more willing member states going ahead with large integration steps. On the other hand, strong impulses, novel proposals and innovative solutions may also be drafted by small member states. Therefore, Switzerland's membership could, from this perspective, also benefit the EU.

Many observers begin from the premise that 'Europe is moving towards ever deeper integration, a process that is not only irreversible but also likely to accelerate in the years to come' (Gabriel & Fanzun 2004b: 611). Therefore, the argument goes, Switzerland is doomed to have to keep pace with these developments. According to such views, the Swiss should even anticipate that further unavoidable integration steps will be taken by the EU and that they should join as soon as possible in order to avoid negotiating under less and less favourable conditions. However, we argue that this is an *ex post* perception that may be proved wrong regarding the future of the EU. Suffice it to mention the crisis into which the French and Dutch referendums of 2005 have plunged the EU's efforts to give itself a constitution. Particularly at this point in time, it appears that nothing assures that the EU will mechanically deepen its integration and even less certain is the argument about the irreversibility of such a process. The trajectory of EU integration has so far indeed shown an upward trend – but not in a linear, mechanical way. The EU has surmounted major crises and the question may be legitimately posed whether the Swiss, if they were part of the EU, could profit from participating in the overcoming of crises and in the shaping of future integration attempts.

At this point, however, let us somewhat provocatively invert the angle from which we have been looking at Switzerland's prospects for EU membership. Let us undertake a thought experiment in which we begin from the assumption that EU membership will successfully pass the referendum hurdle in Switzerland. The next step would be for the twenty-seven EU member states to endorse an amendment of the treaties for allowing Switzerland to join. The penultimate and most important round of enlargement was accommodated by the Nice Treaty of 2001. However, the Irish voters had to vote twice, in two consecutive referendums, before the treaty could come into force. Only then could the EU take on board the ten new member states. Future enlargement may trigger referendums in the EU and nothing prevents a – hypothetical – Swiss eagerness to join the EU from being blocked by a negative outcome in a referendum. One may add that, so far, EU enlargement has mostly proceeded through bundling several countries' demands for joining. To bundle Switzerland's accession demand with those of other countries (for example, countries from the Balkans) could well lead to a scenario in which the hardest part of the accession struggle would not take place in Switzerland, but in Austria, France, Denmark or elsewhere. And even if Swiss membership were submitted to European electorates in isolation from other candidate countries, its success at the European polls cannot be guaranteed. The recent debacles of referendums concerning the Nice Treaty and, in particular, the European Constitution can serve as a warning sign that treaty reform is not to be taken for granted once ratification takes place at the polls (Glencross and Trechsel 2007). If the European Constitution can fall victim to a series of referendums then why not Swiss accession?

To conclude, Switzerland's European trajectory has been neither linear nor unidirectional. However, and in particular over the past decade, it has reached a level of integration that we characterize as 'customized quasi-membership'. It goes without saying that this solution is mostly static compared to the formal membership option, which would lead to a dynamic, continuous integration of Switzerland in most policy areas. However, unilateral adaptation efforts (autonomous implementation) and future rounds of bilateral negotiations may well constitute a functional equivalent to full membership, as the latter option may only be feasible in the (very) long run.

Appendix

Table A1 Elections to the National Council, 1963–2007: percentages of votes

Party	1963	1967	1971	1975	1979	1983	1987	1991	1995	1999	2003	2007
SP	26.6	23.5	22.8	24.9	24.6	22.8	18.4	18.5	21.8	22.5	23.3	19.5
FDP	24.0	23.2	21.5	22.2	24.1	23.3	22.9	21.0	20.2	19.9	17.3	15.8
CVP	23.4	22.1	21.0	21.1	21.5	20.4	19.7	18.3	16.8	15.8	14.4	14.5
SVP	13.2	12.4	10.8	9.9	11.6	11.1	11.0	11.9	14.9	22.6	26.7	28.9
Other traditional	5.8	6.8	6.8	6.8	7.1	5.8	5.4	5.7	6.0	5.5	5.6	5.4
LdU	5.0	9.1	7.6	6.4	4.1	4.0	4.2	2.8	1.8	0.7	–	–
Radical right	–	0.5	7.5	5.5	1.9	3.5	5.8	8.5	9.3	4.9	2.9	2.5
Greens, POCH	–	–	–	1.0	3.4	6.7	9.2	7.6	6.5	5.3	7.9	9.6
Other new	1.8	2.4	2	2.2	1.7	2.4	3.3	5.8	2.7	2.7	2.6	3.8
Total	100	100	100	100	100	100	100	100	100	100	100	100

Table A2 Elections to the Council of States, 1939–2007: distribution of seats

Party	1939	1963	1967	1971	1975	1979	1983	1987	1991	1995	1999	2003	2007
FDP	14	13	14	15	15	11	14	14	18	17	18	14	12
CVP	18	18	18	17	17	18	18	19	16	16	15	15	15
SVP	4	4	3	5	5	5	5	4	4	5	7	8	7
LPS	2	3	3	2	1	3	3	3	3	2	–	–	–
SP	3	3	2	4	5	9	6	5	3	5	6	9	9
LDU	–	–	1	1	1	–	–	1	1	1	–	–	–
Lega	–	–	–	–	–	–	–	–	1	–	–	–	–
Other	3	3	3	–	–	–	–	–	–	–	–	–	3
Total	44	44	44	44	44	46	46	46	46	46	46	46	46

References

Alfonso, Alexandre and Martino Maggetti. 2007. 'Bilaterals II: reaching the limits of the Swiss third way?', in Clive H. Church (ed.), *Switzerland and the European Union*, pp. 215–33. London: Routledge.

Altermatt, Urs. 1991. *Der Weg der Schweizer Katholiken ins Ghetto*, 2nd edition. Zurich: Benziger.

Andrey, Georges. 1986. 'La quête d'un Etat national (1789–1848)', in *Nouvelle Histoire de la Suisse et des Suisses*, pp. 497–598. 2nd edition, Lausanne: Payot.

Armingeon, Klaus. 2001. 'Institutionalizing the Swiss welfare state', in Jan-Erik Lane (ed.), *The Swiss Labyrinth: Institutions, Outcomes and Redesign*, pp. 143–68. London: Frank Cass.

  2004. 'Swiss economic and fiscal policy', in Ulrich Klöti *et al.* (eds.), *Handbook of Swiss Politics*, pp. 633–72. Zurich: Neue Zürcher Zeitung Publishing.

  2007. 'Economic and finance policies of Switzerland', in Ulrich Klöti *et al.* (eds.), *Handbook of Swiss Politics*, 2nd edition, pp. 645–76. Zurich: Neue Zürcher Zeitung Publishing.

Armingeon, Klaus, Fabio Bertozzi and Giuliano Bonoli. 2004. 'Swiss worlds of welfare', *West European Politics* 27, 1: 20–44.

Arvanitis, S., R. Etter, Andres Frick and Heinz Hollenstein. 1992. *Innovationsfähigkeit und Innovationsverhalten der Schweizer Wirtschaft*. Studienreihe Strukturberichterstattung. Berne: Bundesamt für Konjunkturfragen.

Arvanitis, Spyros, M. Bezzola, L. Donzé, Heinz Hollenstein and David Marmet. 2001. *Die Internationalisierung der Schweizer Wirtschaft. Ausmass, Motive, Auswirkungen*. Zurich: vdf Hochschulverlag.

Arvanitis, Spyros, Heinz Hollenstein and David Marmet. 2005. *Internationale Wettbewerbsfähigkeit: wo steht der Standort Schweiz? Eine Analyse auf sektoraler Ebene*. Zurich: vdf Hochschulverlag.

Aubert, Jean-François. 1983. *Exposé des institutions politiques de la Suisse à partir de quelques affaires controversés*, 2nd edition. Lausanne: Payot.

Auer, Andreas and Jean-Daniel Delley. 1986. 'Structure politique des cantons', in Raimund E. Germann and Ernest Weibel (eds.), *Manuel système politique de la Suisse*, vol. 3, pp. 85–106 . Berne: Haupt.

Auer, Andreas and Alexander H. Trechsel (eds.). 2001. *Voter par Internet? Le projet e-voting dans le canton de Genève dans une perspective sociopolitique et juridique*. Basle, Geneva and Munich: Helbing & Lichtenhahn.

Auer, Andreas, Giorgio Malinverni and Michel Hottelier. 2006. *Droit constitutionnel suisse*, vol. 1: *L'Etat*, 2nd edition. Berne: Verlag Stämpfli.

Bächtiger, André and Jürg Steiner. 2004. 'Switzerland: territorial cleavage management as paragon and paradox', in Ugo M. Amoretti and Nancy Bermeo (eds.), *Federalism and Territorial Cleavages*, pp. 27–54. Baltimore: Johns Hopkins University Press.

Badie, Bertrand and Pierre Birnbaum. 1982. *Sociologie de l'Etat*, new edition. Paris: Grasset.

Bairoch, Paul. 1990. 'La Suisse dans le contexte international aux XIXe et XXe siècles', in Paul Bairoch and Martin Körner (eds.), *La Suisse dans l'économie mondiale*, pp. 103–40. Geneva: Droz.

Balthasar, Andreas. 2003. 'Die Prämienverbilligung im Krankenversicherungsgesetz: Vollzugsföderalismus und sekundäre Harmonisierung', *Swiss Political Science Review* 9, 1: 285–308.

Barankay, Iwan, Pascal Sciarini and Alexander H. Trechsel. 2003. 'Institutional openness and the use of referendums and popular initiatives: evidence from Swiss cantons', *Swiss Political Science Review* 9, 1: 169–99.

Barry, Brian. 1975. 'Review article: political accommodation and consociational democracy', *British Journal of Political Science* 5: 477–505.

Barthelmess, Petra Y. 2003. 'Der 11. September und seine Auswirkungen auf die innere Sicherheit: eine sicherheitspolitische und rechtsstaatliche Herausforderung für die Schweiz', in Andreas Wenger (ed.), *Bulletin 2003 zur schweizerischen Sicherheitspolitik*, pp. 129–58. Zurich: Forschungsstelle für Sicherheitspolitik der ETH Zurich.

Bartolini, Stefano. 2000. *The Political Mobilization of the European Left, 1860–1980: The Class Cleavage*. Cambridge: Cambridge University Press.

Battaglini, Monica and Olivier Giraud. 2003. 'Policy styles and the Swiss executive federalism: comparing diverging styles of cantonal implementation of the federal law on unemployment', *Swiss Political Science Review* 9, 1: 285–308.

Beck, Barbara. 2004. 'A special case: a survey of Switzerland', *The Economist*, 14 February 2004.

Berger, Suzanne and Ronald Dore (eds.). 1996. *National Diversity and Global Capitalism*. Ithaca: Cornell University Press.

Bertozzi, Fabio, Giuliano Bonoli and Benoît Gay-des-Combes. 2005. *La réforme de l'Etat social en Suisse. Vieillissement, emploi, conflit travail-famille*. Lausanne: Presses polytechniques et universitaires romandes.

Birnbaum, Pierre. 1997. 'Introduction: dimensions du nationalisme', in Pierre Birnbaum (ed.), *Sociologie des nationalismes*, pp. 1–33. Paris: Presses universitaires de France.

Bobbio, Norberto. 1987. *The Future of Democracy: A Defence of the Rules of the Game*. Minneapolis: University of Minnesota Press.

Bolliger, Christian and Regula Zürcher. 2004. 'Deblokierung durch Kooptation? Eine Fallstudie zur Aufnahme der Katholisch-Konservativen in die schweizerische Landesregierung 1891', *Swiss Political Science Review* 10, 4: 59–92.

Bonjour, Edgar. 1965. *Geschichte der schweizerischen Neutralität: vier Jahrhunderte eidgenössischer Aussenpolitik*, 9 vols. Basle: Helbing & Lichtenhahn.

Bonoli, Giuliano. 1999. 'La réforme de l'Etat social suisse: contraintes institutionnelles et opportunités de changement', *Swiss Political Science Review* 5, 3: 57–78.

Bonoli, Giuliano and André Mach. 2000. 'Switzerland: adjustment politics within institutional constraints', in Fritz W. Scharpf and Vivien A. Schmidt (eds.), *Welfare and Work in the Open Economy: Diverse Responses to Common Challenges*, vol. 2, pp. 131–74. Oxford: Oxford University Press.

  2001. 'The new Swiss employment puzzle', *Swiss Political Science Review* 7, 2: 81–94.

Borner, Silvio, Aymo Brunetti and Thomas Straubhaar. 1990. *Schweiz AG. Vom Sonderall zum Sanierungsfall?* Zurich: Neue Zürcher Zeitung Publishing.

  1994. *Die Schweiz im Alleingang*. Zurich: Neue Zürcher Zeitung Publishing.

Borner, Silvio, Frank Dietler and Stephan Mumenthaler. 1997. *Die internationale Wettbewerbsfähigkeit der Schweiz. Irrungen, Verwirrungen, Auswege*. Chur: Rüegger.

Börzel, Tanja A. and Thomas Risse. 2003. 'Conceptualizing the domestic impact of Europe', in Kevin Featherstone and Claudio Radaelli (eds.), *The Politics of Europeanization*, pp. 57–82. Oxford: Oxford University Press.

Braun, Dietmar. 2000. 'Territorial division of power and public policy-making: an overview', in Dietmar Braun (ed.), *Public Policy and Federalism*, pp. 1–26. Aldershot: Ashgate.

2003. 'Dezentraler und unitarischer Föderalismus. Die Schweiz und Deutschland im Vergleich', *Swiss Political Science Review* 9, 1: 57–89.

Brunner, Hans Peter. 1989. 'L'importance de la neutralité comme moyen d'affirmer l'indépendance suisse dans une Europe intégrée', in Roland Ruffieux and Annik Schachtschneider Morier-Genoud (eds.), *La Suisse et son avenir européen: une analyse des positions suisses face à l'intégration de l'Europe*, pp. 109–18. Lausanne: Payot.

Brunner, Matthias and Pascal Sciarini. 2002. 'L'opposition ouverture-traditions', in Simon Hug and Pascal Sciarini (eds.), *Changements de valeurs et nouveaux clivages politiques en Suisse*, pp. 29–93. Paris: L'Harmattan.

Brunner, Matthias and Lea Sgier. 1997. 'Crise de confiance dans les institutions politiques suisses? Quelques resultats d'une enquête d'opinion', *Swiss Political Science Review* 3, 1: 105–13.

Budge, Ian. 1996. *The New Challenge of Direct Democracy*. Cambridge: Polity Press.

Butler, David and Austin Ranney (eds.). 1994. *Referendums around the World: The Growing Use of Direct Democracy*. Washington, DC: AEI Press.

Bütschi, Danielle. 1993. 'Compétence pratique', in Hanspeter Kriesi (ed.), *Citoyenneté et démocratie directe*, pp. 99–119. Zurich: Seismo.

Bütschi, Danielle and Sandro Cattacin. 1994. *Le modèle suisse du bien-être*. Lausanne: réalités sociales.

Bützer, Michael. 2005. 'Continuity or innovation? Citizen engagement and institutional reforms in Swiss cities', in Herwig Reynaert, Pascal Delwit, Kristof Steyvers and Jean-Benoît Pilet (eds.), *Revolution or Renovation? Reforming Local Politics in Europe*. Bruges: Vanden Broele.

2007a. *Direkte Demokratie in Schweizer Städten. Ursprung, Ausgestaltung und Gebrauch im Vergleich*. Baden-Baden: Nomos.

2007b. 'Civic engagement and uncontrolled ballot votes: evidence from Swiss cities', *Local Government Studies* 33, 2: 215–36.

Bützer, Michael and Sébastien Micotti. 2003. *La démocratie communale en Suisse: vue générale, institutions et expériences dans les villes 1990–2000*. Geneva: Research and Documentation Centre on Direct Democracy (c2d), Université de Genève (also available at http://c2d.unige.ch/publis/rapport_final.pdf).

Calmfors, Lars and John Drifill. 1988. 'Bargaining structures, corporatism and macroeconomic performance', *Economic Policy* 6: 14–61.

Caramani, Daniele. 1993. 'La perception de l'impact des votations fédérales', in Hanspeter Kriesi (ed.), *Citoyenneté et démocratie directe*, pp. 77–98. Zurich: Seismo.

Centlivres, Pierre and Dominique Schnapper. 1991. 'Nation et droit de la nationalité suisse', *Pouvoirs* 56: 149–61.

Christin, Olivier. 1997. *La paix de religion: l'autonomisation de la raison politique au XVIe siècle*. Paris: Editions du Seuil.

Christin, Thomas and Simon Hug. 2003. 'Federalism and conflict resolution: considering selection biases', paper presented at the Annual Meeting of the Midwest Political Science Association, Chicago, 3–6 April.

Christin, Thomas and Alexander H. Trechsel. 2002. 'Joining the EU? Explaining public opinion in Switzerland', *European Union Politics* 3, 4: 415–43.

Christin, Thomas, Simon Hug and Pascal Sciarini. 2002. 'La mobilisation des clivages lors des votations populaires', in Simon Hug and Pascal Sciarini (eds.), *Changements de valeurs et nouveaux clivages politiques en Suisse*, pp. 237–67. Paris: L'Harmattan.

Cox, Gary W. 1997. *Making Votes Count: Strategic Coordination in the World's Electoral Systems*. Cambridge: Cambridge University Press.

Crouch, Colin. 1982. *Trade Unions: The Logic of Collective Action*. London: Fontana.

Crouch, Colin and Wolfgang Streeck (eds.). 1996. *Les capitalismes en Europe*. Paris: Découverte.

Crouch, Colin and Franz Traxler (eds.). 1995. *Organized Industrial Relations in Europe: What Future?* Aldershot: Avebury.

Cusack, Thomas R. 1995. *Politics and Macroeconomic Performance in the OECD Countries*. FS I 95–315. Berlin: Wissenschaftszentrum.

Deleon, Peter. 1999. 'The stages approach to the policy process', in Paul A. Sabatier (ed.), *Theories of the Policy Process*, pp. 19–32. Boulder: Westview Press.

Delgrande, Marina and Wolf Linder. 1997. *Analyse der eidgenössischen Abstimmung vom 8. Juni 1997* (Vox no. 61). Berne: Schweizerische Gesellschaft für praktische Sozialforschung gfs.

Delley, Jean-Daniel, Richard Derivaz, Luzius Mader, Jean-Charles Morand and Daniel Schneider. 1982. *Le droit en action: étude de mise en œuvre de la loi Furgler*. St Saphorin: Georgi.

De Swaan, Abraham. 1988. *In Care of the State*. Cambridge: Polity Press.

Dhima, Giogio. 1991. *Politische Ökonomie der schweizerischen Ausländerregelung*. Chur: Rüegger.

Dupont. Cédric. 1992. 'Succès avec la SDN, échec avec l'EEE? Résistances internes et négociation internationale', in *Schweizerisches Jahrbuch für politische Wissenschaft 'Die Schweiz und Europa/La Suisse et l'Europe'*, pp. 249–72. Berne: Haupt.

Dupont, Cédric and Pascal Sciarini. 2001. 'Switzerland and the European integration process: engagement without marriage', in Jan-Erik Lane (ed.), *The Swiss Labyrinth: Institutions, Outcomes and Redesign*, pp. 211–32. London: Frank Cass.

2007. 'Back to the future: the first round of bilateral negotiations with the EU', in Clive H. Church (ed.), *Switzerland and the European Union*, pp. 202–14. London: Routledge.

Ebbinghaus, Bernhard and Jelle Visser. 1999. 'When institutions matter: union growth and decline in Western Europe 1950–1999', *European Sociological Review* 15, 2: 135–58.

Elazar, Daniel J. 1962. *The American Partnership: Intergovernmental Cooperation in the Nineteenth-Century United States*. Chicago: University of Chicago Press.

Epiney, Astrid and Karine Siegwart. 1998. *Direkte Demokratie und Europäische Union – Démocratie directe et Union européenne*. Freiburg: Universitätsverlag Freiburg.

Epiney, Astrid, Karine Siegwart, Michael Cottier and Nora Refaeil. 1998. *Schweizerische Demokratie und Europäische Union*. Berne: Stämpfli.

Epple-Gass, Rudolf. 1988. *Friedensbewegung und direkte Demokratie in der Schweiz*. Frankfurt: Haag & Herchen.

Ernst, Andreas, 1998. 'Vielsprachigkeit, Öffentlichkeit und politische Integration: schweizerische Erfahrungen und europäische Perspektiven', *Swiss Political Science Review* 4, 4: 225–40.

Esping-Andersen, Gösta. 1990. *The Three Worlds of Welfare Capitalism*. Cambridge: Polity.

(ed.). 1996. *Welfare States in Transition*. London: Sage.

Ettlin, Franz and Serge Gaillard. 2001. 'Die 90er Jahre in der Schweiz: eine wettbewerbsfähige Wirtschaft braucht eine konjunkturstabilisierende Geldpolitik', in Jürg Furrer and Bruno Gehrig (eds.), *Aspekte der schweizerischen Wirtschaftspolitik: Festschrift für Franz Jaeger*, pp. 267–93. Chur: Rüegger.

Federal Council. 1991. *Botschaft zum Beitritt der Schweiz zum Völkerbund*. Berne: Federal Administration (also available at www.ssn.ethz.ch/forschung/amt/Voelkerbundbeitritt.cfm).

1992a. *Botschaft zur Genehmigung des Abkommens über den Europäischen Wirtschaftsraum vom 18. Mai 1992*. Berne: Federal Administration (also available at www.ssn.ethz.ch/forschung/amt/documents/EUWirtschaftsraum.pdf).

1992b. *Bericht über einen Beitritt der Schweiz zur Europäischen Gemeinschaft vom 18. Mai 1992*. Berne: Federal Administration (also available at www.ssn.ethz.ch/forschung/amt/documents/EUBeitrittsbericht.pdf).

1992c. *Volksabstimmung vom 6. Dezember 1992 – Erläuterungen des Bundesrates*. Berne: Federal Administration (also available at www.admin.ch/ch/d/pore/va/19921206/explic/d-pp0164.pdf).

1993a. *White Paper on Neutrality. Annex to the Report on Swiss Foreign Policy for the Nineties of 29 November 1993.* Berne: Federal Administration (also available at www.eda.admin.ch/eda/e/home/recent/rep/neutral/neut93.html).

1993b. *Rapport sur la politique extérieure de la Suisse dans les années 90 du 29 novembre 1993.* Berne: Federal Administration (also available at www.eda.admin.ch/eda/f/home/recent/rep/forpol.Par.0002.UpFile.pdf/rp_931129_foreignpol_f.pdf).

1999a. *Suisse – Union européenne: rapport sur l'intégration 1999 du 3 février 1999.* Berne: Federal Administration (also available at www.europa.admin.ch/europapol/off/ri_1999/f/ri.pdf).

1999b. *Sicherheit durch Kooperation. Bericht des Bundesrates an die Bundesversammlung über die Sicherheitspolitik der Schweiz (SIPOL B 2000) vom 7. Juni 1999.* Berne: Federal Administration (also available at www.vbs-ddps.ch/internet/vbs/de/home/ausdem/publikationen/berichte.Par.0001.DownloadFile.tmp/report-D.pdf).

1999c. *Botschaft zur Genehmigung der sektoriellen Abkommen zwischen der Schweiz und der EG vom 23. Juni 1999.* Berne: Federal Administration (also available at www.europa.admin.ch/ba/off/botschaft/d/ab_mess.pdf).

2001. *Botschaft zur Neugestaltung des Finanzausgleichs und der Aufgaben zwischen Bund und Kantonen (NFA) vom 14. November 2001.* Berne: Federal Administration (also available at www.admin.ch/ch/d/ff/2002/2291.pdf).

2004a. *Die Schweiz und die UNO. Bericht des Bundesrats 2004.* Berne: Federal Administration (also available at www.uno.admin.ch/sub_uno/g/uno/publi/pdf.Par.0028.UpFile.pdf/xy_yymmdd_0123456789_l.pdf).

2004b. *Botschaft zur Genehmigung der bilateralen Abkommen zwischen der Schweiz und der Europäischen Union, einschliesslich der Erlasse zur Umsetzung der Abkommen ('Bilaterale II') vom 01. Oktober 2004.* Berne: Federal Administration (also available at www.europa.admin.ch/nbv/off/botschaft/d/botschaft.pdf).

Federal Department of Economic Affairs. 2002. *Der Wachstumsbericht. Determinanten des Schweizer Wirtschaftswachstums und Ansatzpunkte für eine wachstumsorientierte Wirtschaftspolitik.* Berne (also available at www.seco.admin.ch/imperia/md/content/analysenundzahlen/strukturanalysenundwirtschaftswachstum/rapport_croissance_d.pdf).

2003. 'Finanzkraft der Kantone neue festgelegt – Medienmitteilung vom 5. November', Berne: Eidgenössisches Finanzdepartement (also available at www.efd.admin.ch/d/dok/medien/medienmitteilungen/2003/11/finanzkraft.htm).

Federal Office of Energy. 2003. *Analyse des Meinungsbildungs- und Entscheidungsprozesses zum Elektrizitätsmarkt.* Berne: Bundesamt für Energie (also available at www.energie-schweiz.ch/imperia/ md/content/ energiemrkteetrgertechniken/elektrizittsmarkt/51.pdf).

Federal Statistical Office. 2003. *Bevölkerungsentwicklung in der Schweiz 2003.* Neuchâtel: Bundesamt für Statistik (also available at www.bfs. admin.ch/bfs/portal/de/index/themen/bevoelkerung/ uebersicht/blank/ publikationen.Document.49116.html).

Fischer, Alex. 2003. Die Auswirkungen der Internationalisierung/ Europäisierung auf Schweizer Entscheidungsprozesse. Dissertation. Lausanne: IDHEAP.

Fischer, Alex, Sarah Nicolet and Pascal Sciarini. 2002. 'Europeanization of a non-EU country: the case of Swiss immigration policy', *West European Politics* 25, 4: 143–70.

Fleiner-Gerster. Thomas. 1987. 'Le conseil fédéral: directoire de la confédération', *Pouvoir* 43: 49–64.

Flückiger, Yves. 1997. *La formation continue face aux mutations économiques actuelles.* Geneva: Département d'économie politique, Université de Geneva.

Fluder, Robert. 1998. *Politik und Strategien der schweizerischen Arbeit-nehmerorganisationen. Orientierung, Konfliktverhalten und politische Einbindung.* Chur: Rüegger.

Fluder, Robert and Beat Hotz-Hart. 1998. 'Switzerland: still as smooth as clock work?', in Anthony Ferner and Richard Hyman (eds.), *Changing Industrial Relations in Europe*, pp. 262–82. Oxford: Blackwell.

Franklin, Mark N. 2004. *Voter Turnout and the Dynamics of Electoral Competition in Established Democracies since 1945.* Cambridge: Cambridge University Press.

Freiburghaus, Dieter. 2004. 'Heteronomer Nachvollzug? Oder wie sich die Autonomie verflüchtigt', *Die Volkswirtschaft* 9: 2004 (also available at www.europa.admin.ch/nbv/info_mat/dossiers/d/volkswirtschaft/ vol_09–18d_freiburghaus.pdf).

Froidevaux, Didier. 1997. 'Construction de la nation et pluralisme suisses: idéologie et pratiques', *Swiss Political Science Review* 3, 4: 29–58.

Gabriel, Jürg Martin. 1990. *Schweizer Neutralität im Wandel. Hin zur EG.* Frauenfeld: Verlag F. Huber.

1994. 'Neutralität für den Notfall: der Bericht des Bundesrates zur Aussenpolitik der Schweiz in den 90er Jahren', *Beiträge und Berichte*, no. 221. St Gallen: Institut für Politikwissenschaft der Hochschule St Gallen.

1999. 'Verpasste Chancen: inkohärente Schweizer Politik im Kosovokrieg', *Beiträge der Forschungsstelle für internationale Beziehungen*, no. 25. Zurich: Center for International Studies of the Swiss Federal Institute for Technology.

Gabriel, Jürg Martin and Jon A. Fanzun. 2004a. 'Switzerland in the world', in Ulrich Klöti *et al.* (eds.), *Handbook of Swiss Politics*, pp. 38-48. Zurich: Neue Zürcher Zeitung Publishing.

Gabriel, Jürg Martin and Jon A. Fanzun. 2004b. 'Foreign and security policy', in Ulrich Klöti *et al.* (eds.), *Handbook of Swiss Politics*, pp. 601–32. Zurich: Neue Zürcher Zeitung Publishing.

Gärtner, Heinz and Otmar Höll. 2001. 'Austria', in Erich Reiter and Heinz Gärtner (eds.), pp. 183–94. *Small States and Alliances*. New York: Physica.

Gerber, Elizabeth. 1999. *The Populist Paradox: Interest Group Influence and the Promise of Direct Legislation*. Princeton: Princeton University Press.

Germann, Raimund E. 1975. *Politische Innovation und Verfassungsreform*. Berne: Haupt.

1985. *Experts et commissions de la Confédération*. Lausanne: Presses polytechniques romandes.

1994. *Staatsreform. Der Übergang zur Konkurrenzdemokratie*. Berne: Haupt.

1995. 'Die bilateralen Verhandlungen mit der EU und die Steuerung der direkten Demokratie', *Swiss Political Science Review* 1, 2–3: 35–60.

1996. *Administration publique en Suisse*, vol. 1: *L'appareil étatique et le gouvernement*. Berne: Haupt.

Germann, Raimund E. and Katja Weis. 1995. *Les administrations cantonales: une vue comparative*. Berne: Haupt.

Glencross, Andrew and Alexander H. Trechsel. 2007. 'First or second order referendums? Understanding the votes on the Constitutional Treaty in four EU member states', unpublished manuscript.

Goetschel, Laurent. 1994. *Zwischen Effizienz und Akzeptanz. Die Information der Schweizer Behörden im Hinblick auf die Volksabstimmung über den EWR-Vertrag vom 6. Dezember 1992*. Berne: Haupt.

1995. 'Die EWR-Information der Bundesbehörden', *Swiss Political Science Review* 1, 2–3: 61–91.

1999. 'Neutrality, a really dead concept?', *Cooperation and Conflict* 34, 2: 115–39.

Gruner, Erich. 1977. *Die Parteien in der Schweiz*. Berne: Francke.

Gruner, Erich and Hans Peter Hertig. 1983. *Die Stimmbürger und die 'neue' Politik. Le citoyen et la 'nouvelle' politique*. Berne: Haupt.

Haltiner, Karl W. and Andreas Wenger (eds.). 2004. *Sicherheit 2004. Aussen-, Sicherheits- und Verteidigungspolitische Meinungsbildung im*

Trend. Zurich: Forschungsstelle für Sicherheitspolitik der ETH Zurich und Militärakademie an der ETH Zurich.

Hartmann, Hans and Franz Horvath. 1995. *Heile Welt Schweiz. Die nationalkonservative Bewegung in der Diskussion*. Politik aktuell, vol. 3. Zurich: Realotopia.

Häusermann, Silja. 2007. 'Modernization in hard times. Post-industrial pension politics in France, Germany and Switzerland', unpublished PhD thesis, Department of Political Science, University of Zurich.

Häusermann, Silja, André Mach and Yannis Papadopoulos. 2004. 'From corporatism to partisan politics: social policy making under strain in Switzerland', *Swiss Political Science Review* 10, 2: 33–60.

Helbling, Marc and Hanspeter Kriesi. 2004. 'Staatsbürgerverständnis und politische Mobilisierung: Einbürgerungen in Schweizer Gemeinden', *Swiss Political Science Review* 10, 4: 33–58.

Henneberger, Fred and Alexandre Ziegler. 2001. *Internationalisierung der Produktion und sektoraler Strukturwandel: Folgen für den Arbeitsmarkt*. Strukturberichterstattung no. 8. Berne: Staatssekretariat für Wirtschaft (seco).

Héritier, Adrienne. 1994. *Policy-analyse. Eine Einführung*. Frankfurt: Campus.

Hermann, Michael and Heiri Leuthold. 2003. *Atlas der politischen Landschaften. Ein weltanschauliches Porträt der Schweiz*. Zurich: vdf-Verlag.

Hertig, Hans Peter. 1982. 'Sind Abstimmungserfolge käuflich? – Elemente der Meinungsbildung bei eidgenössischen Abstimmungen', in *Schweizerisches Jahrbuch für politische Wissenschaft 'Medien und politische Kommunikation'*, pp. 35–57. Berne: Haupt.

Hess, Cyrill and Alexander H. Trechsel. 1993. 'Das Ständemehr zwischen Föderalismus und Demokratie. Ein demographisch besser abgestütztes Dreistufenmodell', *Neue Zürcher Zeitung*, 23 June, p. 23.

Hobsbawm, Eric. 1992. 'Introduction: inventing traditions', in Eric Hobsbawm and Terence Ranger (eds.), *The Invention of Tradition*, pp. 1–14. Cambridge: Cambridge University Press.

Hollenstein, Heinz. 2005. 'Determinants of international activities: are SME's different? An empirical analysis based on Swiss survey data', *Small Business Economics* 24: 431–50.

Huber, Evelyne and John Stephens. 2001. *Development and Crisis of the Welfare State: Parties and Policies in Global Markets*. Chicago: University of Chicago Press.

Hug, Simon. 1989. 'L'émergence d'un nouveau parti politique. Cadre théorique et son application au Parti écologiste suisse', MA thesis, University of Geneva Département de science politique.

Hug, Simon and Alexander H. Trechsel. 2002. 'Clivages et identification partisane', in Simon Hug and Pascal Sciarini (eds.), *Changements de valeurs et nouveaux clivages politiques en Suisse*, pp. 207–35. Paris: L'Harmattan.

IDHEAP/BADAC. 2004. *Bestand der Kantonsangestellten 2001*, www.badac.ch/ (consulted on 8 December 2004).

Im Hof, Ulrich. 1991. *Mythos Schweiz. Identität – Nation – Geschichte. 1291–1991*. Zurich: Neue Zürcher Zeitung Publishing.

Immergut, Ellen M. 1992a. *Health Politics: Interests and Institutions in Western Europe*. Cambridge: Cambridge University Press.

    1992b. 'The rules of the game: the logic of health policy-making in France, Switzerland, and Sweden', in Sven Steinmo, Kathleen Thelen and Frank Lonstreth (eds.), *Structuring Politics: Historical Institutionalism in Comparative Perspective*, pp. 57–89. Cambridge: Cambridge University Press.

Independent Commission of Experts Switzerland – Second World War. 2002. *Final Report*. Zurich: Pendo Verlag.

Inglehart, Ronald and Dusan Sidjanski. 1975. 'Electeurs et dimension gauche-droite', in Dusan Sidjanski, Charles Roig, Henry Kerr, Ronald Inglehart and Jacques Nicola (eds.), *Les Suisses et la politique: enquête sur les attitudes d'électeurs suisses (1972)*, pp. 83–124. Berne: Lang.

Interdepartmental Working Group. 2000. *Swiss Neutrality in Practice – Current Aspects. Report of the Interdepartmental Working Group of 20 August 2000*. Berne: Federal Administration.

Iversen, Torben. 1996. 'Power, flexibility, and the breakdown of centralized wage bargaining: Denmark and Sweden in comparative perspective', *Comparative Politics* 26, 3: 399–436.

Jacot-Guillarmod, Olivier. 1990. 'Conséquences, sur la démocratie directe, d'une adhésion de la Suisse à la Communauté européenne', *Beiheft zur Zeitschrift für Schweizerisches Recht* 10: 39–80. Basle.

Jegen, Maya. 2003. *Energiepolitische Vernetzung in der Schweiz. Analyse der Kooperationsnetzwerke und Ideensysteme der energiepolitischen Entscheidungsträger*. Basle: Helbing & Lichtenhahn.

Jegher, Annina. 1999. *Bundesversammlung und Gesetzgebung*. Berne: Haupt.

Jegher, Annina and Wolf Linder. 1998. *Schweizerische Bundesversammlung: ein aktives Gesetzgebungsorgan. Eine empirische Untersuchung des Gesetzgebungsprozesses in den Jahren 1995–97*. Berne: Dokumentationszentrale der Bundesversammlung (also available at www.parlament.ch/ed-pa-gesetzgebungsprozess.pdf).

Jobert, Bruno (ed.). 1994. *Le tournant néo-libéral en Europe*. Paris: L'Harmattan.

Jost, Hans-Ulrich. 1986. 'Menace et repliement 1914–1945', in *Nouvelle histoire de la Suisse et des Suisses*, pp. 683–770. Lausanne: Payot.
1998. 'Der helvetische Nationalismus. Nationale Identität, Patriotismus, Rassismus und Ausgrenzungen in der Schweiz des 20. Jahrhunderts', in Hans-Rudolf Wicker (ed.), *Nationalismus, Multikulturalismus und Ethnizität*, pp. 65–78. Berne: Haupt.

Kappel, Rolf and Oliver Landmann. 1997. *Die Schweiz im globalen Wandel*. Zurich: Neue Zürcher Zeitung Publishing.

Kappeler, Beat. 1996. 'Zuerst das Verhalten ändern, nicht die Institutionen', in Silvio Borner and Hans Rentsch (eds.), *Wieviel direkte Demokratie verträgt die Schweiz?*, pp. 303–6. Chur and Zurich: Rüegger.

Katzenstein, Peter J. 1984. *Corporatism and Change: Austria, Switzerland and the Politics of Industry*. Ithaca: Cornell University Press.
1985. *Small States in World Markets: Industrial Policy in Europe*. Ithaca: Cornell University Press.

Keohane, Robert O. and Helen V. Milner (eds.). 1996. *Internationalization and Domestic Politics*. Cambridge: Cambridge University Press.

Kerr, Henry. 1981. *Parlement et société en Suisse*. Saint-Saphorin: Georg.
1987. 'The Swiss party system: steadfast and changing', in Hans Daalder (ed.), *Party Systems in Denmark, Austria, Switzerland, the Netherlands and Belgium*, pp. 107–92. London: Frances Pinter.

Kersaudy, François. 1987. *Norway 1940*. New York: St Martin's Press.

Kirchgässner, Gebhard, Lars P. Feld and Marcel R. Savioz. 1999. *Die direkte Demokratie. Modern, erfolgreich, entwicklungs- und exportfähig*. Basle: Helbing & Lichtenhahn.

Kissling-Näf, Ingrid. 1997. *Lernprozesse und Umweltverträglichkeitsprüfung – staatliche Steuerung über Verfahren und Netzwerkbildung in der Abfallpolitik*. Basle: Helbing & Lichtenhahn.

Kissling-Näf, Ingrid and Peter Knoepfel. 1992. 'Politikverflechtung dank zentralstaatlichem Immobilismus? Handlungsspielräume kantonaler Vollzugspolitiken im schweizerischen politisch-administrativen System', in Heidrun Abromeit and Werner Pommerehne (eds.), *Staatstätigkeit in der Schweiz*, pp. 43–69. Berne and Stuttgart: Haupt.

Kissling-Näf, Ingrid and Sonja Wälti. 2007. 'The implementation of public policies', in Ulrich Klöti *et al.* (eds.), *Handbook of Swiss Politics*, 2nd edition, pp. 501–24. Zurich: Neue Zürcher Zeitung Publishing.

Kleger, Heinz and Gianni D'Amato. 1995. 'Staatsbürgerschaft und Einbürgerung – oder: Wer ist ein Bürger? Ein Vergleich zwischen Deutschland, Frankreich und der Schweiz', *Journal für Sozialforschung* 35, 3/4: 259–81.

Klöti, Ulrich. 1998. 'Kantonale Parteiensysteme – Bedeutung des kantonalen Kontexts für die Positionierung der Parteien', in Hanspeter Kriesi, Wolf

Linder and Ulrich Klöti (eds.), *Schweizer Wahlen 1995*, pp. 45–72. Berne: Haupt.

2007. 'The government', in Ulrich Klöti *et al.* (eds.), *Handbook of Swiss Politics*, 2nd edition, pp. 145–69. Zurich: Neue Zürcher Zeitung Publishing.

Kollman, Ken. 1998. *Outside Lobbying: Public Opinion and Interest Group Strategies*. Princeton: Princeton University Press.

Kölz, Alfred. 1992. *Neuere schweizerische Verfassungsgeschichte. Ihre Grundlinien vom Ende der Alten Eidgenossenschaft bis 1848*. Berne: Verlag Stämpfli.

2004. *Neuere schweizerische Verfassungsgeschichte. Ihre Grundlinien in Bund und Kantonen seit 1848*. Berne: Verlag Stämpfli.

Koopmans, Ruud, Paul Statham, Marco Giugni and Florence Passy. 2005. 'Contested citizenship: the contentious politics of immigration and ethnic relations in Germany, Britain, France, the Netherlands, and Switzerland', unpublished manuscript.

Körner, Martin. 1986. 'Réformes, rupture, croissances (1515–1648)', in *Nouvelle histoire de la Suisse et des Suisses*, 2nd edition, pp. 333–422. Lausanne: Payot.

Kreid, Harald. 2001. 'The effect of neutral states in the UN – the example of Austria', *Politorbis*, April, special issue: 39–44.

Kriesi, Hanspeter. 1980. *Entscheidungsstrukturen und Entscheidungsprozesse in der Schweizer Politik*. Frankfurt: Campus.

(ed.). 1993. *Citoyenneté et démocratie directe*. Zurich: Seismo.

1998a. *Le système politique suisse*, 2nd edition. Paris: Economica.

1998b. 'Einleitung', in Hanspeter Kriesi, Wolf Linder and Ulrich Klöti (eds.), *Schweizer Wahlen 1995*, pp. 1–17. Berne: Haupt.

1999. 'Note on the size of the public sector in Switzerland', *Swiss Political Science Review* 5, 2: 105–8.

2001. 'The Federal Parliament: the limits of institutional reform', in Jan-Erik Lane (ed.), *The Swiss Labyrinth: Institutions, Outcomes and Redesign*, pp. 59–76. London: Frank Cass.

2005. *Direct Democratic Choice: the Swiss Experience*. Lanham, MD: Lexington.

2006. 'Institutional filters and path dependency: the impact of Europeanization on Swiss business associations', in Wolfgang Streeck, Jürgen R. Grote, Volker Schneider and Jelle Visser (eds.), *Governing Interests. Business Associations Facing Internationalization*, pp. 49–67. London: Routledge.

Kriesi, Hanspeter and Maya Jegen. 2000. 'Decision-making in the Swiss energy policy elite', *Journal of Public Policy* 20, 1: 21–53.

2001. 'The Swiss energy policy elite', *European Journal of Political Research* 39, 2: 251–87.

Kriesi, Hanspeter and Pascal Sciarini. 2004. 'The impact of issue preferences on the voting choices in the Swiss federal elections 1999', *British Journal of Political Science* 34: 725–59.

Kriesi, Hanspeter and Dominique Wisler. 1996. 'Social movements and direct democracy in Switzerland', *European Journal of Political Research* 30: 19–40.

1999. 'The impact of social movements on political institutions: a comparison of the introduction of direct legislation in Switzerland and the United States', in Marco Giugni, Doug McAdam and Charles Tilly (eds.), *How Movements Matter: Theoretical and Comparative Studies on the Consequences of Social Movements*, pp. 42–65. Minneapolis: Minnesota University Press.

Kriesi, Hanspeter, Claude Longchamp, Florence Passy and Pascal Sciarini. 1993. *Analyse de la votation fédérale du 6 décembre 1992* (Vox no. 47). Berne: Schweizerische Gesellschaft für praktische Sozialforschung gfs.

Kriesi, Hanspeter, Ruud Koopmans, Jan-Willem Duyvendak and Marco G. Giugni. 1995. *The Politics of New Social Movements in Western Europe: A Comparative Analysis*. Minneapolis: University of Minnesota Press.

Kriesi, Hanspeter, Boris Wernli, Pascal Sciarini and Matteo Gianni. 1996. *Le clivage linguistique: problèmes de compréhension entre les communautés linguistiques en Suisse*. Berne: Office fédéral de la statistique.

Kriesi, Hanspeter, Romain Lachat, Peter Selb, Simon Bornschier and Marc Helbling (eds.). 2005. *Der Aufstieg der SVP. Acht Kantone im Vergleich*. Zurich: Neue Zürcher Zeitung Publishing.

Kriesi, Hanspeter, Edgar Grande, Romain Lachat, Martin Dolezal, Simon Bornschier and Tim Frey. 2006. 'Globalization and the transformation of the national political space: six European countries compared', *European Journal of Political Research* 45, 6: 921–57.

Krüger, Paul, Alain M. Schoenenberger, Michael Derrer and Claudio Bologna. 2001. *Entschädigung und Infrastruktur der Parlamentsarbeit. Analytisches Profil über den Wert der parlamentarischen Arbeit – Beurteilung der heutigen Entschädigung in Bezug auf ihre Kongruenz zur Leistung – Lösungsvorschläge für die Verbesserung der Arbeitsbedingungen. Gutachten im Auftrag der Parlamentsdienste der Schweizerischen Bundesversammlung* (available at www.parlament.ch/ed-pa-entschaedigung-infrastruktur.pdf).

Krugman, Paul. 1996. *Pop Internationalism*. Cambridge, MA: MIT Press.

Kübler, Daniel. 2001. 'Understanding policy change with the advocacy coalition framework: an application to Swiss drug policy', *Journal of European Public Policy* 8, 4: 623–41.

Kurzer, Paulette. 1993. *Business and Banking: Political Change and Economic Integration in Western Europe*. Ithaca: Cornell University Press.

Kux, Stephan. 1998. 'Zwischen Isolation und autonomer Anpassung: die Schweiz im integrationspolitischen Abseits?', *ZEI Discussion Paper of the Center for European Integration Studies* C3/1998, Bonn: Rheinische Friedrich Wilhelms-Universität Bonn (also available at www.zei.de/download/zei_dp/dp_c03_kux.pdf).

Laakso, Markku and Rein Taagepera. 1979. '"Effective" number of parties: a measure with application to West Europe', *Comparative Political Studies* 12, 1: 3–27.

Lachat, Romain. 2004. 'A heterogeneous electorate: individual-level differences in the process of formation of voting choices in Germany and Switzerland', PhD thesis, Department of Political Science, University of Zurich.

Ladner, Andreas. 1991. 'Direkte Demokratie auf kommunaler Ebene. Die Beteiligung an Gemeindeversammlungen', *Annuaire suisse de science politique* 31: 63–86.

1996. 'Die Schweizer Lokalparteien im Wandel. Aktuelle Entwicklungstendenzen gefährden die politische Stabilität', *Swiss Political Science Review* 2, 1: 1–22.

1998. 'Das Schweizer Parteiensystem und seine Parteien', in Ulrich Klöti et al. (eds.), *Handbuch politisches System der Schweiz*, pp. 211–58. Zurich: Neue Zürcher Zeitung Publishing.

2001. 'Swiss political parties: between persistence and change', in Jan-Erik Lane (ed.) *The Swiss Labyrinth: Institutions, Outcomes, Redesign*, pp. 123–44. London: Frank Cass.

2004. 'Die Politik ist auch im Milizsystem nicht gratis', *Neue Zürcher Zeitung*, no. 160, Tuesday 13 July, p. 15.

Laitin, David D. 1997. 'The cultural identities of a European state', *Politics and Society* 25, 3: 277–302.

Lane, Jan-Erik. 2002. 'The public sector in Switzerland', in Uwe Wagschal and Hans Rentsch (eds.), *Der Preis des Föderalismus*, pp. 55–70. Zurich: Orell Füssli.

Lauvaux, Philippe. 1990. *Les grandes démocraties contemporaines*. Paris: Presses universitaires de France.

Lehmbruch, Gerhard. 1967. *Proporzdemokratie. Politisches System und politische Kultur in der Schweiz und in Österreich*. Tübingen, Mohr.

Lehner, Franz. 1984, 'Consociational democracy in Switzerland: a political-economic explanation and some empirical evidence', *European Journal of Political Research* 12: 25–42.

Leutwiler, Fritz *et al.* 1991. *Schweizerische Wirtschaftspolitik im internationalen Wettbewerb. Ein ordnungspolitisches Programm.* Zurich: Orell Füssli.

Lijphart, Arend. 1977. *Democracy in Plural Societies.* New Haven: Yale University Press.

1979. 'Religious vs linguistic vs class voting: the "Crucial Experiment" of comparing Belgium, Canada, South Africa, and Switzerland', *American Political Science Review* 73: 442–57.

1984. *Democracies: Patterns of Majoritarian and Consensus Government in Twenty-One Countries.* New Haven: Yale University Press.

1999. *Patterns of Democracy.* New Haven: Yale University Press.

Lijphart, Arend and Markus M. L. Crepaz. 1991. 'Corporatism and consensus democracy in eighteen countries: conceptual and empirical linkages', *British Journal of Political Science* 21: 235–56.

Linder, Wolf. 1987. *La décision politique en Suisse. Genèse et mise en œuvre de la legislation.* Lausanne: réalité sociales.

1990. 'Die Zukunft der Demokratie', in *Aufbruch aus der Verspätung.* Zurich: Stiftung für Geisteswissenschaften.

1999. *Schweizerische Demokratie. Institutionen, Prozesse, Perspektiven.* Berne: Haupt.

2007. 'Direct democracy', in Ulrich Klöti *et al.* (eds.), *Handbook of Swiss Politics*, 2nd edition, pp. 101–20. Zurich: Neue Zürcher Zeitung Publishing.

Lipset, Seymour Martin and Stein Rokkan. 1967. 'Cleavage structures, party systems, and voter alignments', (reprinted) in Seimour Martin Lipset, 1985, *Consensus and Conflict: Essays in Political Sociology*, pp. 113–85. New Brunswick: Transaction Books.

Longchamp, Claude. 1991. 'Herausgeforderte demokratische Öffentlichkeit. Zu den Möglichkeiten und Grenzen des politischen Marketings bei Abstimmungen und Wahlen in der Schweiz', in *Schweizerisches Jahrbuch für politische Wissenschaft 'Direkte Demokratie/Démocratie directe'*, pp. 303–26. Berne: Haupt.

Lüthi, Ruth. 1993. *Parlamentarische Entscheidungsprozesse: ein internationaler Vergleich des Einflusses von Institutionen und Akteuren. Ein Literaturbericht.* Berne: Institut für Politikwissenschaft.

1996. 'Die Wirkung von institutionellen Reformen dargestellt am Beispiel der Reform des Kommissionensystems der Schweizerischen Bundesversammlung von 1991', *Swiss Political Science Review* 2, 2: 81–111.

2007. 'The Parliament', in Ulrich Klöti, *et al.* (eds.), *Handbook of Swiss Politics*, 2nd edition, pp. 121–44. Zurich: Neue Zürcher Zeitung Publishing.

Lüthy, Herbert. 1971. *Vom Geist und Ungeist des Föderalismus*, 2nd edition. Zurich: Arche.

Mach, André (ed.). 1999a. *Globalisation, néo-libéralisme et politiques publiques dans la Suisse des années 1990*. Zurich: Seismo.

    1999b. 'L'articulation entre facteurs externes et internes comme clef d'analyse des réformes économiques et sociales', in André Mach (ed.), *Globalisation, néo-libéralisme et politiques publiques dans la Suisse des années 1990*, pp. 419–54. Zurich: Seismo.

    1999c. *Evolution des relations industrielles en Suisse dans les années 90: une lente évolution vers le 'modèle anglo-saxon'?* Lausanne: Département de science politique, Université de Lausanne.

    2006. *La Suisse entre internationalisation et changements politiques internes: législation sur les cartels et relations industrielles dans les années 1990*. Zurich: Rüegger.

Mach, André and Daniel Oesch. 2003. 'Collective bargaining between decentralization and stability: a sectoral model explaining the Swiss experience during the 1990s', *Industrielle Beziehungen* 10, 1: 160–82.

Mach, André, Silja Häusermann and Yannis Papadopoulos. 2003. 'Economic regulatory reforms in Switzerland: adjustment without European integration, or how rigidities become flexible', *Journal of European Public Policy* 10, 2: 302–19.

Mair, Peter and Ingrid van Biezen. 2001. 'Party membership in twenty European democracies, 1980–2000', *Party Politics* 7, 1: 5–21.

Manow, Philip. 2002. '"The Good, the Bad, and the Ugly": Esping-Andersens Sozialstaats-Typologie und die konfessionellen Wurzeln des westlichen Wohlfahrtsstaats', *Kölner Zeitschrift für Soziologie und Sozialpsychologie*, 54, 2: 203–25.

Mänz, Marcus and Alexander H. Trechsel. 2004. 'Multi-level e-governance – the impact of ICTs on social security implementation within a federal state', e-DC e-Working Paper, 2004, 2 (also available at http://edc.unige.ch/publications/e-workingpapers/Manz_Trechsel.pdf).

Marques de Bastos, Guilhermina. 1993. 'La sélectivité de la participation', in Hanspeter Kriesi (ed.), *Citoyenneté et démocratie directe*, pp. 167–88. Zurich: Seismo.

Marquis, Lionel and Gerald Schneider. 1996. 'Wer kommt als Vermittler zum Zuge? Überschätzte und unterschätzte Anforderungsfaktoren für Mediationstätigkeiten', *Swiss Political Science Review*, 2, 3: 69–82.

Marquis, Lionel and Pascal Sciarini. 1999. 'Opinion formation in foreign policy: the Swiss experience', *Electoral Studies* 18, 4: 453–71.

Mauer, Victor. 2003. 'Die Europäische Sicherheits- und Verteidigungspolitik: eine janusköpfige Entwicklung', in Andreas Wenger (ed.), *Bulletin 2003 zur schweizerischen Sicherheitspolitik*, pp. 43–68. Zurich: Forschungsstelle für Sicherheitspolitik der ETH Zurich.

Mayntz, Renate. 1989. 'Föderalismus und die Gesellschaft der Gegenwart', Discussion paper 89/3. Cologne: Max-Planck-Institut für Gesellschafts-forschung.

McKay, David. 2001. *Designing Europe: Comparative Lessons from the Federal Experience*. Oxford: Oxford University Press.

Mendelsohn, Matthew and Andrew Parkin (eds.). 2001. *Referendum Democracy: Citizens, Elites and Deliberation in Referendum Campaigns*. London: Palgrave.

Mény, Yves. 1992. *Politique comparée. Les démocraties: Allemagne, Etats-Unis, France, Grande-Bretagne, Italie*, 3rd edition. Paris: Montchrestien.

Merrien, François-Xavier and Giuliano Bonoli. 2000. 'Implementing major welfare state reforms: a comparison of France and Switzerland – a new-institutionalist approach', in Stein Kuhnle (ed.), *Survival of the European Welfare State*, pp. 128–45. London: Routledge.

Morand, Charles-Albert. 1987. 'La formation et la mise en œuvre du droit', *Pouvoir* 43: 73–86.

Moravcsik, Andrew. 1998. *The Choice for Europe: Social Purpose and State Power from Messina to Maastricht*. Ithaca: Cornell University Press.

Moser, Peter. 1991. *Schweizerische Wirtschaftspolitik im internationalen Wettbewerb. Eine ordnungspolitische Analyse*. Zurich: Orell Füssli.

1996. *Die Haltung der Schweizer Stimmberechtigten zu Fragen der Aussen- und Aussenwirtschaftspolitik unter besonderer Berücksichtigung der Integrationspolitik. Eine Synthese der Resultate von Repräsentativbefragungen, Schlussbericht*, Zurich: Institut für Politikwissenschaft der Universität Zurich.

Mottier, Véronique. 1993. 'La structuration sociale de la participation aux votations fédérales', in Hanspeter Kriesi (ed.), *Citoyenneté et démocratie directe*, pp. 123–44. Zurich: Seismo.

Nabholz, Ruth. 1998. 'Das Wählerverhalten in der Schweiz: Stabilität oder Wandel? Eine Trendanalyse von 1971–1995', in Hanspeter Kriesi, Wolf Linder and Ulrich Klöti (eds.), *Schweizer Wahlen 1995*, pp. 17–44. Berne: Haupt.

Nagel, Joan. 1999. 'Ethnic troubles: gender, sexuality and the construction of national identity', in Hanspeter Kriesi, Klaus Armingeon, Hannes

Siegrist and Andreas Wimmer (eds.), *Nation and National Identity. The European Experience in Perspective.* pp. 85–108. Chur: Rüegger.

Nef, Rolf. 1989. 'Armeeabschaffungs-Initiative: soyons réalistes, demandons l'impossible? – Konzeptionelle Überlegungen und empirische Analysen zum politischen Gehalt einer 'Wegmarke'', *Schweizerische Zeitschrift für Soziologie* 15, 3: 545–82.

Neidhart, Leonard. 1970. *Plebiszit und pluralitäre Demokratie: eine Analyse der Funktion des schweizerischen Gesetzesreferendums.* Berne: Francke.

Nicolet, Sarah, Pascal Sciarini and Alex Fischer. 2003. 'Seeking consensus: a quantitative analysis of decision-making processes in Switzerland', unpublished manuscript. Lausanne: IDEAP.

Nüssli, Kurt. 1985. *Föderalismus in der Schweiz. Konzepte, Indikatoren, Daten.* Grüsch: Rüegger.

Oberer, Thomas. 2001. *Die innenpolitische Genehmigung der bilateralen Verträge Schweiz-EU: Wende oder Ausnahme bei Aussenpolitischen Vorlagen. Analyse der Argumente und Strategien im Genehmigungsverfahren und in der Referendumskampagne.* Baslerschriften zur europäischen Integration no. 52/53. Basel: Europainstitut der Universität Basel (also available at www.europa.unibas.ch/fileadmin/pdf/BS52–53.pdf).

Obinger, Herbert. 1998. *Politische Institutionen und Sozialpolitik in der Schweiz.* Berne: Peter Lang.

Ochsner, Alois. 1987. *Die schweizerische Bundesversammlung als Arbeitsparlament: Vollanalyse der parlamentarischen Kommissionen einer Legislaturperiode.* Entlebuch: Huber Druck.

OECD. 2004. *OECD Economic Studies – Switzerland.* Paris: OECD.

OECD Reviews of Regulatory Reform. 2006. *Switzerland. Seizing the Opportunities for Growth.* Paris: OECD.

Oesch, Daniel. 2004. 'Redrawing the class map: stratification and institutions in Britain, Germany, Sweden and Switzerland', PhD thesis, Department of Political Science, University of Zurich.

　2006. *Redrawing the Class Map: Stratification and Institutions in Britain, Germany, Sweden and Switzerland.* Basingstoke: Palgrave.

Papadopoulos, Yannis. 1991. 'Quel rôle pour les petits partis dans la démocratie directe?', *Annuaire suisse de science politique* 31: 131–50.

　1994a. 'Les votations fédérales comme indicateur de soutien aux autorités', in Yannis Papadopoulos (ed.), *Elites politiques et peuple en Suisse. Analyse des votations fédérales: 1970–1987*, pp. 113–60. Lausanne: Réalités sociales.

　(ed.). 1994b. *Elites politiques et peuple en Suisse. Analyse ds votations fédérales: 1970–1987.* Lausanne: réalités sociales.

1995. 'Analysis of functions and dysfunctions of direct democracy: top-down and bottom-up perspectives', *Politics and Society* 23, 4: 421–48.

1996. 'Les mécanismes du vote référendaire en Suisse: l'impact de l'offre politique', *Revue française de sociologie*, 37: 5–35.

1997. *Les processus de décision fédéraux en Suisse*. Paris: L'Harmattan.

1998. *Démocratie directe*. Paris: Economica.

2005. 'Implementing (and radicalising) art. I-47.4 of the Constitution: is the addition of some (semi-)direct democracy to the nascent consociational European federation just Swiss folklore?', *Journal of European Public Policy* 12, 3: 448–67.

Passy, Florence. 1993. 'Compétence et décision politique', in Hanspeter Kriesi (ed.), *Citoyenneté et démocratie directe. Compétence, participation et décision des citoyens et citoyennes suisses*, pp. 213–31. Zurich: Seismo.

Poitry, Alain-Valéry. 1989. *La fonction d'ordre de l'Etat. Analyse des mécanismes et des déterminants sélectifs dans le processus législatif suisse*. Berne: Lang.

Rennwald, Jean-Claude. 1994. *La transformation de la structure du pouvoir dans le canton du Jura (1970–1991). Du séparatisme à l'intégration au système politique suisse*. Courrendlin: Communication jurassienne et européenne (CEJ).

Rich, Georg. 2005. 'Die Schweizer Wirtschaft wächst schneller, als es scheint. "Zusatzverdienst" im Ausland und Reformdruck im Inland', *Neue Zürcher Zeitung, Internationale Ausgabe*, no. 152, 2/3 July, p. 19.

Richardson, Jeremy, Gunnel Gustafsson and Grant Jordan. 1982. 'The concept of policy style', in Jeremy Richardson (ed.), *Policy Styles in Western Europe*, pp. 1–16. London: George Allen and Unwin.

Righart, Hans. 1986. *De katholieke zuil in Europa*. Amsterdam: Boom.

Riklin, Alois. 1991. 'Funktionen der schweizerischen Neutralität', in Bernard Prongué *et al.* (eds.), *Passé pluriel*, pp. 361–94. Fribourg: Editions universitaires.

1992. 'Schweizerische Neutralität vor der europäischen Herausforderung', *Beiträge und Berichte* 177. St Gallen: Institut für Politikwissenschaft.

Riklin, Alois and Silvano Möckli. 1991. 'Milizparlament?', in Madeleine Bovey Lechner, Martin Graf and Annemarie Huber-Hotz (eds.), *Das Parlament – Oberste Gewalt des Bundes? – Festschrift der Bundesversammlung zur 700-Jahr-Feier der Eidgenossenschaft*, pp. 145–63. Berne: Haupt.

Riklin, Alois and Alois Ochsner. 1984. 'Parliament', in Ulrich Klöti *et al.* (eds.), *Manuel du système politique Suisse*, pp. 77–115. Berne: Haupt.

Rokkan, Stein. 1970. *Citizens, Elections, Parties*. Oslo: Universitetsforlaget.

Rougemont, Denis de. 1965. *La Suisse ou l'histoire d'un peuple heureux*. Lausanne: L'âge d'homme.

Sager, Fritz. 2003. 'Kompensationsmöglichkeiten föderaler Vollzugsdefizite. Das Beispiel der Alkoholpräventionspolitiken', *Swiss Political Science Review* 9, 1: 309–33.

Sardi, Massimo and Eric Widmer. 1993. 'L'orientation du vote', in Hanspeter Kriesi (ed.), *Citoyenneté et démocratie directe*, pp. 191–212. Zurich: Seismo.

Sartori, Giovanni. 1976. *Parties and Party Systems: A Framework for Analysis*, vol. I. Cambridge: Cambridge University Press.

1987. *The Theory of Democracy Revisited*. London: Chatham House.

Scharpf, Fritz. 1988. 'The joint-decision trap: lessons from German federalism and European integration', *Public Administration* 66, 3: 239–78.

1994. *Optionen des Föderalismus in Deutschland und Europa*. Frankfurt: Campus.

Scharpf, Fritz W. and Vivien A. Schmidt. 2001. 'Introduction', in Fritz Scharpf and Vivien A. Schmidt (eds.), *Welfare and Work in the Open Economy*, vol. II: *Diverse Responses to Common Challenges*, pp. 1–18. Oxford: Oxford University Press.

Schattschneider, E. E. 1960 (1988). *The Semisovereign People: A Realist's View of Democracy in America*. London: Thomson Learning.

Schindler, Dietrich. 1990. 'Neutralität am Wendepunkt?', *Neue Zürcher Zeitung*, 22/23 September.

Schmidt, Manfred G. 1985. *Der Schweizer Weg zur Vollbeschäftigung*. Frankfurt: Campus.

1995. 'Vollbeschäftigung und Arbeitslosigkeit in der Schweiz. Vom Sonderweg zum Normalfall', *Politische Vierteljahresschrift* 36, 1: 35–48.

1998. 'Die Gesundheitsausgaben und die Staatsquote. Befunde des Vergleichs demokratisch verfasster Länder', unpublished manuscript.

Schmitter, Philippe C. and Jürgen R. Grote. 1997. 'Der korporatistische Sysiphus: Vergangenheit, Gegenwart und Zukunft', *Politische Vierteljahresschrift* 38, 3: 530–54.

Schmitter, Philippe C. and Wolfgang Streeck. 1981. *The Organization of Business Interests. A Research Design*. Revised and extended version. Discussion paper IIMV/LMP 81–13. Berlin: Wissenschaftszentrum.

Schmitter, Philippe C. and Alexander H. Trechsel (eds.). 2004. *The Future of Democracy in Europe: Trends, Analyses and Reforms*. Strasbourg: Council of Europe Publishing.

Schneider, Gerald and Cyrill Hess. 1995. 'Die innenpolitische Manipulation der Aussenpolitik: die Logik von Ratifikationsdebatten in der direkten Demokratie', *Swiss Political Science Review* 1, 2–3: 93–111.

Schumann, Klaus. 1971. *Das Regierungssystem der Schweiz*. Cologne: Karl Heymans Verlag KG.

Schumpeter, Joseph A. 1947. *Capitalism, Socialism and Democracy*. New York: Harper and Brothers.

Schwartz, Herman. 2001. 'Round up the usual suspects! Globalization, domestic politics, and welfare state change', in Paul Pierson (ed.), *The New Politics of the Welfare State*, pp. 17–44. Oxford: Oxford University Press.

Schweizer, Paul. 1895. *Geschichte der schweizerischen Neutralität.* Frauenfeld: Verlag F. Huber.

Sciarini, Pascal. 1994. *Le système politique suisse face à la Communauté européenne et au GATT: le cas-test de la politique agricole.* Geneva: Georg.

   1995. 'Réseau politique interne et négociations internationales: le GATT, levier de la réforme agricole suisse', *Swiss Political Science Review* 1, 2–3: 225–52.

   2004. 'The decision-making process', in Ulrich Klöti *et al.* (eds.), *Handbook of Swiss Politics*, 2nd edition, pp. 509–62. Zurich: Neue Zürcher Zeitung Publishing.

   2007. 'The decision-making process', in Ulrich Klöti *et al.* (eds.), *Handbook of Swiss Politics*, 2nd edition, pp. 465–500. Zurich: Neue Zürcher Zeitung Publishing

Sciarini, Pascal and Sarah Nicolet. 2005. 'Internationalization and domestic politics: evidence from the Swiss case', in Hanspeter Kriesi, Peter Farago, Martin Kohli and Milad Zarin-Nejadan (eds.), *Contemporary Switzerland: Revisiting the Special Case*, pp. 221–38. London: Palgrave-Macmillan.

Sciarini, Pascal and Alexander H. Trechsel. 1996. 'Démocratie directe en Suisse: l'élite politique victime des droits populaires?', *Swiss Political Science Review* 2: 201–32.

Sciarini, Pascal, Sarah Nicolet and Alex Fischer. 2002. 'L'impact de l'internationalisation sur les processus de décision en Suisse: une analyse quantitative des actes législatifs 1995–1999', *Swiss Political Science Review* 8, 3–4: 1–34.

Senti, Martin. 1994. *Geschlecht als politischer Konflikt.* Berne: Haupt.

Serdült, Uwe and Walter Schenkel. 2006. 'Intergovernmental relations and multi-level governance', in Ulrich Klöti *et al.* (eds.), *Handbook of Swiss Politics*, 2nd edition, pp. 525–45. Zurich: Neue Zürcher Zeitung Publishing.

Sidjanski, Dusan. 1987. 'La Suisse face à la Communauté européenne', *Pouvoirs* 43: 139–49.

Siegenthaler, Hansjörg. 1993. 'Supranationalität, Nationalismus und regionale Autonomie: Erfahrungen des schweizerischen Bundesstaates – Perspektiven der Europäischen Gemeinschaft', in Heinrich A. Winkler and Hartmut Kaelble (eds.), *Nationalismus – Nationalitäten – Supranationalität*, pp. 309–33. Stuttgart: Klett-Cotta.

Smith, Anthony D. 1986. *The Ethnic Origins of Nations*. Oxford: Basil Blackwell.

1991. *National Identity*. London: Penguin.

Stepan, Alfred. 1999. 'Federalism and democracy: beyond the US model', *Journal of Democracy* 10, 4: 19–34.

Streeck, Wolfgang. 1981. *Gewerkschaftliche Organisationsprobleme in der sozialstaatlichen Demokratie*. Königstein: Athenäum.

Streeck, Wolfgang and Philippe C. Schmitter (eds.). 1985. *Private Interest Government: Beyond Market and State*. London: Sage.

Suter, Andreas. 1999. 'Neutral seit Marignano? Zur Realität einer Staatsmaxime in der Schweiz der Frühen Neuzeit', in *Neue Helvetische Gesellschaft, Jahrbuch 1998/99*, pp. 193–216.

Swanson, David L. and Paolo Mancini. 1996. 'Patterns of modern electoral campaigning and their consequences', in David L. Swanson and Paolo Mancini (eds.), *Politics, Media, and Modern Democracy: An International Study of Innovations in Electoral Campaigning and their Consequences*, pp. 247–76. London: Praeger.

Tanquerel, Thierry. 1991. 'La Suisse doit-elle choisir entre l'Europe et la démocratie directe?', *Revue de droit suisse* 110, 2: 188–220.

Theiler, Tobias. 2004. 'The origins of Euroscepticism in German-speaking Switzerland', *European Journal of Political Research* 43: 635–56.

Tilly, Charles. 2004. *Contention and Democracy in Europe, 1650–2000*. Cambridge: Cambridge University Press.

Trachsler, Daniel. 2004. 'Gute Dienste – Mythen, Fakten, Perspektiven', in Andreas Wenger (ed.), *Bulletin 2004 zur schweizerischen Sicherheitspolitik*, pp. 33–64. Zurich: Forschungsstelle für Sicherheitspolitik der ETH Zurich.

Traxler, Franz. 1982. *Evolution gewerkschaftlicher Interessenvertretung*. Vienna: Braunmüller.

Trechsel, Alexander H. 1994. 'Clivages en Suisse. Analyse des impacts relatifs des clivages sur l'électorat suisse lors des élections fédérales', MA thesis, Département de science politique, University of Geneva.

2000. *Feuerwerk Volksrechte. Die Volksabstimmungen in den schweizerischen Kantonen 1970–1996*. Basle: Helbing & Lichtenhahn.

2004. 'Limits of participatory democracy: direct democracy reassessed', paper presented at the ECPR Joint Sessions of Workshops, Uppsala, Sweden.

2005. 'How to federalize the European Union . . . and why bother', *Journal of European Public Policy* 12, 3: 401–18.

2006. 'Popular votes', in Ulrich Klöti *et al.* (eds.), *Handbook of Swiss Politics*, 2nd edition, pp. 435–61. Zurich: Neue Zürcher Zeitung Publishing.

2007a. 'E-voting and electoral participation', in Claes de Vreese (ed.), *Dynamics of Referendum Campaigns – An International Perspective*, pp. 159–82. London: Palgrave.

2007b. 'Direct democracy and European integration – A limited obstacle?', in Clive H. Church (ed.), *Switzerland and the European Union*, pp. 36–51. London: Routledge.

Trechsel, Alexander H. and Hanspeter Kriesi. 1996. 'Switzerland: the referendum and initiative as a centrepiece of the political system', in Michael Gallagher and Pier Vincenzo Uleri (eds.), *The Referendum Experience in Europe*, pp. 185–208. London: Macmillan.

Trechsel, Alexander H. and Fernando Mendez (eds.). 2005. *The European Union and E-voting: Addressing the European Parliament's Internet Voting Challenge*. London: Routledge.

Trechsel, Alexander H. and Pascal Sciarini. 1998. 'Direct democracy in Switzerland: do elites matter?', *European Journal of Political Research* 33, 1: 99–123.

Trechsel, Alexander H. and Uwe Serdült. 1999. *Kaleidoskop Volksrechte. Die Institutionen der direkten Demokratie in den schweizerischen Kantonen 1970–1996*. Basle: Helbing & Lichtenhahn.

Tresch, Anke. 2008. *Öffentlichkeit und Sprachenvielfalt. Medienvermittelte Kommunikation zur Europapolitik in der Deutsch- und Westschweiz*. Baden-Baden: Nomo.

Vatter, Adrian. 2002. *Kantonale Demokratien im Vergleich: Entstehungsgründe, Interaktionen und Wirkungen politischer Institutionen in den Schweizer Kantonen*. Opladen: Leske & Budrich.

Vatter, Adrian. 2007a. 'Federalism', in Ulrich Klöti *et al.* (eds.), *Handbook of Swiss Politics*, 2nd edition, pp. 77–99. Zurich: Neue Zürcher Zeitung Publishing.

Vatter, Adrian. 2007b. 'The cantons', in Ulrich Klöti *et al.* (eds.), *Handbook of Swiss Politics*, 2nd edition, pp. 197–225. Zurich: Neue Zürcher Zeitung Publishing.

Vatter, Adrian and Fritz Sager. 1996. 'Föderalismusreform am Beispiel des Ständemehr', *Swiss Political Science Review* 2, 2: 165–200.

Vogel, Steven K. 1996. *Freer Markets, More Rules: Regulatory Reform in Advanced Industrial Countries*. Ithaca: Cornell University Press.

Von Wyss, Moritz. 2003. 'Die Namensabstimmung im Ständerat: Untersuchung eines parlamentarischen Mythos', in *Nachdenken über den demokratischen Staat und seine Geschichte: Beiträge für Alfred Kölz*, pp. 23–47. Zurich: Schulthess.

Wagschal, Uwe and Herbert Obinger. 2000. 'Der Einfluss der Direktdemokratie auf die Sozialpolitik', *Politische Vierteljahresschrift* 41, 3: 466–97.

Wagschal, Uwe, Daniele Ganser and Hans Rentsch. 2002. *Der Alleingang.* Zurich: Orell Füssli.

Wälti, Sonja. 2001. *Le fédéralisme d'exécution sous pression: la mise en œuvre des politiques à incidence spatiale dans le système fédéral suisse.* Basle: Helbing & Lichtenhahn.

——— 2003. 'L'effet des rapports financiers sur la dynamique fédérale: la qualité médiative du fédéralisme Suisse', *Swiss Political Science Review* 9, 1: 91–108.

Werder, Hans. 1978. *Die Bedeutung der Volksinitiativen in der Nachkriegszeit.* Berne: Francke.

Wernli, Boris, Pascal Sciarini and José Barranco. 1994. *Analyse des votations fédérales du 12 juin 1994* (Vox no. 53). Berne: Schweizerische Gesellschaft für praktische Sozialforschung gfs.

Wheare, Kenneth C. 1946. *Federal Government.* London: Oxford University Press.

Widmer, Paul. 2003. *Schweizer Aussenpolitik und Diplomatie. Von Charles Pictet de Rochemont bis Edouard Brunner.* Zurich: Verlag Ammann.

Wimmer, Andreas. 2002. *Nationalist Exclusion and Ethnic Conflict. Shadows of Modernity.* Cambridge: Cambridge University Press.

Wittmann, Walter. 1992. *Marktwirtschaft für die Schweiz.* Frauenfeld: Huber.

Z'graggen, Heidi and Wolf Linder. 2004. *Professionalisierung der Parlamente im internationalen Vergleich. Studie im Auftrag der Parlamentsdienste der Schweizerischen Bundesversammlung.* Berne: Institut für Politikwissenschaft der Universität Bern.

Zaller, John R. 1992. *The Nature and Origins of Mass Opinion.* Cambridge: Cambridge University Press.

Zbinden, Martin. 1992. 'Das EWR-Projekt: eine Wiederholung des Assoziationsversuches von 1961 bis 1963?', in *Schweizerisches Jahrbuch für politische Wissenschaft 'Die Schweiz und Europa'*, pp. 221–48. Berne: Haupt.

Zervudacki, Denis. 1999. *Patronats dans le monde.* Paris: Presses universitaires de France.

Index